Names in Stone

Some there be, which have no memorial;
who are perished, as though they had never been;
and are become as though they had never been born;
and their children after them.
Ecclesiasticus, Chapter 44, verse 9

Names in Stone

Forgotten Warriors
of
Bradford-on-Avon and District
1939-45

Jonathan Falconer

BED & BOLSTER PUBLISHING

Holt War Memorial. *Author*

First published in 2009

A catalogue record for this book is available from the British Library.

ISBN 978 0 9563423 0 0

Published by Bed & Bolster Publishing,
10 Frome Road, Bradford-on-Avon,
Wiltshire BA15 1LB.

Designed by Annie Falconer-Gronow.
Page build by James Robertson.

Printed and bound in Great Britain by
JF Print Ltd, Sparkford, on paper supplied by
Denmaur Paper Ltd.

Contents

Acknowledgements

A great many people and organisations have been generous in providing me with information and photographs, not to mention their time and helpful advice, during the research and writing of this book. It is difficult to single out any particular individuals for special thanks, but I would still like to put on record my gratitude to the following: my neighbour Marian Webb, whose encyclopaedic knowledge of Bradford people has been invaluable in helping my research along; Charley Morgan and Victoria Ashford of the *Wiltshire Times* editorial team, for their unstinting interest and support for this project; my friend of many years, Paul Weeks, for his frank but constructive critique of my first manuscript draft; and my friend and former colleague Jim Crawley for his wise suggestions on literary style.

I also owe debts of thanks to Peter Leach, Managing Director of JF Print Ltd of Sparkford, for generously underwriting the production and printing costs for this book; my wife Annie Falconer-Gronow for her page and cover designs; James Robertson for the page-build; and Tracey and Jon Williams of Winsley, for kindly sponsoring the cost of the page-build in memory of family members who have served in HM Forces.

Acknowledgement is made to the Imperial War Museum, London; Australian War Memorial, Canberra; U-Boat Archive, Cuxhaven, Germany; and the Bundesarchiv, Freiburg, Germany, for kind permission to reproduce photographs from their collections.

I should also like to thank the following museums, institutions and associations for their help: Army Medical Services Museum (Capt P.H. Starling); British Airways Archives and Museum Collection (Keith D. Hayward); Devon and Dorset Regiment Museum, Dorchester; DCLI Museum, Bodmin, (Major Hugo White); Firepower: the Royal Artillery Museum, Woolwich (Paul Evans); Fleet Air Arm Museum, Yeovilton (Jerry Shore, Dave Morris and Susan Deering); Force 'Z' Survivors incorporating the HMS *Prince of Wales* and HMS *Repulse* Survivors' Association (POWRSA); Guy's and St Thomas's NHS Foundation Trust (Bethan Adams); New Zealand Defence Force Personnel Archives; RGBW (Salisbury) Museum (David Chilton); RAF Halton Aircraft Apprentices Association and Museum (Gp Capt Min Larkin); RAF Museum, London, (Peter Elliott); RN Submarine Museum, Gosport (Debbie Corner and George Malcolmson); Thailand and Burma Railway Company Museum, Kanchanaburi, Thailand (Terry Manttan); The Tank Museum, Bovington, Dorchester, Dorset, (David Fletcher, Janice Tait); Welch Regiment Museum, Caernarvon; the Salvation Army Archives.

My grateful thanks are also due to the following individuals, many of whom invited me into their homes and poured out their family histories to a complete stranger. Thank you, all of you, for your candour and kindness: Tony Allard, sole survivor of the Lancaster crash at RAF Hullavington; Paul Baillie, TNA researcher; Tony Banham of the Hong Kong War Diary; Jill Bennett, niece of Fred Green; Paul and Jane Bentley, who visited Ancona War Cemetery, Italy, on my behalf and photographed the grave of Joseph Groves; Rita Boswell, archivist, Harrow School; John and Phil Cooch, brother and nephew of Charlie Cooch; Peter and Jayne Curnock, nephew and niece by marriage of Sam Curnock; and Bob and Dick Curnock, brothers of Sam Curnock; Theo James, daughter of William James; Cdr Brian Darch, RN, nephew of Brian Darch, for kind permission to reproduce photographs and extracts from his uncle's letters; David Dobson, son of Len Dobson, and nephew of Arthur Dobson; Mina Dudley and Joan Stickland from Winsley, who helped me with information about Reggie Miller, Jack Harker and Ronald Perkins; Søren C. Flensted from Billund, Denmark, for help with information and photographs of Reggie Miller's crashed Hampden bomber; Ken Ford, author and Second World War historian; Mike Garbett and Brian Goulding, aviation historians and authors of the 'Lancaster at War' series of books; Eunice and Ruth Godfrey, daughter and granddaughter of Nelson Webb; Yvonne Gosselin (nee Willmer), daughter of 'Bunny' Willmer; Caroline Hall, daughter of Tony Hall; Major Bill Hanna, ex-Somerset Light Infantry, National Inventory of War Memorials researcher; Chris Hobbs, Sheffield historian, for help with Reg Collins' story; Dick and Phyl Huntley for help with information about Dick's twin brother Fred, and the Harker brothers; Michael Hurst, MBE, Director of the Taiwan POW Camps Memorial Society, for help in discovering the fate of Leslie Davis; Pamela Joyce, daughter of Roy Heavyside; Alan Matthews, Chairman, *Prince of Wales* and *Repulse* Survivors Association; John and Rene Maundrell (son-in-law and daughter of Philip Margetts); Beryl Mayell, daughter of Sidney Pratten; Dr Alex Moulton, childhood friend of Ronnie Perkins; Philip 'Nobby' Oliver and Tracy Bridges, son and granddaughter of Herbert Oliver; Nigel Orton, nephew of Michael Orton, and Aileen Johnson, Michael's sister; Air Cdre Graham Pitchfork, author and RAF historian; Marilyn Schofield, Frances Davis, David Rogers and Elizabeth Holland (all of whom are relatives or friends of Leslie Davis; David 'Danny' Sheppard, son of Albert Sheppard; Golda Sheppard and Jerry Bray, sister and brother of Ronald Bray; Eileen Sheppard (nee Sadd), and Brian Lyewood, sister and nephew of Eric and Ronald Sadd; Chris Shores, aviation historian and author; my friend Jak Mallmann Showell for picture research on my behalf at the U-Boat Archive; Fred Strudwick, former able seaman, HMS *Orion*; my friend Dr Simon Trew, Senior Lecturer in War Studies, Royal Military Academy, Sandhurst; Pamela Ward, sister of Albert Jones; Kay West, HMS *Orion* Association; Enid Wicheard (niece of Albert and Len Dobson) and Joyce Wicheard (billettee with the Harker family).

To all of you a very big 'thank you', and in particular to the families of those men who are remembered in the pages that follow – this is your book.

Jonathan Falconer
Bradford-on-Avon, July 2009

IN
EVERLASTING MEMORY
OF THE MEN OF
BRADFORD-ON-AVON
WHO FELL
IN THE GREAT WAR
1914-1918.
INFORMATION

INTRODUCTION

'One feels that so much was given for absolutely no recognition, and here suddenly is a sign that all is not forgotten by the world at large.'
Graham Powell, whose Halifax bomber pilot brother Gordon was killed in action over Germany in February 1945

Names in stone. In so many cases just a surname and an initial. This is how the dead of two world wars are commemorated on war memorials all over Britain. Behind the plain inscriptions lie stories of men who marched away to war never to return; ordinary men caught up in extraordinary events almost a lifetime ago. They are tales that have resonance in communities the world over. Bradford-on-Avon and its neighbouring Wiltshire villages are no different.

We have largely lost sight of the identities of these men – and one woman – whose stories are recounted in this book. Indeed, many of the accounts you will read have never been told before, and the individuals and events described are now all but forgotten. Thankfully many are still remembered by their families, but as the years pass the memories have dimmed of who these men *really* were.

Since moving to the Bradford area in 1972 I have often wondered how many times I have walked past the town's war memorial in Westbury Gardens. Although I knew well enough what it was and what it represented, I had never found the need to stop and read the long lists of names recorded on its three bronze panels. That is, not until the summer of 1999 when I began the research for this book.

You could say that until then I had taken its presence for granted. The stone memorial is part of the street scene that we often take for granted – much like the park benches and bus shelters – and in any case Bradford's war memorial is not particularly memorable in architectural terms. But when Lord Long unveiled it in August 1922 it became the focus of remembrance for more than one hundred grieving local families. The 'war to end wars' had come to an end little more than four years earlier and the loss of loved ones was still gnawing at their minds, their emotions still raw.

When Hitler launched his blitzkrieg on Poland in September 1939, Britain and France declared war on Germany through their treaty obligations to the Poles. In June 1941 Germany invaded Soviet Russia and the Japanese attacked Pearl Harbor in December, drawing the two great powers of Russia and the USA into the conflict, turning what had been essentially a European war into a truly global conflagration.

Bradford-on-Avon of the 1930s was a country market town of some 4,700 inhabitants. Today it is home to more than 9,000 people. ***Marian Webb collection***

Britain's armed forces were involved in fighting across Europe and Asia. Bradford and district's war casualties were sustained in North West Europe, Italy and Sicily, Greece, North Africa and the Far East, in the air and at sea. The Second World War witnessed the growth of the RAF, with Bradford's casualties across the three armed services reflected in a different relative split to those of the First World War: 35 Army, 17 Royal Navy and 15 RAF. Of the 73 who died, 33 are buried overseas, and 13 in the UK; 3 remain untraceable; and of the 23 who have no known grave, 17 were lost at sea, 5 airmen were lost without trace, and 1 soldier was lost in battle. After the blood letting of the Second World War another panel was added containing 42 more names, and the memorial was reinvigorated by their sacrifice as a focus for remembrance.

Bradford-on-Avon in the 21st century is far away in time, place and values from the carnage of the Somme or a burning Lancaster bomber over Germany. For many the war memorial represents times passed that, at best, have little relevance to their present existence. Yet our war memorials are tangible links with the defining events of two world wars that have shaped our lives today.

For those who want to discover more about these forgotten men there seems very little information to go on. So, how do you make that quantum leap from names carved in stone or cast in bronze, to the real-life stories of the living, breathing men they recall?

In some cases it is not difficult – a trawl through archives at the County Record Office, or a 'Google' search on the Internet; but for many families and researchers the trail of a living connection in the 21st century is stone cold. It is as if these men had never lived.

Bradford-on-Avon War Memorial. *Author*

Luck and coincidence have both played important parts in the research for this book, as some of the stories reveal. Most have been pieced together from a variety of different sources; for many it has been a jigsaw puzzle, but without the benefit of a picture on the box to show how the pieces are meant to fit together. Like old jigsaws, inevitably there are still some with the key pieces missing.

The journeys of research and discovery are compelling, and at times addictive. There is a strong sense of raking over ground that has lain undisturbed since the war. Once you have set off along the road, the further you travel the more you feel driven to try and explain why things happened in a certain way and how they turned out as they did.

During the war these men and their families were known in the town and villages; the loss of sons and fathers, brothers and husbands would have been the talk of the local community. After the war some families moved away from the Bradford area and lost contact with the local community; and there were others for whom the family name died out with the loss of an only son in battle.

Three or more generations have been born and raised since 1945. Firsthand recollections of those lost men and the dramatic events in which they were caught up have long since vanished from family conversations and pub chat.

With the passage of time it will probably be impossible to discover the full stories behind all the names. New records may come to light at some time in the future; or someone might come forward with firsthand knowledge of an individual and events (although as the years pass the latter will become increasingly unlikely).

For some families, my discoveries about the fate of their relatives have been their first proper news in more than sixty years. It seems hard to believe that they have lived in ignorance of the fates of their loved ones for more than half a century.

I hope this book will reinstate in the present and future lives of the town and surrounding villages the names of these largely forgotten warriors, and that each individual will be honoured and remembered again.

Author's note

The following abbreviations have been used for local memorials and cemeteries: AR = Avon Rubber Co. memorial; BOA C = Bradford-on-Avon Cemetery; BOA WM = Bradford-on-Avon War Memorial; CC = Christ Church, Bradford-on-Avon; HT = Holy Trinity, Bradford-on-Avon; WM = War Memorial.

Chapter One

Last Stands

'Suddenly I had the sensation that I was being watched, and looking up I saw six Ju87 dive-bombers fanning out to attack. Down, *Down,* DOWN they screamed, straight at *me.* About two hundred feet up they started to pull out, clearing the ground by not more than fifty feet. Big black lumps fell from under their bellies, and these came straight for *me.*' 'Summer 1940' from *Infantry Officer: A Personal Record* (Batsford, 1943)

When British and French troops were cut off by the German army at Dunkirk in 1940, the evacuation to England of 338,226 Allied soldiers from the beaches of France between 26 May and 4 June 1940 was hailed as a miracle. It was the second in a series of humiliating routs suffered by British forces overseas that began with the expulsion of the BEF from Norway in April 1940, then the evacuation of W Force from Greece in April 1941, and culminating in the fall of Singapore to the Japanese in February 1942. They were dark times indeed for Britain and her allies.

FIRST TO FALL

Gunner Albert John Sheppard, 76 Field Regiment, Royal Artillery – Bradford-on-Avon

Albert Sheppard has the sad distinction of being the first Bradford-on-Avon serviceman to die in the Second World War through enemy action. The reason why the thirty-eight year-old gunner was travelling on a road in northern France in June 1940 and how he came to be fatally injured are not clear, nor probably ever will be, but it almost certainly happened in the chaos leading up to the fall of France.

A trawl of the Commonwealth War Graves Commission's online records quickly gave details of Albert's regiment, when he died and where he was buried, but for the events that led to his death at a hospital in the Loire, I had to cast my net wider.

A friend who knew of my research told me that Albert's son, David, worked at the local Mace convenience store so I wrote to David, care of George Stone, the proprietor. (Although I didn't know who he was at the time, for many years I used to see David early each morning in his white pick-up truck delivering the milk and daily papers.) David replied to my letter and said he was happy to meet and talk about his father, so I arranged to visit him at his home – coincidentally just a few hundred yards from my own.

Over afternoon tea I talked to David and his brother and sister, who told me about

Gnr Albert Sheppard, RA, from Bradford-on-Avon, seen here in 1939. *David Sheppard*

Albert Sheppard's headstone in the small village cemetery at Le Grand-Luce, near Le Mans in France's Loire valley. *David Sheppard*

their father, showed me photographs and his last letters home from France. They also handed me a small bundle of handwritten letters from a nursing sister to Albert's wife, Rosina. It is amazing that the nurses who cared for Albert at two different British military hospitals in France found the time to write home to Rosina Sheppard, giving news of her husband's deteriorating condition – especially with the German Army drawing ever closer and scores of wounded BEF troops admitted every day to field hospitals

The Sheppard family had carefully preserved their father's papers in a plastic wallet, but the one thing they couldn't tell me was how he had died in 1940. In the absence of any known official documents or eyewitness statements, my account of Albert's final few weeks have been pieced together from a variety of published sources. It is, at best, informed conjecture, but probably the best we can now hope for. This is what I believe happened to Albert Sheppard.

During much of May 1940 the roads in northern France and Belgium were in chaos, choked with frightened refugees fleeing before the German Army's relentless drive towards the Channel ports. Troops of the British Expeditionary Force (the BEF), and French and Belgian troops, were bravely attempting to hold the frontline. Faced with the overwhelming strength of the German Army and the Luftwaffe they were forced to retreat westwards towards the Channel coast and Dunkirk. The Luftwaffe spread fear and panic on the roads by indiscriminate machine-gunning and dive-bombing of refugees and military vehicle columns. Albert may have been travelling in a vehicle convoy that was caught on the open road and machine-gunned by roving German fighter-bomber aircraft, killing and maiming its passengers.

On 28 May 1902, Albert John Sheppard was born to Rose Ena Sheppard, a woollen cloth worker, at 20 St Margaret's Hill in Bradford-on-Avon. In June 1916 Albert went to work at the rubber factory of Spencer, Moulton & Co, by which time the family were living at 14 Bridge Street in the centre of the town.

Albert must have thought there was more to life than working in a rubber factory, so he lied about his age to enlist in the Regular Army at Trowbridge on 3 July 1919, claiming he was two years older than he actually was. He signed on for a period of six years service as a gunner with the Royal Artillery and was posted overseas to India on 11 December 1919, where he served with his regiment on garrison duties. In search of adventure to escape from a humdrum life, he was not the first to conceal his true age from a recruiting sergeant, and he was certainly not the last.

In November 1925 Albert came home to Bradford-on-Avon and left the Army. He was placed on the Reserve List and returned to his old job in the town as a rubber worker with Spencer, Moulton & Co. On Boxing Day 1927 Albert married Rosina May Wicheard at Holy Trinity parish church. They went on to raise three children – Jean, John and David.

When the Second World War broke out in September 1939, Albert was called up straight away into 76 Field Regiment, Royal Artillery, which went over to France on 15 January 1940 to reinforce the British Expeditionary Force (BEF). By this time the Sheppard family had moved to a cottage in Bradford-on-Avon a few hundred yards further along the road at 1 St Margaret's Steps.

Initially 76 Field Regiment was part of the 51st Highland Division, but in March 1940 it was transferred to General Bernard Montgomery's 3rd Infantry Division garrisoned near Louvain in Belgium.

When the Germans unleashed their Blitzkrieg against the Low Countries on 10 May, the Highland Division was holding the northern flank of the BEF line along the western banks of the River Dyle, from just north of Louvain to Wavre some 22 miles to the southwest.

Albert was at home on leave when he received an urgent telegram that ordered him to return to his regiment in France. On a road in Belgium, on the way to rejoin his unit, he sustained serious multiple gunshot wounds to the legs, knees and thighs. Albert was rushed to No 6 Casualty Clearing Station, just inside the French border at Bailleul. The next day the Germans mounted their first concerted attacks on the BEF's front line, but were quickly repulsed in the north by a 3rd Division counter-attack. On the 16th the BEF received the order to retreat from Belgium into France.

On 19 May Albert was transferred to No 10 General Hospital in the Channel port town of Dieppe, but was moved inland on 25 May to No 9 General Hospital at Le Mans on the edge of the Loire Valley. Here he remained in a very serious condition and under constant medical care, but his health continued to deteriorate and on 7 June Albert died of gas gangrene and pneumonia.

Not long after I met David Sheppard I learned that he had been taken seriously ill at work and faced major surgery. Like his father, David is a fighter. I was fortunate to meet him when he was fit and strong and still able to tell me about his father.

Gunner Albert John SHEPPARD

Service No: 1044616; 76 Field Regiment, Royal Artillery; *Died:* 7 June 1940 aged 38; *Buried:* Le Grand-Luce War Cemetery, Sarthe, France, Row B, Grave 6; *Commemorated:* BOA WM; HT; AR.

RETREAT TO THE BEACHES

Lance Corporal William Leslie James, 2 Reserve Motor Transport Company, Royal Army Service Corps – Bradford-on-Avon

When France fell in June 1940, William James was crammed onboard one of the last ships to sail from the Breton port of St Nazaire, carrying home to England the tired and desperate remnants of the BEF. Evacuation had begun on 16 June when a five-mile queue of weary men inched its way slowly forward to board vessels at the dockside, or were ferried out to waiting ships anchored in the approaches to the harbour. Complete military hospitals and convalescent depots were emptied of patients and staff and became part of the mass exodus. Loading went on all through the night and throughout the next day.

William may have witnessed Britain's worst ever-maritime disaster while he was awaiting evacuation. The White Star liner-turned-troopship SS *Lancastria*, crammed with more than 6,000 troops and civilians desperate to escape the invaders, was sunk by German dive-bombers on 17 June while laying at anchor off St Nazaire. More than 3,000 men, women and children died. Churchill suppressed news of the disaster, fearing it would damage morale at such a critical time in the war for Britain, when the fear of invasion was at its greatest.

L/Cpl Leslie James, RASC, from Bradford-on-Avon. *Theo James*

Phaleron War Cemetery in the suburbs of Athens is the last resting place of Leslie James. *Theo James*

Between 14 June and the Armistice on the 22nd when France capitulated, 124,000 British servicemen were evacuated from France on board a motley collection of lighters, tenders, ferries and destroyers. The government propaganda machine turned 'the miracle of Dunkirk' into a heroic victory won against the odds, but in reality it was a humiliating defeat for the British Army.

Ten months later William was again caught up in a futile attempt to stem another German invasion in Europe, only this time on mainland Greece and with another expeditionary force – 'W' Force. In the confusion of the sea-borne evacuation of Allied forces to Crete, German dive-bombers harried 'W' Force and caused many casualties while they waited to be taken off Greek quaysides and beaches.

William Leslie James was born in 1902 at Eton, Berkshire, the son of Theodore W. and Alice James, the husband of Lilian Violet James, and the father of a son (Clive) and daughter (Theodora) of Bradford-on-Avon. William's father, originally from London, had worked at the Royal Botanical Gardens, Kew, before moving west to raise his young family in Bath.

Before the war William worked in the Nestlé factory at Staverton. As an Army reservist he was called up a few days before war was declared and went to France in September 1939 with the BEF. William was posted to North Africa in November 1940 from where his motor transport unit was sent to Greece in the following March with 'W' Force.

Like the BEF in France, 'W' Force was a military expeditionary force intended to help the Greeks defend their country against a German and Italian invasion. When German forces marched through Yugoslavia almost unopposed and invaded Greece on 6 April 1941, Greek resistance was crushed in three weeks. The German advance was rapid and decisive, causing the under resourced 'W' Force to beat a hasty retreat south. On 20 April the Greek Army surrendered; by the 24th the Allied forces had begun their evacuation.

In convoy with an odd assortment of other road vehicles, the lorries of William James's 2 Reserve Motor Transport (RMT) Company carried soldiers, sailors and airmen, consular staff and ex-patriot British subjects, as well as nurses and walking wounded, in their trek south. During the chaotic retreat to the ports and beaches of southern mainland Greece, men and women became separated from the main body of troops and were forced to make their own way to freedom – or into captivity.

As each road convoy approached the coast, the men wrecked their vehicles to prevent them from falling into enemy hands and then marched down to the waterfront to join waiting troop columns. Others provided a rearguard, covering the harbours and beaches where troops waited patiently for nightfall when small boats and caiques would steal in to ferry them out to waiting destroyers laying offshore. Some men were told by their commanding officers that they had the choice of taking to the hills, or making good their escape by boat.

German reconnaissance aircraft appeared overhead and directed dive-bombers, which attacked Allied troops and shipping. Enemy aircraft regularly over flew the evacuation areas, but those troops who were lucky enough to find shelter in the surrounding olive groves by day remained largely undetected until they could be taken off in boats under the cover of darkness.

The desperate evacuation of 'W' Force was completed by 28 April, first to Crete and eventually to Egypt. William James died on 28 April, possibly while waiting to be ferried out to a ship. Because of the chaos that existed in southern Greece during those last desperate days, we will probably never know for sure how he met his death. By 30 April, the last of some 60,000 British, Greek, Australian and New Zealand troops had been evacuated.

Lance Corporal William Leslie JAMES

Service No: 25014; 2 Reserve Motor Transport Company, Royal Army Service Corps; *Died:* 28 April 1941 aged 38; *Buried* Phaleron War Cemetery, Greece, Grave 12.E.5; *Commemorated* BOA WM.

Chapter Two

In Which We Serve

The Royal Navy at War

'O Eternal Lord God, who alone spreadest out the heavens, and rulest the raging of the sea; who hast compassed the waters with bounds until day and night come to an end: Be pleased to received into thy almighty and most gracious protection the persons of us thy servants, and the Fleet in which we serve.'
'Prayer to be used in His Majesty's Navy every day', from The Book of Common Prayer

When war broke out in September 1939, Britain's overstretched peacetime Royal Navy was forced into a huge expansion programme, building and buying aircraft carriers and escort carriers, frigates and corvettes, forging a strong submarine service, and recreating its naval air arm that had been taken from it in 1918.

A great fleet action on the high seas by the German Navy was unlikely, but unrestricted U-boat warfare and surface raiders soon proved powerful weapons against the British war effort. German U-boats came close to starving Britain into submission in the Battle of the Atlantic, but the Royal Navy and the RAF eventually won through in a desperate war of attrition.

Not only was the Royal Navy expected to patrol the North Atlantic and protect Arctic convoys to Russia, it also had to maintain control of the Mediterranean singlehandedly after the fall of France. Escorting convoys to besieged Malta, disrupting Axis supply lines between Italy and North Africa, and supporting allied land forces in North Africa and in Greece required huge resources in ships, submarines and manpower. When the Japanese attacked Pearl Harbor in December 1941 the war became truly global, and the Royal Navy had to confront the great naval might of Japan in Far Eastern waters.

From the small prewar Royal Navy of 129,000 men, 12 battleships, 7 aircraft carriers and 100 destroyers, by 1944 the fleet had swelled to 863,000 men, 61 battleships, 59 aircraft carriers and 846 destroyers, making it one of the most powerful in the world.

THE 'MIGHTY *HOOD*'

Able Seaman Albert Frank Webb, RN, HMS *Hood* – South Wraxall

The 42,462-ton battle cruiser HMS *Hood* was the pride of the Royal Navy. Launched at Clydeside in 1918, she packed a devastating punch with her main armament of eight 15-inch guns. As the flagship of Vice-Admiral L.A. Holland, *Hood* was a powerful reminder to any would-be aggressor of the might of Britain's Navy. Able Seaman Albert Webb, 39, from South Wraxall, was one of the 1,418 officers and men who crewed the 'mighty *Hood*' – as she was popularly known – which was commanded by Capt Ralph Kerr, RN.

Albert Frank Webb was born near Melksham on 16 May 1902, the first son and second child of Frank and Sally Webb. During the First World War Albert's father had served in the Army as batman to Capt Pinckney from Bradford-on-Avon. When peace came he went to work for Pinckney at Duckmead House, but things were different now the war was over and the job didn't work out. Instead, Frank went to work for another local worthy, Sir Charles Hobhouse, at his family home in Monkton Farleigh.

Albert Webb's family always knew him as 'Alb'. When he left school Alb worked as an under-gardener for several years before deciding to join the Royal Navy. He enlisted at Portsmouth on 23 May 1918 as a 16-year-old boy seaman. Alb was promoted to ordinary seaman on his eighteenth birthday, at which time he signed on for twelve years regular service. Between then and September 1931 Alb served on the 28,000-ton battleship HMS *Revenge*, the cruiser *Dido* (5,600 tons) and the 25,000-ton battleship *Iron Duke*, until the

Bismarck* fires a salvo at HMS *Hood* during the action in the Denmark Strait on 24 May 1941. The photograph was taken from the German battle cruiser *Prinz Eugen*. *IWM HU381

The 'mighty *Hood*' as she was popularly known in the early war period. *Author's collection*

latter was paid off for a major refit. The next ten years of Alb's Navy career are not known, but he was probably re-engaged in 1932 for a further spell, and the year 1941 found him serving on the battle cruiser HMS *Hood*.

Alb's record of service describes him as standing 5ft 6¾in tall, with a 34½-inch chest, brown hair, brown eyes and a fresh complexion. His character and ability were assessed predominantly as being 'very good' and 'satisfactory' to 'superior'.

In 1935 Alb married Olive ('Olie') Cainey (1912-90) at South Wraxall church. They made their home at 35 Lower Village, South Wraxall and had three children – Janet (who died in infancy), Rex and Alan.

German Grand-Admiral Raeder envisaged the 41,673-ton battleship *Bismarck* and the heavy cruiser *Prinz Eugen* (16,974 tons) as a convoy raiding force in the Atlantic, with the potential to wreak havoc on Allied merchant shipping and its naval escorts. In fact the threat was more potent than the reality, but it led to the Royal Navy tying up ships and men on the off chance that the two Nazi warships might go on a hunting spree.

At midnight on 22 May 1941, HMS *Hood*, the battleship *Prince of Wales* and six destroyers weighed anchor and sailed from the naval base at Scapa Flow in the Orkneys. Reports had been received that the *Bismarck* and *Prinz Eugen* had left the Baltic port of Gdynia and were en-route to the Atlantic to harry British convoys.

On the morning of the 24th in the North Atlantic, the British force encountered the German warships in the Denmark Strait. High winds and heavy seas hampered *Hood*'s fire control teams and Vice-Admiral Holland had forbidden the use of radar by his warships in case the Germans picked up their transmissions.

Soon after 5.55am on the 24th, just as the British warships were turning to port to engage the German vessels, *Bismarck*'s fifth salvo landed alongside *Hood*'s starboard quarter. One or more 15-inch shells penetrated and detonated in one of the battle cruiser's aft magazines. Her stockpiles of ammunition were ignited and the conflagration spread almost instantaneously to the other after-magazines. *Hood* was quickly ripped apart by a huge explosion. Massive damage was caused to the hull, breaking the ship's back. Wreathed in smoke, *Hood* rolled over to port and began to sink by the stern, which then broke off and the forward part of the great warship reared upwards before its rapid descent into the ocean. A second massive internal explosion tore apart the bow and forward hull as it left the surface.

With two such catastrophic explosions, it is no wonder that *Hood* went down in little more than three minutes. She lies at the bottom of the Denmark Strait between Iceland and Greenland in more than 9,000ft of water, at position 63°20'N, 31°50'W. All but three men from *Hood*'s crew of 1,418 were lost. It is surprising, even, that three men survived this cataclysm. Alb Webb was one of the many hundreds who perished.

It was not long before the Admiralty issued a press communiqué and the BBC reported the loss of the *Hood* to a stunned nation. Alb's nephew, Tony Young, remembers:

> 'News of her sinking came through on the BBC a few days later, at teatime. Mother heard it and went down the road to see Olive who was laid up in bed as she was expecting their third child. Although we didn't know it at the time, there were only three survivors. I remember it because *Hood* was sunk on Empire Day, the 24th of May.
>
> 'I remember the last time he was home on leave; I suppose it would have been in the January before the *Hood* was sunk. Alb said "cheerio" as he went off, but then he came back up to the house and said it again. My mother [Alb's sister] said afterwards that this was odd, as he had never said "goodbye" twice before. Maybe he'd felt this was the last time he'd ever see her? He'd left his medals at home, too.'

The loss of HMS *Hood*, which had epitomised the strength of the Royal Navy, was the single worst Royal Navy ship loss of the Second World War. It represented a massive blow to British morale and the nation's image as the world's premier naval power.

Two days later on the 26th, *Bismarck* was fatally damaged by Swordfish torpedo bombers from HMS *Ark Royal*, and by warships that included the *Rodney*, *King George V*, and *Norfolk*. She was finished off by torpedoes fired from HMS *Dorsetshire* and sank in the eastern Atlantic at 10.40am on 27 May, in 16,000ft of water. From *Bismarck*'s crew of 2,131, *Dorsetshire* was able to rescue only 110 men.

Able Seaman Albert Frank WEBB

Service No: P/J 89697; *Ship:* HMS *Hood*, Royal Navy; *Died:* 24 May 1941 aged 39; *Commemorated:* Portsmouth Naval Memorial, Panel 49, Column 3; South Wraxall church; South Wraxall churchyard.

HOSTAGE TO FORTUNE

Able Seaman Frederick Charles Green, RN, HMS *Prince of Wales* – Bradford-on-Avon

Able Seaman Fred Green, RN, from Bradford-on-Avon. *Jill Bennett*

Speaking after the Second World War on the sinking by Japanese torpedo bombers in 1941 of HMS *Repulse* and *Prince of Wales*, Winston Churchill said: 'In all the war I never received a more direct shock.' The loss of these two capital ships contributed to the fall of Singapore and the end of British naval supremacy in the Far East until 1945. Able Seaman (AB) Fred Green of Bradford-on-Avon had survived the sinking of two other warships in the previous two years, but in a case of third time *un*lucky it was on *Prince of Wales* that his luck finally ran out.

Frederick Charles Green was born on 10 January 1917, one of eight sons to Harry Edwin (b.1877, Bradford-on-Avon), rubber worker, and Annie Green of 49 Whitehill, Bradford-on-Avon.

HMS *Prince of Wales* arrives in Singapore on 4 December 1941. Six days later on 10 December she was sunk by Japanese torpedo bombers with the loss of 327 lives. *IWM A6784*

He attended Holy Trinity School and worked for a short spell in Trowbridge before joining the Royal Navy in 1934 at Plymouth.

On completion of his training in 1936, Fred's first ship was the Royal Navy's 1,375-ton 'D' class destroyer HMS *Diamond* (Lt-Cdr N.L. Dwane, RN) on which he saw service in the Far East on the China Station with the Navy's 8th Flotilla.

Before the outbreak of war in September 1939, Fred had been drafted to the aircraft carrier HMS *Courageous* (Capt W.T. Makeig-Jones, RN). On 17 September he survived the sinking of *Courageous* in the North Atlantic, south west of Ireland, when the 22,500-ton aircraft carrier was struck on her port side by two torpedoes fired from the German U-boat *U-29* (*Kapitänleutnant* Otto Schuhart), fatally damaging her. She sank fifteen minutes later with the loss of 518 lives; 742 men were saved. In May 1941 Fred was rescued from a destroyer in the Mediterranean that was sunk by enemy action in the battle for Crete.

Returning home on survivor's leave, Fred was later drafted to the 35,000-ton 'King George V' class battleship HMS *Prince of Wales* (Capt John Leach, RN). On 25 October 1941 Fred sailed with *Prince of Wales* from Greenock in Scotland as part of Force 'Z' accompanied by the battlecruiser HMS *Repulse* and the destroyers HMS *Electra* and *Express*. *Prince of Wales* was flagship of the Eastern Fleet under the command of Admiral Sir Tom Phillips. She reached Singapore in early December.

Also onboard was Royal Marine Maurice Edwards who recalled the last time that *Prince of Wales* left British shores: 'It wasn't made clear to us that we'd be going to Singapore, and the first place I recall stopping at was Freetown. You must remember the lower decks weren't very well informed on what was going on, and I suppose the same could be said for all but the highest ranking of officers.'

Force 'Z' was sent to Singapore to deter the Japanese from attacking Malaya and the East Indies, but the Japanese were not at all deterred and launched their invasions on 8 December, the same day that they attacked Pearl Harbor on the other side of the International Date Line.

Lieutenant Haruki Iki, of the Japanese Kanoya Air Corps, wrote about the arrival in Singapore of *Repulse* and *Prince of Wales*.

> 'On 28 November 1941 the Japanese armed forces received information that the *Prince of Wales* and *Repulse* would enter port in Colombo and then head for Singapore. The Commander of our combined fleets, Isoroku Yamamoto, decided to send 36 warplanes of the type known as the "Betty" equipped with torpedoes to reinforce those already in Indo-China.... On 30 November my own fleet, known as the Kanoya Naval Force, was unofficially told to attack the *Prince of Wales* and *Repulse* using the "Betty". We immediately began training day and night to maximise the potential of our aircraft. And on 3 December a reconnaissance plane discovered the ships at Singapore.'

Admiral Phillips decided to try and intercept the Japanese landing fleets. *Prince of Wales* and *Repulse* set out from Singapore on 8 December with the destroyers HMS *Electra*,

Men frantically abandon *Prince of Wales* as she heels over and begins to sink. The destroyer HMS *Express* has come alongside to take off as many as possible. This photograph was taken from the bridge of *Express* by her captain, Lt-Cdr Francis Cartwright. The destroyer, which survived the Japanese attack, took the survivors back to Singapore where many subsequently became prisoners of war. *IWM HU2675*

Express, *Tenedos*, and HMAS *Vampire*, to try and find the Japanese vessels. They were not successful and the Japanese submarine *I-65* spotted them as they returned to Singapore.

Japanese aircraft and submarines shadowed Force 'Z' in the South China Sea off the east coast of Malaya. At 11.44am on 10 December, without any protective air cover from RAF or Fleet Air Arm aircraft, *Prince of Wales* and *Repulse* were attacked by 86 Japanese bombers and torpedo bombers from the 22nd Air Flotilla based at Saigon. *Prince of Wales* was hit by at least one aerial torpedo that did serious damage to her machinery, causing her to lose full control. At 12.23pm she suffered two more torpedo hits, followed by another two at 12.24pm. In a further high-level attack she sustained at least one more hit.

Ordinary Seaman (OS) Alan McIvor onboard *Prince of Wales* remembers the frightening events of that day:

> 'I was standing at the open entrance to our turret; suddenly there were three tremendous explosions, the force of which threw me back inside. I soon realised I'd been very lucky, for the shock of these detonations lifted our gun turret off its trunion, and I'm certain if I hadn't been sheltered from the main blast, I wouldn't be here today.

'As a result of this attack, I'd cut my head quite severely, and was losing a lot of blood. This was noticed by Petty Officer Crowther, who made me cross over the gangplank to the relative safety of HMS *Express*, which was now tied up alongside the Prince. It was the last I ever saw of him. I've no-idea if he survived the sinking.'

By 1.10pm the *Prince of Wales* was settling rapidly in the water, and at 1.20pm she turned over and sank. From a crew of 1,612 men and 20 officers, 280 sailors (including Fred Green) and 27 marines were lost. Among the dead were Admiral Sir Tom Phillips, Commander-in-Chief of the Eastern Fleet, and the *Prince*'s commander Capt John Leach.

Able Seaman Frederick Charles GREEN

Service No: D/SSX 15896; *Ship:* HMS *Prince of Wales*, Royal Navy; *Died:* 10 December 1941 aged 25; *Commemorated:* Plymouth Naval Memorial, Panel 47, Column 1; BOA WM; HT.

WHEN LUCK RUNS OUT

Petty Officer Leslie Victor Millard, RN, HMS *Bonaventure* – Bradford-on-Avon

Bonaventure was a lucky ship. In the fateful summer of 1940, with a German invasion of Britain looking increasingly likely, a large shipment of Britain's gold reserves left Greenock in Scotland for Canada on 5 July aboard three passenger liners, the battleship HMS *Revenge* and the cruiser *Bonaventure*. Serving onboard the 5,450-ton 'Dido' class cruiser HMS *Bonaventure* was Petty Officer (PO) Leslie Millard from Bradford-on-Avon. This fast convoy with its precious cargo reached Halifax, Nova Scotia, one week later.

Later that same year while serving with the Home Fleet, *Bonaventure* had been on escort duties with Convoy WS5a in the North Atlantic. On Christmas Day 1940 she was attacked by the German pocket battleship *Admiral Hipper*, although the cruiser suffered no damage. Several days later *Bonaventure* was ordered to the Mediterannean. On 28 December she intercepted the German blockade runner *Baden* (8,204 tons) about 325 nautical miles north-east of Ponta Delgada, in the Azores. The ship was en route from Santa Cruz de Tenerife to France, but due to bad weather a capture was not possible so *Bonaventure* sank *Baden* with a torpedo.

When *Bonaventure* was part of Force 'F' during the Operation 'Excess' convoy to Malta in January 1941, she was attacked by Italian torpedo boats *Circe* and *Vega* south of Pantellaria, but she succeeded in sinking *Vega* in a sharp dawn action on 10 January.

On 23 February *Bonaventure* supported an unsuccessful assault by commandos on the Dodecanese island of Castellorizo. The landing was attempted again on the night of the 27th–28th with *Bonaventure* supplying supporting firepower.

In March she escorted a convoy to Malta, and while at the island on 22 March was damaged by near misses from raiding bombers. Then she became involved in the ill-fated Greek campaign.

Leslie Victor Millard was born on 3 June 1907 at Bradford-on-Avon, one of four children, and the only son, to Albert Victor Millard (b.1885, Bradford-on-Avon), a cloth worker, and Mary Millard; and the husband of Dorothy L. Millard of Rickmansworth,

The 'Dido' class cruiser HMS *Bonaventure. Author's collection*

Hertfordshire. Leslie's father Albert was killed in action serving with the Tank Corps during the First World War on 29 September 1917.

Leslie worked as a labourer before joining the Royal Navy at Devonport on 30 November 1923 as a boy seaman on HMS *Ganges*. He was promoted to ordinary seaman on 3 June 1925 and engaged for a period of 12 years, serving on HMS *Benbow*, *Ramillies*, *Berwick*, and *Kent* (Petersfield).

Leslie's naval record of service for the period 1929-41 is not currently open to the public, but it is likely that on completion of his 12-year engagement in 1937 he signed on for a further period of service. But events overtook him when war was declared in September 1939 and he was committed to service with the Royal Navy 'for the duration of hostilities'.

Leslie's record of service describes him as standing 5ft 4in tall, with a 37-inch chest, fair hair, blue eyes and a fresh complexion. He had a scar at the side of his right eye. His character and ability were assessed as being 'very good' and 'satisfactory'.

Following the initial stages of Italy's Greek offensive in the autumn of 1940, Allied troop and supply convoys had run regularly between Greece and Egypt. Military transport and store ships of 'Lustre' Force were soon included in these convoys, as well as special fast convoys (coded 'AG' northbound and 'GA' southbound), and troop carriers that included navy cruisers.

On 27 March 1941 it became plain that a major naval action was brewing in the Mediterranean between the Italian and British fleets. Convoy GA8, which included *Bonaventure*, was held at Piraeus to avoid it straying into the threatened area. In the night action at Cape Matapan on 28-29 March, the Royal and Australian Navies conclusively beat an Italian naval force, sinking three cruisers and two destroyers, and losing none of their own ships.

On the evening of 29 March Convoy GA8 was finally allowed to leave Piraeus, accompanied by the warships *Stuart*, *Hereward* and *Griffin*, fresh from their action at Matapan. The next day *Bonaventure* joined the escort at sea and the convoy proceeded southeast across the Mediterranean to Alexandria.

At about 9.00pm on the 30th the Italian submarine *Dagabur* intercepted *Bonaventure* and launched an unsuccessful attack on the cruiser, but none of the torpedoes struck their mark. (*Dagabur* was sunk on 12 August 1942 north of Algiers by HMS *Wolverine*.)

Once night had fallen, danger returned. The Italian coastal submarine *Ambra*, commanded by Lt Mario Arilio, intercepted the convoy and proceeded to shadow the clutch of vulnerable merchant vessels with its naval escort. Not long before 3.00am on the 31st, midway between Crete and Alexandria, the watch party on *Stuart*'s bridge were brought to alert by two heavy explosions on the far side of the escort screen.

Bonaventure had strayed into the patrol area of *Ambra*, which attacked her at 2.44am 90 miles south of Crete. The cruiser sank almost immediately at position 33°20'N, 26°35'E, north of Sollum; the destroyer HMS *Hereward* rescued 310 survivors (she herself was later sunk by enemy aircraft off Crete on 29 May), but Leslie was lost with *Bonaventure*.

Stuart and *Hereward* made seven depth-charge attacks *on Ambra* after they had rescued survivors from *Bonaventure*. The submarine broke surface soon after *Stuart*'s second depth charge attack, then crash-dived and escaped. (*Ambra* was later scuttled at La Spezia on 9 September 1943 after the Italian Armistice.) The convoy reached Alexandria late in the afternoon of 31 March without further difficulty.

(Leslie's uncle, Frank Millard (b.1890, Bradford-on-Avon), also died on the Western Front on 9 April 1917 serving with the 2nd Battalion Wiltshire Regiment.)

Petty Officer Leslie Victor MILLARD

Service No: D/J 109047; *Ship:* HMS *Bonaventure*, Royal Navy; *Died:* 31 March 1941 aged 33; *Commemorated:* Plymouth Naval Memorial, Panel 45, Column 3; BOA WM; HT.

DEAD IN THE WATER

Able Seaman Frederick George Farrant, RN, HMS *Wryneck* – Westwood

Saturday 27 April 1941 was a disastrous day for Allied forces in the Mediterranean. It was the day on which the Greek capital, Athens, fell to the Germans; and the day that two British destroyers and a former Dutch passenger liner, the latter requisitioned as a troopship, were sunk by German bomber aircraft with massive loss of life. When German forces captured Crete on 31 May, mainland Greece and its islands finally collapsed under the weight of Axis occupation. Things could not have looked darker for the Allies.

The fast escort destroyer HMS *Wryneck*. *Author's collection*

Men of the Australian 6th Division Signals stand on the deck of HMS *Wryneck* on their way from Greece to Crete, 25 April 1941. Some 620 troops were evacuated to Crete by *Wryneck*, which replaced the Dutch liner turned troop transport *Pennland*, sunk by Ju88 bombers the day before. On the 27th, *Wryneck* was sunk by German dive bombers. *Australian War Memorial P02053.003*

In late April 1941, 41-year-old AB Frederick George Farrant from Westwood was on the destroyer HMS *Wryneck* that was involved in the hurried evacuation of Allied forces from Greece. Frederick, who was married to Violet Mabel Farrant and who lived at Freshford, had made the Royal Navy his career. Born on 26 March 1900 at Eastbourne, Sussex, Fred was the son of George and Mary Farrant. On 18 August 1915, the 15-year-old joined the Royal Navy at Portsmouth as a boy seaman and entered HMS *Ganges*, reputedly the toughest training ship in the Navy. Frederick was drafted to HMS *Lancaster* on 5 March 1916 and promoted to the rank of ordinary seaman on 26 March 1918, when he signed on for 12 years regular service in the Navy. Fred's record of service describes him as standing 5ft tall, with a 32-inch chest, light brown hair, grey eyes and a fresh complexion. His character and ability were assessed predominantly as being 'very good' and 'satisfactory'.

Between March 1918 and January 1929 Fred served on the following Navy ships: HMS *Euryalus*, *Geranium* (*Hydrangea*), *Tama*r, *Victory I*, *Columbine* (*Vectis*), *Cormorant*, Motor Launch *291* (*ML473*), and *Cormorant* (*Tourmaline*).

On 26 April 1919, Fred was promoted to able seaman, but during his early naval service he was twice charged with petty misdemeanours: on *ML291* for the unlawful possession of three coat hangers, and on HMS *Cormorant* for creating a disturbance.

In the absence of access to his record of service, it is not clear whether Fred left the Navy in 1930 on completion of his period of engagement, and was called up in 1939; or if he continued his service with the Navy.

In 1941, Fred was serving on the 1,300-ton 'V & W' class fast escort destroyer HMS *Wryneck* (Cdr R.H.D. Lane, RN). In the climate of confusion that followed the German invasion of Greece on 6 April 1941, British warships and transports were used to evacuate British, Commonwealth and Greek forces to Crete and Egypt.

At 4.15am on 27 April the 11,800-ton former Dutch liner *Slamat*, which had been requisitioned by the Ministry of War Transport, sailed from the Greek port of Navplion. Sailing in convoy with HM ships *Calcutta, Hotspur*, and *Isis*, the troopship SS *Khedive Ismail*, and HMS *Diamond*, she was carrying over 700 British, Australian and New Zealand troops south towards the relative safety of Crete. The convoy cleared the Gulf of Navplion at 6.00am and headed out into the open sea.

At 5.00am, 60 German bombers and fighter-bombers of *III. Stukageschwader 2 (III./StG2), Stab, II.* and *III. Jagdgeschwader 77 (Stab, II.* and *III./JG77)* and *III. Stukageschwader 77 (III./StG77)* had taken off from Almyros airfield on mainland Greece, their mission to sink the Allied troop convoys sailing south from the Greek ports of Navplion and Akra Taineron. At 6.45am the convoy was spotted by the bombers and over the next three hours the force of Messerschmitt Bf109s, Dornier Do17s, Junkers Ju87 Stukas and Ju88s pressed home a series of devastating attacks using bombs and cannon fire.

Slamat's size and distinctive appearance made her an easy target for the attackers to single out. The former liner was bombed and set on fire at 7.10am. Her commander, Capt Tjalling Luidinga, gave the order to abandon ship and the British 'Defender' class destroyer HMS *Diamond* (Lt Cdr P.A. Cartwright, RN) soon came alongside to take off her crew and troops. By about 8.00am she had taken some 600 men off the blazing liner, which by now was dead in the water. It took all Cartwright's skill to dodge the hail of bombs and bullets as he pulled away.

At about 9.00am three more destroyers joined the convoy and *Wryneck* was sent to help with the rescue work, reaching *Diamond* at about 10.00am. At 10.25am *Wryneck* signalled for fighter protection and both ships sailed together to the area where *Slamat* had been attacked to pick up any remaining survivors, then *Diamond* torpedoed the burning wreck of the liner to sink her.

It was not long before the Luftwaffe returned to attack *Diamond* and *Wryneck*. Just before 1.30pm, nine Stuka dive-bombers made a surprise attack on the two destroyers. In their first pass they machine-gunned the ships and on the second pass bombs were dropped.

Two bombs made a hole in *Diamond*'s hull and wrecked her engine room, causing the destroyer to sink within 8 minutes. The men from *Slamat* that she had rescued only a few hours before were plunged back into the sea and machine-gunned by the Stuka crews.

Wryneck managed to rescue some of these men before she, too, was hit. A bomb that

This Ju87 Stuka dive-bomber of *I./Stukageschwader 1* operated from Sicily during May 1941. German bombers including the feared Stukas of this unit were responsible for sinking the *Wryneck* and other Royal Navy ships in the Mediterranean. *Bundesarchiv*

fell on her port side crushed the hull, causing many deaths. Her 4-inch guns had been put out of action in the attack and their crews killed instantly, so they never had the chance to return fire. The second and third bombs to hit struck the destroyer's engine room and the bridge. *Wryneck* was fatally damaged. She rolled over onto her port side and sank within fifteen minutes.

Fred Farrant died on *Wryneck*, but whether he met his end on board as a result of the enemy bombs and bullets, or drowned when the destroyer sank, we may never know.

Both *Diamond* and *Wryneck* sank at 1.30pm about one mile apart, 20 miles east of Cape Maleas, off the south-eastern tip of Greece (in position 36°30'N, 23°34'E).

Twelve hours had passed since the air attacks on the convoy when at 2.30am on the 28th, HMS *Griffin* arrived from Suda Bay at the spot in the ocean where the two destroyers had been sunk. The scream of men's voices was heard coming from out of the darkness and two Carley floats were soon spotted, with fourteen survivors from *Wryneck* clinging to them. They were picked out of the water and taken by *Griffin* to Suda Bay in Crete.

A sloop containing twenty-three survivors from *Wryneck* and *Slamat* drifted in the ocean for two days and nights until an Allied ship picked it up on the morning of the 29th. Its exhausted occupants were also taken to Crete.

One officer and forty-one ratings were rescued from *Wryneck*'s crew of 146, and eight soldiers from *Slamat*. There were no survivors from *Diamond*. Approximately 253 officers and crew, as well as 700 embarked troops, were lost from both vessels. The loss of the transport *Slamat* became the worst maritime disaster in Dutch history.

Able Seaman Frederick George FARRANT

Service No: P/J43714; *Ship:* HMS *Wryneck*, Royal Navy; *Died:* 27 April 1941 aged 41; *Commemorated:* Portsmouth Naval Memorial, Panel 47, Column 3; St Mary's Church, Westwood.

OFFICIAL SECRET

Ordinary Seaman Lionel Henry Harris, RN, Westwood
Leading Stoker Robert Scrine, RN, Holt – HMS *Neptune*

In the week before Christmas 1941, two local men became victims of one of the worst – but least known – maritime disasters of the Second World War. At their homes in Westwood and Holt, the Scrine and Harris families celebrated Christmas Day the best they could without their sons around the festive table, raising glasses to their safe return at some time in the future. It was not until several months later that each family received the dreaded Post Office telegram that began: 'The Admiralty regrets to inform you …'.

The mining and sinking of the Royal Navy cruiser HMS *Neptune* in the Mediterranean on 19 December 1941 – of whose crew only one man is known to have survived – was the second most serious loss of life suffered by a Royal Navy ship in the whole of the Mediterranean campaign, and is up there among the heaviest crew losses suffered in any naval theatre of the Second World War.

Official accounts of the loss say that *Neptune* ran into an unexpected minefield in a depth of water and at a distance from mainland Libya that made it totally unexpected.

However, it is probable that the Royal Navy's higher commanders in the Mediterranean already knew that the minefield was there, but whether *Neptune*'s captain was actually aware of its existence, or indeed whether he had been fully briefed at all about its location and extent, seems to have been successfully obscured by officialdom. These are questions that today still need truthful answers from the Ministry of Defence.

Lionel Henry Harris was born in 1923 at Tetbury, Gloucestershire, the son of William J. and Dorothy E. Harris (nee Cook), latterly of Iford and Bradford-on-Avon. William Harris was a gardener at Iford Manor and lived with his family in a tied cottage that can be found on the steep bend towards the bottom of Iford Hill. Lionel had not long celebrated his 18th birthday when *Neptune* went down.

Able Seaman Robert Scrine, RN, from Holt. *Holt Village Hall*

The 'Achilles' class cruiser HMS *Neptune*. *Author's collection*

Robert Scrine was born at Bradford-on-Avon in 1913, the son of Edward P. Scrine (b.1882, at Holt, d.1959), a stonemason, and Gertrude Scrine (nee Dunford, 1895–1920).

We know nothing of Lionel's early life, and very little about Robert's, except that the latter had probably joined the Royal Navy as a boy seaman in the late 1920s. In 1941 both men were part of *Neptune*'s 750-man crew – Lionel Harris was barely out of training; Robert Scrine was an experienced hand in the engine room.

HMS *Neptune* (Capt Rory O'Conor, RN), a 7,175-ton 'Achilles' class cruiser, was the leader of a British cruiser raiding squadron, Force 'K'. Its task was to destroy German and Italian shipping convoys carrying troops and supplies across the Mediterranean from Italy to Libya, in support of Rommel's Afrika Korps in North Africa. In the early evening of 18 December the squadron left Malta to intercept an important enemy convoy bound for the Libyan port of Tripoli.

In command of *Neptune* was 43 year-old Capt Rory O'Conor. A career naval officer with a reputation for being attentive to the welfare of the sailors under his command, he was a keen sportsman and a one-time captain of the Navy's rugby team. In the Far East during the Nanking Incident in 1926, the timely gun action taken by HMS *Emerald* saved the lives of thousands of people thanks largely to her gunnery officer, Lt-Cdr Rory O'Conor. In 1933 he was appointed second-in-command of the battleship HMS *Hood* and later, as a captain, was given command of HMS *Neptune* in May 1940. O'Conor was destined for high office in the Royal Navy.

Neptune had arrived in the Mediterranean in July 1941 where she joined the 7th Cruiser Squadron and soon became involved in the transport of troops to Cyprus. In the last week of October she took part in the bombardment of enemy positions along the Libyan coast, prior to the British offensive in the Western Desert in November.

On 21 October, Force 'K' arrived at Malta from England. It comprised of the cruisers *Aurora* and *Penelope*, and the destroyers *Lance* and *Lively*. Working alongside submarines and aircraft, Force 'K' became the scourge of the enemy's convoys and completely disrupted Axis shipping traffic across the Mediterranean to Tripoli. During October, nearly 63 per cent of enemy shipping sailing from Italy to Tripoli was sunk in transit; this figure rose to 77 per cent in November. The enemy hit back with heavy air attacks on Malta.

On 27 November the *Ajax* and *Neptune*, accompanied by the destroyers *Kimberley* and *Kingston*, sailed from Alexandria to reinforce Force 'K'. Four days later, on 1 December, *Neptune* shared in the sinking of an ammunition ship, a tanker and an Italian destroyer.

On 18 December Allied photo-reconnaissance planes had revealed that Axis convoys were likely to arrive at Benghazi and Tripoli during the night. Force 'K' sailed from Malta at high speed to try and intercept the convoy off Tripoli.

The three cruisers of Force 'K', comprising *Neptune*, *Aurora* and *Penelope*, supported by the destroyers *Kandahar*, *Lance*, *Lively* and *Havock*, were steaming south in single line-ahead on a stormy night, when at 1.06am *Neptune* (which was leading) exploded a mine on one of her paravanes, north of Tripoli. For an instant she appeared silhouetted against a bright flash of flame.

Able Seaman Norman Walton, who was onboard the cruiser, recalls: 'We had been at action stations since 8.00pm, when just after midnight there was an explosion off our starboard bow. The captain stopped engines and went astern but we hit another mine, blowing away the screws and most of the stern. Then we were hit abaft the funnel [at 01.00hrs]. We were ordered up top and [the ship] had a bad list to port and [we] were down in the stern.'

In the darkness, the cruiser force had blundered into an enemy minefield. Comprising some 1,800 sea mines, the enormous minefield had been laid by the Italians in May and June 1941 and extended from between three to thirteen miles from the Libyan coast. Postwar researchers have reckoned *Neptune* struck the minefield about twelve miles from land, although the officially recorded position is about 20 miles. The Royal Navy had already lost the submarine *Undaunted* in this minefield on 13 May, and then two more submarines (*P32* and *P33*) in August 1941. After that the Navy kept clear of the area until December when Force 'K' became trapped.

Without her propellers and rudder, *Neptune* came to a standstill and was now dead in the water. In a brave attempt to reach *Neptune* and tow her out of danger, the destroyers *Kandahar* and *Lively* entered the minefield. Capt Nicholl was also cautiously edging the cruiser *Penelope* towards *Neptune* when at 3.18am *Kandahar* struck a mine. Capt O'Conor of *Neptune* flashed a warning: 'Keep away', and the *Kandahar* made a similar signal to the *Lively*.

Norman Walton again: '*Kandahar* then hit a mine and slewed off. Then we hit a fourth mine [04.03hrs] and we were lifted up and dropped back again.'

The fourth mine had exploded amidships under *Neptune*'s bridge. It was the *coup de grâce* for the already badly damaged cruiser because five minutes later she rolled over and sank. *Neptune*'s survivors abandoned ship in heavy seas.

'We saw the ship capsize and sink and gave her a cheer as she went down,' remembers Walton. 'We picked up Capt O'Conor who was clinging to what looked like an anchor buoy, and he and three other officers finished up on a cork raft attached to ours. The sea was thick with oil and most of us had swallowed a lot of it.'

About thirty-four survivors from *Neptune* were clinging to a Carley float. In the chill water of the Mediterranean in winter, men succumbed to exhaustion and hypothermia before daybreak and by sunrise just sixteen were left. In desperation, two officers tried to swim towards the *Kandahar* but never made it.

As dawn broke *Kandahar* was still afloat, but settling in the sea by the stern and awash from abaft the funnel. Scanning the ocean, *Kandahar*'s crew could see no survivors from *Neptune*. All day they watched and waited for signs of life. With the darkness of another night the sea rose, carrying *Kandahar* clear of the minefield.

At 4.00am the destroyer *Jaguar* appeared from out of the darkness, sent to the rescue from Malta. Because the sea was still so rough, *Jaguar* dared not go alongside for fear of sustaining serious damage. She positioned herself upwind of *Kandahar* and the ship's company jumped in the water. As *Jaguar* drifted slowly down towards the survivors, a total of eight officers and 170 crew were pulled from out of the sea, but 73 men were lost.

Unseen and with their situation becoming more hopeless by the hour, on the fourth day only four of *Neptune*'s crew were still left alive clinging to the raft, including Capt O'Conor who died that night.

With dawn breaking *Jaguar* fired a torpedo into *Kandahar*, sending her to the bottom, and then returned to Malta.

> 'I was in the water for three days before being able to find room aboard the raft. Most of the lads just gave up the ghost. By Christmas Eve on the fifth day there was only Price [AB Albert Price] and myself left. I saw an aircraft, waved to it, and an hour later an Italian torpedo boat came alongside and threw me a line. I collapsed when I got on board and woke up on Christmas Day in a Tripoli hospital. They told me Price was dead.'

Lionel Harris and Robert Scrine were also dead. Had they been dragged down into the depths of the Mediterranean when *Neptune* capsized? Or had they managed to escape, to number among the pathetic knot of humanity clinging to the rafts and flotsam, only to die later in the water? We may probably never know what fate befell them, but Leading Seaman (LS) Norman Walton was the only man to survive from *Neptune*'s ship's company of 763 officers and men, including 150 of the Royal New Zealand Navy.

The higher command of the Royal Navy in the Mediterranean probably knew of the existence of this minefield, but whether they recognized or understood its full extent is questionable. For reasons best known to them, the Navy kept secret the circumstances surrounding *Neptune's* loss for some time after her sinking. The next-of-kin eventually received a telegram from the Admiralty stating simply that their husbands or sons were 'missing on active war service'. *Neptune*'s loss was one of the worst disasters to befall the Royal Navy in the Second World War.

Neptune was the thirteenth British cruiser, and the *Kandahar* the fifty-ninth British destroyer, lost during the first twenty-eight months of the war. Their sinking followed closely on the heels of the losses of the *Repulse* and *Prince of Wales* off Malaya. Within a few hours of the sinking of *Neptune* and *Kandahar*, the battleships *Queen Elizabeth* and *Valiant* were severely damaged in harbour at Alexandria by Italian 'human torpedoes' and put out of action for some time. It was a bleak time indeed for Britain and her fortunes.

Ordinary Seaman Lionel Henry HARRIS

Service No: D/JX 182102; *Ship:* HMS *Neptune*, Royal Navy; *Died:* 19 December 1941 aged 18; *Commemorated:* Plymouth Naval Memorial, Panel 49, Column 2; St Mary's Church, Westwood.

Leading Stoker Robert SCRINE

Service No: D/KX 81506; *Ship:* HMS *Neptune*, Royal Navy; *Died:* 19 December 1941 aged 28; *Commemorated:* Plymouth Naval Memorial, Panel 52, Column 2; Holt WM.

Michael Orton, whose family home was on Winsley Hill, pictured as a newly appointed midshipman in the Royal Navy. *Aileen Johnson*

Lt Michael Faber, RN, the commander of HM submarine P48. *RN Submarine Museum*

THE FINAL DIVE

Sub-Lieutenant Michael Swaffield Orton, RN, HM Submarine *P48* – Bradford-on-Avon

Tracing descendants of submariner Michael Orton was a frustrating – and seemingly fruitless – task. Like the submarine in which he served, any trace of Michael and his family seemed to have vanished. For some time I struggled to corroborate the 'Orton, M.' on Bradford War Memorial with the Commonwealth War Graves Commission's forty-eight listings under this surname. The most likely match was a Sub-Lt Michael Swaffield Orton of Henfield in Sussex. Clearly, Henfield was not Bradford-on-Avon, but was Michael Swaffield Orton the right man and had he any links with Bradford?

There were no reports of his loss in the *Wiltshire Times*, nor in the *Bath and Wilts Chronicle* of the period. On the off-chance I tried *The Times* personal columns, which is where eventually I found a brief death notice for Michael that established the link to Bradford-on-Avon that I needed. A further check through old telephone directories revealed that in 1939 Aileen Orton had moved to a house on Winsley Hill called The Woodlands.

In one of those serendipitous moments that can sometimes happen when trawling the Internet, I stumbled across an Orton family tree compiled by Australian academic Dr John Cameron Ward. I contacted Dr Ward who put me in touch with a cousin of Michael Orton in England, who in turn kindly introduced me to Michael's younger sister, Aileen, who lives in Hampshire. Subsequently, in the course of several conversations with Aileen I found the missing pieces to the Orton family puzzle that helped me complete Michael's story.

Michael Swaffield Orton and his twin sister Rosemary were born in 1920 at Broadstairs, Kent. Before the First World War their father, Charles James Swaffield Orton MBE (b.1879, Normanton-on-Stour), had been a civil engineer with the Canadian Pacific Railway at Montreal. He returned to England on the outbreak of war to work in London for the Ministry of Munitions, which was responsible for overseeing and coordinating the production and distribution of munitions for the war effort.

While their family was still young, Charles and Aileen Orton (nee Shannon, b.1891, India) chose to move away from London to Gloucestershire for the education of their children – Owen, Michael, Rosemary and Aileen – where they made their home at Douro Court in the Regency spa town of Cheltenham. Michael was educated at Cheltenham Boys' College where he took up fencing and competed in many schoolboy championships in which he excelled. He was a keen sportsman and particularly enjoyed rowing, which may have drawn him towards a career in the Royal Navy.

When Charles Orton died at the beginning of the Second World War, Aileen decided to move her family to be nearer an aunt who lived in Bath. She took a liking to Bradford-on-Avon which was where she bought a house called The Woodlands, off Winsley Hill. After the war Aileen moved away to the Sussex village of Henfield, to be with her sister, where she lived until the mid-1960s.

Michael's twin sister Rosemary joined the WRNS on the outbreak of war, rising to the rank of Third Officer. She later married the Reverend Philip Barry, vicar of Holy Trinity, Bradford-on-Avon.

On 1 January 1939, Michael joined the Royal Navy as an officer cadet, having sat and passed the special entrance examination. He underwent basic training in the shore establishment HMS *Norfolk* at Devonport and two days before war was declared Michael was promoted to midshipman and appointed to the 'Hunt' class minesweeper HMS *Quorn*, followed by a further appointment to HMS *Berwick*. Michael was promoted to sub-lieutenant on 1 February 1941 and on 9 November he volunteered for the submarine service, joining the submarine course at HMS *Elfin* in Blyth, Northumberland, for basic training as a submarine officer. He then joined the submarine depot ship HMS *Cyclops* at Rothesay on the River Clyde in Scotland, on 10 February 1942. *Cyclops* was the old, uncomfortable depot ship for the Royal Navy's 7th (Training) Submarine Flotilla. She was primarily the training base for Royal Navy submariners, and mother ship to a mixed bag of geriatric First World War 'H' and 'L' class submarines that were no longer considered fit for operational patrols. Michael spent time sea training around the craggy coasts of western Scotland and Northern Ireland on the 'H' class submarine *H33*. Despite their cramped size and lack of a deck gun, the 'H' class had been enormously popular amongst submariners during the First World War. At the outbreak of the Second World War they were obsolete, but were retained in training and coastal warfare roles to help the Royal Navy cope with heavy losses to its submarine fleet during the early stages of the war.

Joel Blamey, in his book *A Submariner's Story*, remembers his time training on the 'H' class:

> 'To say that I had qualms about diving in one of these small uncomfortable little submarines would be an understatement. I can't say that I suffered from claustrophobia any more than the average person when shut up in a small space, but these were single hulled boats that rolled and pitched like the very devil in any sort of sea. Then there was the ever present smell of diesel fuel permeating throughout the boat, mingling with the acid stench of battery gas. We trainees, being additional to the crew, made space even more restricted, and when on the surface the noise of the main engines in this steel shell was deafening.'

On 22 May Michael was appointed to the newly commissioned submarine *P48* as her torpedo and gunnery officer. The 630-ton 'U' class submarine had been launched a month earlier on 15 April at Barrow in Furness, and was commissioned two months later on 18 June, joining the 3rd Submarine Flotilla at Lerwick.

Known officially as 'War Emergency 1940 and 1941 programmes, short hull', the British 'U' class comprised forty-nine small submarines built just before and during the Second World War. They carried a crew of between twenty-seven and thirty-one men, and were armed with up to ten torpedoes and a single 3-inch deck gun.

Most of the 'U' class served with the Royal Navy's 10th Submarine Flotilla that was based on the Mediterranean island of Malta. Nineteen of the class were lost during the war: thirteen boats in the Mediterranean and the remainder in the North Sea and Atlantic Ocean. They proved to be capable vessels in the confined waters of the North Sea, but were particularly successful in the warmer waters of the Mediterranean. Thirty-four more boats were ordered in 1940 and 1941, forming the third group of 'U' class boats (which included *P48*). They were similar to the second group, and to improve streamlining their hulls were lengthened by 5ft.

In 1940, in view of the high number of submarines likely to be ordered, the decision was taken to suspend the practice of naming them. These boats were initially labelled *P31* to *P39*, *P41* to *P49*, and so on, instead of receiving names. However, at the end of 1942 the Prime Minister, Winston Churchill, personally ordered that all submarines were to receive names, but eight boats, including *P48*, were lost in service with the Royal Navy before they could be named.

P48's first war patrol was from Lerwick on 18 July when she sailed with Lt Michael

A rare photograph of HMS *P48*, seen on her acceptance trials prior to commissioning in May 1942. *RN Submarine Museum*

The Royal Navy's 10th Submarine Flotilla was based on Malta. Photographed in January 1943, here are HMS *United* (left) with HMS *Unison* (centre). The bows of HMS *Unseen* are in the foreground. *IWM A14512*

Faber as her commander for a patrol area off Trondheim Zenit. It proved an uneventful eleven days at sea, the highlight for the crew being the sighting of dozens of sea mines floating in the North Atlantic. During August, *P48* and her crew left Britain for the warmer waters of the Mediterranean and the 10th Submarine Flotilla at Malta.

Rommel's Afrika Korps, which was fighting the British 8th Army in North Africa, was reliant on supplies delivered by shipping convoys to ports in North Africa. The island of Malta lay on the ocean supply routes between North Africa and Italy, so Axis merchant shipping targets and their naval escorts were numerous. Within a short time of weighing anchor in Malta and sailing on patrol, the submarines of the Royal Navy's 10th Flotilla would be in action against the convoys and suffering the inevitable depth charge counter-attacks.

P48 sailed from Gibraltar on 31 October to carry out submarine beacon duties at 'B' Sector, Algiers, in preparation for the impending Allied landings. On 4 November Faber carried out a night and day reconnaissance of the five sector beaches from the submarine, and four days later *P48* landed a beach working party. Faber and *P48* were part of a screen of British submarines that guided in the 340-strong invasion fleet with infra red signal beams. Faber was then ordered to sail to Libya to patrol off Bizerta, which is where *P48* arrived on 12 November with submarines *Ursula* and *P45* for a patrol off Marittimo. A frustrating couple of days followed in which Faber made torpedo attacks on several enemy merchant ships and their destroyer escorts, but his torpedoes missed their mark. *P48* returned to Malta on 18 November before sailing on the 26th for her second war patrol to cover the approaches to Tunis, and in the Tyrrhenian Sea. It proved to be yet another frustrating patrol in which *P48* attacked enemy shipping targets but without scoring any hits.

Following the landings at Oran, 29-year-old Lt Michael Elliot Faber, had become concerned about his boat's lack of success. Born in Sussex but raised in London, Michael Faber had entered the Royal Naval College Dartmouth in 1929 at the age of 14. He served on the antiquated submarine depot ship HMS *Lucia* (2nd Submarine Flotilla) at Devonport before promotion to lieutenant in 1938 and his first submarine appointment to HMS *Starfish* (she was destined to be lost in 1940). During the Second World War Faber was mentioned in despatches.

On *P48* Faber had a capable first lieutenant in 22-year-old volunteer reservist Stephen Spring-Rice. Known as 'Sprice' to everyone, he had been a King's Scholar at Eton, and an exhibitioner at King's College Cambridge, before volunteering for the Royal Navy in 1940. He had recently transferred from *P48*'s sister submarine *Ursula*. Twenty-two year-old Lt Peter Caddy from Horsell, Surrey, was the fourth officer on *P48*. He had joined the Navy in 1938 as an officer cadet and first saw service on the battleship *Malaya*. Under Faber's command there was a first class ship's company of thirty men.

Since her commission in June, *P48* had completed three 'blank' patrols in which she had sunk nothing. Faber felt anxious about letting his crew down. John Wingate, a fellow submariner on the 10th Flotilla and a friend of Faber since schooldays, recalls how *P48*'s captain confided in him and told him how he felt responsible for this perceived poor result. 'We talked far into the night on 10 December: it was clear that Faber was suffering all the stress that goes with bolstering the morale of others while he was suffering from a lack of self-confidence. That was the last time I saw him.'

Capt Simpson, commanding the 10th Flotilla at Malta, wanted to keep as many of his submarines as possible in harbour for Christmas. It fell to the newest arrivals *P48* and *P51* (Lt M.L.C. Crawford), with HMS *Ursula* who had just returned for her second commission, to spend Christmas out on patrol.

On 21 December *P48* sailed from Malta on her third Mediterranean patrol, heading for the 'billet' recently vacated by HMS *P44* in the mouth of the Gulf of Tunis. She never returned, but we know from Italian naval records how she may have met her end:

> 'The Italian "Fortunale" class torpedo boats *Ardente* and *Ardito* sailed from Palermo on 24 December, escorting two merchant ships, *XXI Aprile* and *Carlo Zeno*. At 11.20am on Christmas Day, 12 miles northwest of the island of Zembra in the Gulf of Tunis, a submarine asdic contact was obtained at 2,600 metres. Twelve depth charges were dropped. The senior officer in *Ardente*, after waiting for a quarter of an hour for the disturbed water to subside, then regained contact.
>
> 'After the third attack with another twelve depth charges, the bridge sighted a confused boiling on the sea. Thinking that the submarine was about to surface, all guns were trained on this spot. But the boiling slowly subsided and when the echo from the submarine was again obtained, the target's position was stationary at a depth of 200 metres.'

To make absolutely certain of its kill, *Ardente* carried out a fourth and final attack, dropping twelve more depth charges. Reassured of their success, *Ardente* and *Ardito* then rejoined their convoy and escorted it to Bizerta.

There were no other British submarines operating in the Gulf of Tunis on Christmas Day 1942, so *Ardente*'s kill was almost certainly *P48*. The Admiralty declared HMS *P48* overdue on 5 January 1943, lost with all thirty-four hands, which included Michael Orton. Her estimated position at the time of loss was 37°15'N,10°30'E. When news broke that *P48* had been lost, the luckiest man in Malta was the boat's Asdic operator who had been loaned to *P48*'s sister submarine, HMS *Unbroken*, to replace their own man.

The official statement of Royal Navy losses published in 1947 lists the date of *P48*'s loss as 4 January 1943, the cause as 'lost, possibly mined, Gulf of Tunis'. The Commonwealth War Graves Commission gives the date of Michael Orton's death as 5 January 1943; but the Royal Navy lost no submarines on that day.

Ardente's days were also numbered. She had been launched at Genoa only a month after *P48*, but less than three weeks after sinking the 'U' class submarine the *Ardente* collided with the Italian destroyer *Grecale* on 12 January and sank. Her commander, Lt Rinaldo Ancillotti, was lost.

Sub-Lieutenant Michael Swaffield ORTON

Ship: HM Submarine *P48*, Royal Navy; *Died:* 5 January 1943 aged 23; *Commemorated:* Portsmouth Naval Memorial, Panel 73, Column 1; BOA WM; HT; Henfield Club Memorial, Sussex.

'COURAGE, SKILL AND DETERMINATION'

Commissioned Engineer John William Heavyside DSC, RN, HMS *Eclipse* – Holt

The pursuit and sinking of the German destroyer *Z26* on 29 March 1943 by the Royal Navy destroyer HMS *Eclipse* is one of the epic stories of the Arctic convoys. *Eclipse*, whose chief engineer was John Heavyside from Holt, was part of the naval escort for Convoy PQ13. Throughout the action *Eclipse* was handled with great skill and determination, in very severe weather conditions with one of her guns out of action owing to ice. Spray, which swept over the guns and bridge, immediately froze upon anything it touched; gun decks were icy and gun wells full of water and ice. The use of binoculars by the destroyer's bridge and director personnel was almost impossible.

For their bravery in this action, nineteen of *Eclipse*'s crew were recommended for awards by their captain, Lt-Cdr Edward Mack, DSO, DSC, RN. They included a Distinguished Service Cross (DSC) to John Heavyside. His award was gazetted on 23 June 1942, 'for great courage, skill and determination in action with the enemy whilst escorting a convoy'. In his recommendation to the Rear Admiral Home Fleet on 7 April 1942, Mack wrote: 'Mr Heavyside's previous untiring work was undoubtedly responsible for the efficient running of all machinery during the action. After damage had been received, he behaved with great calm and competence and was the greatest assistance to me.'

John William Heavyside was born at Trowbridge on 14 July 1899, the son of John Henry (b.1874, Bootle, Merseyside), a leather dresser, and Florence Heavyside (b.1875, Lydney, Gloucestershire) of the Common, Holt; and the husband of Emily Heavyside. John joined the Royal Navy as a boy seaman at the age of 15½ on 3 January 1915. His initial training was at Devonport Barracks (HMS *Vivid)* followed by trade specialisation at the mechanical training establishment, HMS *Indus,* in Chatham. John's naval record of service notes that on enlistment he was slightly built at 5ft 0½in tall, with brown hair, grey-blue eyes and a fresh complexion. The rigours of boy seaman training clearly improved his physique because when he was engaged in the Navy (as M11340) for 12 years service as an artificer on 14 July 1917 – his eighteenth birthday – he had grown 2½in in height, and his chest had expanded from 31¼in to 37in.

Between 1915 and 1929, John served on HMS *Vivid* (seven times), *Indus*, *Lion*, *Greenwich*, *Columbine, Warspite*, *Egmont II*, *Osprey*, *Heather,* and *Comus*. On 1 November 1926 he was promoted to engine room artificer second class.

During the twelve years he spent as a rating, John's personal character was rated as being 'very good' and his ability 'excellent'. He was clearly a prime candidate to be offered a commission in the Royal Navy – which he was on 15 March 1929.

Between 1 October 1931 and 1939 John served as a warrant engineer on the following Royal Navy ships: HMS *Malaya* (31,100-ton battleship) 1932; *Medway* (submarine depot ship) 1934; *Skipjack* (minesweeper) 1937; *Forth* (submarine depot ship) 1938; *Cardiff* (4,200-ton cruiser) 1938.

Commissioned Engineer John Heavyside, DSC, RN, from Holt. *Holt Village Hall*

John was appointed to the 'E' class destroyer HMS *Eclipse* in 1939 as a commissioned engineer (which was the equivalent of a sub-lieutenant in the Engineering Branch). *Eclipse* was one of many Royal Navy warships that escorted Arctic merchant shipping convoys carrying essential supplies of war materials to Russia. These convoys and their escorts not only had to endure appalling weather, but they also had to fight off determined attacks by enemy warships, submarines and aircraft.

On 10 March 1942, Convoy PQ13 sailed from Loch Ewe in Scotland destined for Murmansk in north Russia, carrying war supplies. Nineteen merchantmen were escorted by a large force of Royal Navy warships, including a close escort provided by the destroyers HMS *Eclipse* and *Fury*, and the cruiser *Trinidad.*

Severe gales, high seas and snowfall scattered the convoy and its escort. On 29 March three warships of the German 8th Destroyer Flotilla, stationed at Kirkenes in north Norway, encountered the escort in the Arctic Ocean off North Cape, and north of the Russian port of Murmansk. In atrocious weather conditions *Eclipse* fought a gun and torpedo action with the three 'Narvik' class destroyers, *Z24, Z25* and *Z26,* which began at 9.50am in snow and poor visibility. In company with HMS *Fury* and the cruiser *Trinidad*, *Eclipse* pursued the 2,600-ton destroyer *Z26* (*Korvettenkapitän* Georg Ritter von Berger) in the Barents Sea, hitting her six times with 4.7in shells. She inflicted further damage on *Z26* until the German destroyer was fully ablaze and lying dead in the water, her stern awash. During the action the cruiser *Trinidad* was hit and disabled by one of her own torpedoes.

Eclipse was about to finish off *Z26* with a torpedo attack when the two other German destroyers suddenly appeared from out of the snow squalls and shelled *Eclipse*, which was hit and her crew suffered heavy casualties. She in turn fired a salvo that hit one of the enemy vessels (which luckily did not pursue her), but in view of her damaged

Sister destroyers HMS *Eclipse* and HMS *Echo* at speed off the coast of Iceland in March 1942. *IWM A8089*

condition her captain, Lt-Cdr Mack, decided to break off the action and proceed alone to Murmansk. *Eclipse* arrived alongside at 2.00pm on 30 March, holed twice above the waterline and with her stern a mess, short of fuel and carrying nine men onboard in need of urgent medical attention.

Later in 1943 *Eclipse* was deployed from the North Atlantic to the Mediterranean. On 23 July she was jointly responsible with HMS *Laforey* for sinking the Italian 'Ardua' class submarine *Ascianghi* 10 miles off Augusta, Sicily. The submarine had torpedoed and seriously damaged the cruiser HMS *Newfoundland*, but had then been forced to the surface by depth charges from *Eclipse* and *Laforey*. *Ascianghi* was then sunk by gunfire from the destroyers.

Eclipse was responsible on her own for attacking and badly damaging two German torpedo boats, *TA12* and *TA10*, on 22 August and 23 September respectively. Also on 23 September, she sank the Italian 2,428-ton transport MV *Gaetano Donizetti* east of Rhodes, which was sailing under the German flag and carrying Italian PoWs. Badly damaged by gunfire, the transport capsized and went down with the loss of her entire crew of about 220, and more than 1,500 Italian servicemen.

In late October 1943, *Eclipse* sailed from Alexandria carrying 200 soldiers of the 4th Battalion Royal West Kent Regiment (The Buffs) to reinforce the British garrison on the Greek island of Leros. On 23 October at around midnight, east of the Dodecanese island of Kalymnos, *Eclipse* struck a mine that detonated under her forward boiler room and set the fuel tanks ablaze. She quickly took on a heavy list and broke in two, spilling burning fuel into the sea. Within three minutes she sank in position 37°01'N, 27°11'E.

There was heavy loss of life on the destroyer: 135 soldiers died along with 135 of the ship's company that included John Heavyside.

Commissioned Engineer John William HEAVYSIDE

Ship: HMS *Eclipse*, Royal Navy; *Died:* 23 October 1943 aged 44; *Commemorated:* Plymouth Naval Memorial, Panel 78, Column 2; Holt WM.

IN SEARCH OF TONY

Paymaster Midshipman Guy Anthony Brereton Underwood, RN, HMS *Orion* – Bradford-on-Avon

At its highest point the volcanic island of Pantelleria towers 2,743ft over the waters of the Mediterranean. Lying midway between Sicily and Tunisia the rocky outcrop once belonged to Italy, but during the Second World War it was of strategic interest to the Allies. Pantelleria was considered crucial to their plans for the invasion of Sicily, as well as being a potential supply base for Allied forces in the Middle East and Malta. When German forces in Tunisia surrendered, the island became a target for British and American bombers and warships.

In the spring of 1943, 19-year-old Tony Underwood from Bradford-on-Avon was serving as a Royal Navy paymaster midshipman on the 7,270-ton 'Leander' class light cruiser HMS *Orion*. (Paymasters were in the Accountant Branch of the Navy, which was later renamed the Supply and Secretariat Branch. They carried out a range of administrative roles on board ship, including secretary to the captain, supervision of ship's writers, payment of wages and salaries to the crew, and management of ship's supplies.)

As a warship of the Royal Navy's 15th Cruiser Squadron of the Mediterranean Fleet based in Malta, *Orion* was deployed with other vessels of the squadron to intercept enemy supply convoys sailing between Italy and North Africa, and for the protection of Allied shipping convoys.

Orion was chosen to support the planned military operation to invade Pantellaria. During May and June enemy positions on the island were subjected to continuous bombardment from the sea and air culminating in the invasion of the island on 10 June.

Guy Anthony Brereton Underwood, who was known to his family as Tony, was born in 1924 in the comfortable West London suburb of Kensington, the son of Charles Guy (b.1882, London), and Grace Audrey Antoinette Underwood (nee Griffith, b.1892, Steyning, Sussex), of Belcombe House, Bradford-on-Avon. Tony's father Charles had been a lawyer in London before moving to Bradford-on-Avon, where he entered local politics as a town councillor and set up in Bath as a solicitor.

A personal announcement in *The Times* stated that Tony Underwood had died on active service in Malta as a result of an accident. Another source noted that his death and that of a petty officer from the same ship was due to an air crash. Working from the assumption that more than two people died in this air crash (because neither man was an airman, nor was actually piloting an aircraft, therefore someone else must have been) it is not unreasonable to assume that any other casualties may have been buried in the same cemetery on Malta as Tony Underwood.

I checked the cemetery records for Malta (Capuccini) Naval Cemetery and found that

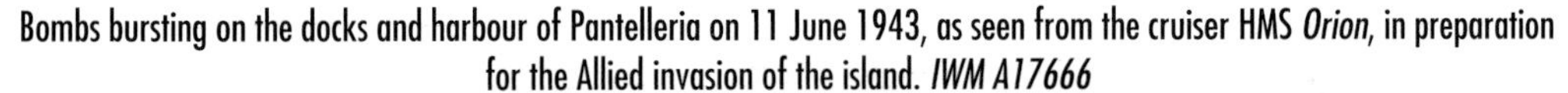

Bombs bursting on the docks and harbour of Pantelleria on 11 June 1943, as seen from the cruiser HMS *Orion*, in preparation for the Allied invasion of the island. *IWM A17666*

the pilot and navigator of a 108 Squadron RAF Beaufighter had died on the same day and were buried in the cemetery.

The Beaufighter was a two-man aircraft so it was most unlikely to have been carrying two naval personnel as passengers. Could the aircraft have crashed and killed people on the ground? A request to the RAF Museum for accident record cards of RAF aircraft that had crashed in Malta on 5 May 1943 revealed that a 108 Squadron Beaufighter had crashed and burned on take-off from RAF Luqa. Was Tony Underwood ashore near Luqa when the aircraft crashed, and could it have been a tragic case of him being in the wrong place at the wrong time? I was not convinced.

Not entirely satisfied with this line of enquiry I contacted the HMS *Orion* Association whose secretary, Kay West (whose late husband had been a Royal Marine on the cruiser during the war), placed a request for me in the association's newsletter. I asked for anyone who recalled Tony Underwood or the events of 5 May 1943 (whatever they might have been) to contact me. Two months passed before I received an email from an excited Kay saying 'the newsletter has only just gone out and I've had a reply from a member about your enquiry'. I phoned Kay and she gave me the telephone number of former Able Seaman Fred Strudwick, who was serving on *Orion* in May 1943 and who said he recalled the incident in which Tony Underwood had lost his life. I telephoned Fred at his home in Croydon and this is what he told me:

> 'Around the time when Midshipman Underwood was killed I know we were at sea. It was when we were bombarding the islands of Pantellaria and Lampedusa. May 1943 was a very busy time for *Orion*.
>
> 'When we went to sea we used to wonder where to put the midshipmen. The fellows were always taking the Mickey out of them because they were so young, but the truth was we were all mates together and we got on well.
>
> 'I was what was called a layer rating, inside the gun turret elevating and training the guns. On 5 May we were at action stations and I was closed up inside the twin 4-inch turret (called F2) on the starboard side. Something hit the ship and there was this bump. It wasn't the sound that was normally made by a shell hit. I heard later that it was a dud from an enemy shore battery that had gone straight through the starboard side and into the gunroom where Tony Underwood was. It didn't go off but the shell hit him and it killed him. The damage to the ship was above the waterline and was minimal.
>
> 'There aren't many of us left now that remember this incident, but it has always remained in my mind. It's just something you don't make up. When I returned to Malta this year [2008] for a reunion I went to the Cappuccini Cemetery to find his grave. I saw a lot of other sailors' graves, but it made me feel real good when I found him. It was a funny feeling. He was one of "ours" and I put a few flowers on his grave.'

Paymaster Midshipman Guy Anthony Brereton UNDERWOOD
Ship: HMS *Orion*, Royal Navy; *Died:* 5 May 1943 aged 19; *Buried:* Malta (Capuccini) Naval Cemetery, Prot Sec (Officers') Plot E, Collective Grave 10; *Commemorated:* BOA WM; HT.

A DEADLY HARVEST

Commander Erlysman Patrick Hamilton Pinckney, RN, HMS *Hannibal* – Monkton Farleigh

Cdr Patrick Pinckney, RN, from Monkton Farleigh.
John Pinckney

On 23 October 1943, Commander Patrick Pinckney sailed on the minesweeper HMS *Cromarty* from the newly established British naval base at Taranto in southern Italy. That same day *Cromarty* hit a mine and sank taking many of her crew down with her, including Patrick Pinckney.

Erlysman Patrick Hamilton Pinckney ('Patrick') was born at 72 St George's Road, Belgravia, London, on 3 June 1902, the son and first of two children (his sister, Frances Jeanie Helena, 1905–62) to Capt Erlysman Charles Pinckney, mechanical engineer, (b.1872, Charlcombe, Bath; d.1954, Trowbridge), and Agnes Ponsonby Pinckney (nee Adair, b.1867, Scotland; d.1932, Bradford-on-Avon), latterly of Duckmead House, Bradford-on-Avon. Capt Pinckney JP later became a chairman of the Bradford-on-Avon bench of magistrates.

Patrick went to the Royal Naval Colleges at Osborne, Isle of Wight, and Dartmouth, in Devon. It is possible that he saw active service in the First World War as a boy seaman; indeed, the *Wiltshire Times* reported that 'he served as a midshipman on various cruisers and was in action against the German Fleet', but it has not been possible to corroborate this.

Patrick was promoted midshipman on 15 September 1919 and his first appointment was to the battleship HMS *Benbow* (25,000 tons) where he remained until 3 July 1920 when he was appointed to another battleship, the 23,000-ton *Centurion*. He was promoted to sub-lieutenant on 15 September 1922, lieutenant on 15 June 1924, and lieutenant commander in June 1932.

Appointments to a succession of ships in Home Waters, the Atlantic, Mediterranean and the Far East followed: *Walrus* (torpedo-boat destroyer), 15 August 1923; *Newark* (minesweeper), 3 February 1926; *Venomous* (destroyer, 4th Flotilla, Mediterranean Fleet), 9 April 1926; *Sesame* (destroyer, Atlantic Fleet), 17 October 1928; *Whirlwind* (destroyer, 5th Flotilla, Atlantic Fleet), 8 September 1930; *Berwick* (cruiser, 5th Cruiser Squadron, China Station), 31 October 1934.

On 22 November 1937 Patrick was given his first seagoing command in the guise of the 510-ton fishery protection patrol vessel HMS *Kingfisher*. Here he remained for nine months until leaving to command the 593-ton armed trawler *Lilac* on 15 June 1939, as Fisheries Liaison Naval Officer English Channel.

Framed in the supports of the main block ship sunk by the Germans in Tripoli harbour, HMS *Cromarty* makes her way into the harbour in February 1943. *IWM E22406*

After the outbreak of the Second World War Patrick served with distinction on the base ship HMS *Paragon* at Hartlepool, where he was Senior Officer Auxiliary Patrol. His duties placed him in charge of the Inner Coastal Patrol off the English northeast coast, with a motley collection of minesweepers and converted trawlers under his command. Once war had begun, to rapidly increase its numerical strength in vessels the Royal Navy created 'auxiliary patrol boats' by commandeering trawlers and drifters and arming them with guns. These vessels were used for minesweeping and other coastal patrol duties.

On 27 January 1941 Patrick was appointed to HMS *Boscawen* at Portland Naval Base on the south coast as Port Minesweeping Officer. Here he remained until 18 April 1943 when he went overseas to Gibraltar and was placed in command of the Royal Navy's minesweeping activities for the Mediterranean. He was serving at HMS *Hannibal*, the shore-based Headquarters (HQ) of the Royal Navy Mediterranean Fleet at Allied HQ – initially at Algiers, and from late September 1943 at Taranto in Italy – when he met his death.

Following the invasion of Italy on 9 September, the 14th Minesweeping Flotilla was ordered to the Straits of Bonefaccio between Corsica and Sardinia for minesweeping operations. Patrick Pinckney was a passenger on the flotilla commander's ship, the 'Bangor' class minesweeper HMS *Cromarty*, which hit a mine in the straits on 23 October and blew up. Four officers and sixteen ratings died from the 50-man crew, including Pinckney, whose body was never recovered. The minesweeper *Seaham* sailed into the minefield and picked up survivors including *Cromarty*'s badly injured captain, Lt-Cdr Charles 'Bunty' Palmer, RNZNVR.

Patrick Pinckney is also commemorated on a memorial in the chancel of St Peter's parish church in the village of Charlton St Peter, near Upavon, Wiltshire. Patrick's grandfather, Erlysman Pinckney, MA, JP, had been born at Berwick St James, near Salisbury, in 1838.

Commander Erlysman Patrick Hamilton PINCKNEY

Ship: HMS *Hannibal,* Royal Navy; *Died:* 23 October 1943 aged 41; *Commemorated:* Portsmouth Naval Memorial, Panel 72, Column 3; St Peter's Church, Monkton Farleigh; St Peter's Church, Charlton St Peter, Wiltshire.

SNOWBLIND

Lieutenant-Commander Antony Francis Hall, RN, 781 Naval Air Squadron – Monkton Farleigh

By the time he celebrated his thirty-fifth birthday, Antony Hall had been wedded to the Royal Navy for the greater part of his life. He had joined the Senior Service in 1922 as a thirteen year-old cadet at Dartmouth and within fourteen years he was a qualified Fleet Air Arm fighter pilot as well as second-in-command of a navy destroyer.

Antony Francis Hall was born on 24 January 1909 at Transvaal, South Africa, the second child and son of the Rev Mildmay Francis Hall MA (Oxon) (d.1948), and Lilian Hall (nee Mordaunt, 1882–1969). At the time of his birth, Antony's father had recently moved on from his living as priest in charge at Wakkerstroom, South Africa, to become rector of Potchefstroom. The family returned to England in 1912 when Mildmay was appointed rector of Badgworth, Somerset, where he remained until 1929. From then until 1944 he was rector of Monkton Farleigh. Antony married Albertine Isabel Briggs (1907–82) and they had two children, Caroline and Julian.

In September 1922 Antony entered the Royal Naval College Dartmouth. As a cadet and midshipman from 1926 to 1929 he served on the 'Queen Elizabeth' class sister battleships HMS *Barham* and *Warspite*, joining *Warspite* in January 1929.

Lt-Cdr Tony Hall, RN, 'performing a difficult feat of navigation' (as he wrote on the back of this photograph). *Caroline Hall*

Hawker Sea Hurricane aircraft similar to that in which Lt-Cdr Antony Hall, RN, died in a crash in 1944.
Author's collection

He was promoted sub-lieutenant on 16 December 1929 and on completing his exams for lieutenant in 1930 was appointed to the destroyer *Tetrarch.*

In 1931 he was selected for pilot training and learned to fly with No 20 Naval Pilots' Course at Leuchars in Scotland. On graduation in April 1932 he was awarded his naval pilot's wings (he had been promoted lieutenant on 19 September 1931).

From 1932 to 1936 Antony served as a Fleet Air Arm pilot on the carriers *Furious, Glorious* and *Courageous*, at home and in the Mediterranean, and also in 1935 on the 29,150-ton battleship *Ramillies.* From 1936 to 1938 Antony was made second-in-command successively of the destroyers *Witch* and *Garland.*

On 8 July 1938, Antony was posted to 822 Naval Air Squadron (NAS) which was embarked on the 22,890-ton carrier HMS *Furious*, followed by promotion to lieutenant commander on 16 September 1939. After the outbreak of war *Furious* was employed on hunting German U-boats in the Atlantic. On 15 April 1940 Antony was posted to 767 NAS, a deck landing training unit, on the carrier *Argus* (15,750 tons, originally the liner *Conte Rosso*), and then to the carrier *Eagle* on 29 March 1941.

The 22,200-ton aircraft carrier was assigned to Freetown on the West African coast. Her Sea Hurricanes, flying from Port Sudan, attacked Italian ships at Massawa en route. *Eagle* arrived at Freetown in early May where she remained until October 1941.

Returning to Britain for a refit she rejoined the Mediterranean Fleet early in 1942 and in February she carried much needed aircraft for defence of the beleaguered island of Malta, an operation that was repeated again in May and twice in June. Between 12 and 16 June, *Eagle* also provided air cover for the convoy of Operation 'Harpoon' to Malta.

Tony left *Eagle* for a shore-based posting to HMS *Condor* at Arbroath, Scotland, on 27 July 1942. He was posted to another shore base on 23 March 1943 when he joined HMS *Daedlus* at Lee-on-Solent, Hants, as a staff officer. Later that year when Tony was onboard ship, he was seriously injured after an aircraft that was landing on deck struck a stanchion, which collapsed on top of him. He sustained serious head injuries and spent many months in hospital undergoing treatment that included skin grafts. Tony's return to health was long and painful, but eventually he was allowed to fly again, albeit not operationally.

On 28 Febuary 1944, Tony was piloting a Hawker Sea Hurricane Mk Ib, V7352, of 781 NAS, HMS *Daedlus*, on a flight to Scotland when it flew into high ground en route in a heavy snowstorm, 2 miles east of the ancient Northumbrian market town of Wooler, on Fowberry Moor. Tony was killed in the crash.

Lieutenant-Commander (pilot) Antony Francis HALL

Unit: 781 Naval Air Squadron, HMS *Daedalus; Died:* 28 February 1944 aged 35; *Buried:* Biddestone Churchyard Extension, Wiltshire, near south boundary; *Commemorated:* St Peter's Church, Monkton Farleigh.

THE FINAL WAVE-OFF

Petty Officer Bernard Kenneth Blissett, RN, 852 Naval Air Squadron – Bradford-on-Avon

The weather in the North Atlantic off the west coast of Scotland was particularly awful on 29 July 1944. Grumman Avenger Mk I, FN841, of 852 Naval Air Squadron, had completed an anti-submarine patrol and was returning to the 'Ruler' class escort carrier HMCS *Nabob*. At the controls of the single-engine torpedo bomber was pilot Sub-Lt D. Cash, and his crew of observer Sub-Lt Cecil Wheeler RNVR, and air gunner Petty Officer Bernard Blissett, the latter from Bradford-on-Avon.

Nabob was a Canadian ship with a Canadian crew, but she had a Royal Navy Avenger squadron embarked. As the Avenger approached the pitching flight deck of the carrier intending to 'land on', Sub-Lt Cash was given an early 'wave-off' by the deck-landing officer who must have considered the aircraft to be either too high or too fast to catch one of the deck arrester wires. The rough weather conditions he was experiencing would have made it more difficult for Cash to accurately judge his height and approach speed. In giving him a 'wave-off' the deck-landing officer was indicating that he should 'go round' and try his approach again.

The Avenger passed up the starboard side of the ship at about 400ft but then crashed into the sea ahead of the carrier. The aircraft was carrying two depth charges that exploded when the plane hit the water. Sub-Lt Cash was pulled from the sea, but it proved impossible to rescue PO Bernard Blissett and the 22-year-old observer, Sub-Lt Cecil Wheeler, both of whom were lost without trace.

Bernard Kenneth Blissett was born in 1924 at Bradford-on-Avon, the son of Frank Blissett, and Clara Emma Blissett (nee Sheppard, b.1898, Bradford-on-Avon), of St Margaret's Place, Bradford-on-Avon. Before he joined the Royal Navy, Bernard worked

A Grumman Avenger torpedo bomber of the type flown by PO Bernard Blissett, RN. *Andy Thomas collection*

for Spencer, Moulton & Co and was also a Scout patrol leader in the town. He played a prominent part in the Christ Church Crusaders boys' club and was a regular member of the Football and Cricket XI's. 'He was particularly successful as secretary of both Football and Cricket,' recorded the *Bradford-on-Avon Churchman*, the parish magazine for Holy Trinity and Christ Church. 'He was amazingly keen and it was astounding from where he accumulated his fixtures.'

Petty Officer Bernard Kenneth BLISSETT

Service No: FAA/FX 95691; *Unit:* 852 Naval Air Squadron, Royal Navy, HMCS *Nabob; Died:* 29 July 1944 aged 20; *Commemorated:* Lee-on-Solent Memorial, Hampshire, Bay 5, Panel 1; BOA WM; HT; AR.

Chapter Three

Convoy Killers

Wolf Pack Victims

'Though *U-230* was continually shaken by hard breakers, she moved inexorably into firing position. Far on port, three sweepers patrolled rigorously, while two escorts swept the surface astern. Ahead of us steamed one of the largest convoys ever to sail the Atlantic. Shadow after shadow crawled through the lenses of my TBY [target bearing transmitter], and their masts stuck up along the horizon like a heavy picket fence.' ***Herbert Werner, Executive Officer,*** U-230

In the first few years of war Germany's spectacularly successful campaign of unrestricted U-boat warfare against Atlantic convoys nearly resulted in Britain's defeat. By 1941, the 'grey wolves' had cost the allies more than 700 ships totalling 3.4 million tons. Their success continued almost unchecked until 1943 when the tide began to turn. Allied developments in countermeasures – radar, long range maritime patrol aircraft, new weapons, new destroyers and better convoy tactics – helped them to regain the initiative and beat the U-boats. Even so, Britain's Atlantic lifeline came at a terrifyingly high cost in human lives, ships and cargoes.

GREATER LOVE

Aircraftman 1st Class Lawry Brimson Mortimer, RAF – Holt

In the small hours of 5 July 1941 the German Type VII U-boat, *U-96*, commanded by *Kapitänleutnant* Heinrich Lehmann-Willenbrock, was alerted to the presence of Convoy WS9B in the Atlantic Ocean in a contact report received from a patrolling Focke Wulf Fw200 *Kondor* aircraft. In thick fog *U-96* pursued the convoy on the surface, enabling her to make better speed with her diesel engines than with her electric motors had she been submerged. At daybreak her lookouts on the conning tower, scanning the horizon through their powerful binoculars, finally spotted the ships about 300 miles north of the Azores as they emerged from the early morning sea mist.

Twenty-nine year-old Lehmann-Willenbrock ordered the U-boat's tanks to be blown and dived *U-96* to periscope depth to make his attack. The Type VII U-boat was carefully trimmed so she remained just below the surface of the ocean, but out of sight of the convoy. At 8.29am with the convoy firmly in his sights, Lehmann-Willenbrock fired a salvo of four torpedoes at the unsuspecting merchant vessels.

AC1 Lawry Mortimer, RAF, from Holt. *Holt Village Hall*

This is the sight that Lawry Mortimer would have had of the convoy in mid-Atlantic from the deck of the *Anselm*. The line of ships stretches as far as the eye can see. *IWM A5113*

Eighteen-year-old Aircraftman 1st Class (AC1) Lawry Mortimer from Holt was a passenger onboard the former Booth Line liner SS *Anselm,* commanded by Master Andrew Elliott. The 5,954-ton troopship was sailing with Convoy WS9B from Gourock, Scotland, to Freetown, Sierra Leone, with 1,300 British servicemen on board. Lawry was on his way to join an RAF unit at Takoradi, West Africa.

Before the war, the *Anselm* had been operated by the Booth Line as a cargo and passenger liner on the route from Liverpool to South America. In 1939 she was taken over by the British government for service as an auxiliary troop transport.

A letter written to an RAF padre in 1965 speaks of the SS *Anselm* in very negative terms: 'We were too slow. The ship could manage about six knots, and even in 1941 a U-boat could do better than that underwater, and 1941, in the spring, was high season for U-boats, you will recall! Anyway, we were given the comforting news that the ship was unsafe to proceed – then deflation: we sailed ...'

Lawry Brimson Mortimer was born on 28 January 1922, the second son of four children (Dorothy, Gladys, Bernard and Lawry) to Howard, a coal merchant, and Grace Gladys Mortimer of Garland Farm, Holt. Lawry, who was a pupil at Fitzmaurice Grammar School from 1934 to 1938, decided on a career in the RAF. He volunteered for the RAF in January 1939 aged 17 and joined No 1 School of Technical Training at Halton, near Aylesbury in Buckinghamshire, with the 39th Entry. He passed out from Halton in 1941 as a Fitter 2E – 'fitter, aero engines'– the *crème de la crème* of technical graduates from Halton.

On 5 July, *Anselm* was in mid-Atlantic with six other vessels – the survey ship HMS

Challenger, the auxiliary merchant cruiser HMS *Cathay*, and three 'Flower' class corvettes *Petunia*, *Lavender* and *Starwort*.

Lehmann-Willenbrock thought he had scored hits on the *Cathay* and *Challenger* with his first salvo, but in fact two of his torpedoes had hit the *Anselm*. The troopship settled rapidly by the head and sank within 22 minutes at position 44°25'N, 28°35'W, with her crew managing to launch all but one of their lifeboats.

Dave Everett, an eyewitness aboard *Anselm*, recalls the moment of impact from the torpedoes:

> 'The alarm sounded. By instinct, we headed for the lifeboat station. I witnessed chaos and panic beyond anything I could imagine. Despair and hopelessness was written on everyone's face. I heard screams and howls from the guys trapped down below. I watched guys fighting each other, seemingly for no reason at all. The destroyer *Challenger* nosed in towards the back of the ship, catching servicemen dropping from the stern.'

The three corvettes counter-attacked *U-96* with depth charges, but their attacks brought them close to the survivors of *Anselm* in the water and so were forced to break off their action. The Master, 93 crew, 3 gunners and about 970 RAF and military personnel from *Anselm* were rescued by *Challenger* and *Starwort*, who later were transferred to the *Cathay* and then landed at Freetown. However, 4 crew and about 250 service personnel were lost at sea, among them Lawry Mortimer. It is likely that many were killed or badly injured by the explosion of the torpedoes, which struck the ship immediately beneath the accommodation space below the waterline, and destroyed their means of escape.

An RAF padre, Sqn Ldr the Revd Herbert Cecil Pugh, RAFVR, was a passenger

The hunted: former Booth Line passenger liner SS *Anselm*. *Author's collection*

The hunter: *Kapitänleutnant* Heinrich Lehmann-Willenbrock, commander of the German U-boat *U-96*, at the periscope. *Jak Showell collection*

aboard the *Anselm*. He performed one of the most quietly inspiring acts of heroism of the war for which he was posthumously awarded the George Cross. The official award citation published in the *London Gazette* on 1 April 1947, describes what happened:

> 'Mr Pugh came up on deck in a dressing gown and gave all the help he could. He seemed to be everywhere at once, doing his best to comfort the injured, helping with the boats and rafts (two of these were rendered unserviceable as a result of the explosion) and visiting the different lower sections where the men were quartered. When he learned that a number of injured airmen were trapped in the damaged hold, he insisted on being lowered into it with a rope.
>
> 'Everyone demurred because the hold was below the water line and already the decks were awash and to go down was to go to certain death. He simply explained that he must be where his men were. The deck level was already caving in and the hold was three parts full of water, so that when he knelt to pray the water reached his shoulders. Within a few minutes the ship plunged and sank and Mr Pugh was never seen again. He had every opportunity of saving his own life but, without regard to his own safety and in the best tradition of the Service and of a Christian minister, he gave up his life for others.'

Padre Pugh was awarded the George Cross posthumously in 1947, but had it not been for *The News of the World* newspaper he may never have been honoured at all. In October 1946

Sqn Ldr the Rev Herbert Pugh was posthumously awarded the George Cross for his selfless act of courage when the *Anselm* was sinking. *Author's collection*

a Flt Sgt Sharp wrote to the paper asking why the Padre's bravery had never been acknowledged. This letter caused a flood of correspondence lending further support, which led to the Air Ministry looking into the case. Here is an extract from one of the letters sent in 1946:

> 'I was one of the more fortunate members of the troops on board, and in actual fact came out the same hold as the one the RAF Padre entered. I didn't see him enter, although while in the lifeboat waiting to be picked up by the escorting corvette I heard several members of the boat remark to the effect that they did see the Padre enter the hold containing the trapped personnel. He must have known full well that it was impossible to come out again alive, in view of the fact that the hold when I left was covered in at least 5ft of water which was still gushing in. Only a few moments after I left the *Anselm* it gave one definite plunge and passed below the water out of sight in few seconds. In view of this I doubt very much if the Padre could have survived more than a few moments in that hold of death. Whilst I was scrambling out I passed literally dozens of screaming men with their heads fastened between the rungs of the connecting ladder. It was horrible to hear their screams and to pass them by, knowing full well that it was absolutely hopeless for them to get out alive.'

U-96 had been badly damaged by the depth charge attacks from the convoy escort vessels. She was forced to abort her patrol and head for her homeport of St Nazaire in France, where she duly arrived on 9 July.

The commander of *U-96*, Heinrich Lehmann-Willenbrock, became one of the top scoring and most highly decorated German U-boat aces of the Second World War, sinking 24 ships for a total of over 170,000grt. He survived the war and later joined the German merchant navy. In 1959 the former U-boat captain showed great courage as the skipper of the freighter *Inga Bastian*, when he and his crew saved 57 survivors from the burning Brazilian ship *Commandante Lyra*. He died at Bremen in 1986 aged 74.

Aircraftman 1st Class Lawry Brimson MORTIMER

Service No: 575923; *Service:* Royal Air Force; *Died:* 5 July 1941 aged 18; *Commemorated:* Commonwealth Air Forces Memorial, Runnymede, Panel 57; Holt WM.

ADRIFT AND ALONE

Chief Petty Officer Steward Harold Edward John Gane, RN, HMS *Dunedin* – Bradford-on-Avon

Bradford-on-Avon man, Chief Petty Officer Harold Gane, was on HMS *Dunedin* when she captured the Nazi supply ship *Lothringen* on 15 June 1941 in what was probably the high point of the Royal Navy cruiser's career. *Dunedin,* commanded by Capt Richard Lovatt, RN, OBE, was a Royal Navy 4,850-ton 'D' class cruiser with a crew of 492. Working with aircraft from the carrier HMS *Eagle*, *Dunedin* found the 10,746-ton *Lothringen* in mid-Atlantic and was able to capture her and take her to Bermuda as a prize. She was later taken into Merchant Navy service as the *Empire Salvage*.

The *Lothringen* was one of several Kriegsmarine ships in the Atlantic that were responsible for replenishing the battleship *Bismarck* and patrolling U-boats. *Lothringen*'s key role was to supply four U-boats with fuel, torpedoes and new crewmembers. Thanks to Enigma decrypts supplied by the code-breakers at Bletchley Park, the Royal Navy was able to track down and capture or sink a number of the supply ships.

As well as dealing a significant blow against the German surface and U-boat fleets by taking out a key supply vessel, *Dunedin*'s prize crew also found crucial documents onboard the *Lothringen* that helped Bletchley Park in its ongoing battle to keep abreast of the secret German naval codes. *Dunedin*'s commander, Capt Richard Lovatt, was awarded the OBE for his part in the capture of the *Lothringen*.

Harold Edward John Gane was born on 1 July 1902 at South Wraxall, the son of Henry Charles (b.1875, Monkton Farleigh), a quarryman, and Annie M. Gane (nee Dore, b.1872, Poole, Dorset); and the husband of Dorothy Emily Gane, of Bradford-on-Avon.

Harold had worked at Spencer, Moulton & Co in Bradford-on-Avon before he joined the Royal Navy as a boy seaman aged 16 on 1 February 1919. He trained on HMS *Pembroke I*, *Attentive II*, *Pembroke V*, *Pembroke II*, and *Dragon*, before he was promoted to ordinary seaman on 15 March 1922 and signed on for 12 years service in the Navy. Between 1922 and 1929 Harold served on HMS *Victory II*, *Conquest*, *Excellent*, and *Osprey*. Because of today's government rules concerning public access to military records of service after 1920, the period 1929 to 41 is currently not open to scrutiny. However, it is likely that on completion of his 12-year engagement in 1934 Harold signed on for a further period of service, but events overtook him when war was declared in September 1939 and he was committed to service with the Royal Navy 'for the duration of hostilities'.

Harold's pre-1920 record of service describes him as standing 5ft 4 ½in tall, with a 34½in chest, light brown hair, brown eyes and a fresh complexion. His character and ability were assessed as being 'very good' and 'superior'.

Following the capture of the *Lothringen, Dunedin* spent some time in the South Atlantic on patrol. In November 1941 the Admiralty received further intelligence based on Enigma decrypts that the Germans were planning to attack allied shipping near Cape Town in South Africa. The plan involved four U-boats, the armed merchant raider *Atlantis* and a supply ship, *Python*. HMS *Dunedin*, *Devonshire* and *Dorsetshire* were ordered independently to track them down. On 24 November, *Devonshire* came upon *U-126* and

The 4,850-ton 'D' class cruiser HMS *Dunedin. Author's collection*

HMS *Dunedin* captured the Nazi supply ship *Lothringen* in mid-Atlantic on 15 June 1941 in what was probably the high point of the Royal Navy cruiser's career. *Author's collection*

Atlantis. She sank the armed merchant raider but stayed far enough away from *U-126* to avoid being attacked.

That same day, *U-124* (*Kapitänleutnant* Johann Mohr) was on its way to rendezvous with *Python*. Some 900 miles west of Freetown, Sierra Leone, near St Paul's Rock, just south of the equator, Mohr sighted *Dunedin* and gave chase. At 1.26pm he launched three torpedoes at the cruiser, two striking her in rapid succession. The first wrecked the W/T office so no distress signal could be sent; the second caused fatal damage to the ship.

Dunedin heeled over to 90 degrees and, realising the futility of the situation, Capt Lovatt gave the order to abandon ship. Crewmembers leapt into the sea but it proved impossible to float off the ship's boats before *Dunedin* sank. Only six Carley floats and one flottanet were deployed and crammed to capacity with survivors, floating slightly submerged in the ocean swell.

Shortly before *Dunedin* disappeared from sight beneath the waves, the U-boat broke surface close by. Royal Marine William Gill, a survivor, told of the experience in a book written by his son, *Blood in the Sea*. He describes what happened next:

> 'The men's shouting quietened as the submarine manoeuvred around us, stalking and mocking us. We were silent now, all our gazes fixed on the conning tower and the two deck guns fore and aft, our desperate bids to clamber on board rafts and debris suspended temporarily as we wondered what would happen next.
>
> 'We watched in disgust as the grey impostor strutted where once Dunedin had sailed. We were close enough to hear the coughing of her diesel engines and our noses filled with her contemptuous exhaust fumes. She passed slowly within fifty yards of us, almost coming to a stop… What did she want? Why didn't she get it over with? Was this really the end?
>
> 'Then something happened which, if we saw it in a movie today, would be barely believable. Slowly, hardly perceptibly, someone on my raft began to sing. It was hard to understand at first, hard to believe what I was hearing. Within a few seconds others had joined in, tentatively at first, then loudly and defiantly enveloping our tiny band of desperate men. I sang too, the words of "There'll Always be an England" ringing out triumphantly and rhythmically, our bodies sweating and thrusting with every word, every last breath.'

The U-boat circled the survivors several times, but made no attempt to intimidate them further before finally moving away to the north and diving again. The cruiser finally sank seventeen minutes after the first torpedo strike, at position 03°N 26°W.

Most of the rafts carried some badly wounded men among their occupants, many of whom died during the first night. Over the next few days in the equatorial heat more of the men suffered from delirium and exposure, and in their delusory state many drowned easily. As well as suffering from an extreme shortage of food and fresh water, the survivors were repeatedly attacked each night by ferocious barracuda-like fish that caused several deaths.

One hour before sunset on the fourth day, the American merchant vessel SS *Nishmaha*, en route from Takoradi to Philadelphia, came upon *Dunedin*'s survivors and her lifeboats were lowered to pick them up. The men were very weak and many required urgent medical attention. This is an extract from the official report of the rescue, filed by the master of the *Nishmaha*, Capt Olsen:

> '... we started to take the ship-wrecked men aboard. In all we had 72 men – some of whom were able to climb aboard by the pilot ladder, others were so weak that we were obliged to hoist them to the ship's deck. Some were unconscious, delirious and hysterical. Some were badly burned from fractured steam pipes, some suffered from splinter wounds, others were in bad shape from sunburn, dog fish and Barracuda bites, and all were more or less smeared [with] fuel oil. All were practically naked.'

Of the 72 men who survived from a crew of almost 500, five died of exposure within eighteen hours of rescue. The *Nishmaha* landed the survivors at Port of Spain, Trinidad, on 7 December 1941, nine and a half days after *Dunedin*'s sinking.

It is not possible to say with any degree of certainty what happened to Harold Gane: he may have died onboard *Dunedin* when *U-124*'s torpedoes struck; he might have drowned when abandoning the sinking cruiser; or he could have succumbed later on one of the life rafts. Whichever way he met his end, Gane's body was never recovered.

Dunedin's assailant, *U-124*, her captain Johann Mohr and his 53-man crew, lived to fight on for another fourteen months. On 2 April 1943, *U-124* was lost with all hands in the Atlantic west of Oporto in position 41°02'N, 15°39'W, sunk by depth charges from the Royal Navy corvette HMS *Stonecrop*, and the sloop HMS *Black Swan*.

Chief Petty Officer Steward Harold Edward John GANE

Service No: P/L 12028; *Ship:* HMS *Dunedin*, Royal Navy; *Died:* 24 November 1941 aged 39; *Commemorated:* Portsmouth Naval Memorial, Panel 58, Column 1; BOA WM; CC.

STRANGER THAN FICTION

Marine David Rupert Nelson Ledbury, 40 (Royal Marines) Commando – Holt

The tale of HMS *Fidelity* and her maverick commander is one of the strangest stories to come out of the Second World War. In June 1940, after the fall of France, the French armed merchantman *Le Rhin* was handed over to the Royal Navy at Gibraltar by her captain, *Lieutenant-de-Vaisseau* Claude Costa, with her entire crew and a top secret cargo of plastic explosive. She was sailed to the UK and converted to a special service vessel for the Royal Navy. In return for handing over his ship with its secret cargo, Costa was rewarded with the rank of acting lieutenant-commander in the Royal Navy and the *nom de guerre* of Jack Langlais, and allowed to remain in command of his ship that had now been renamed HMS *Fidelity*.

Before the war Costa had been involved in clandestine activities for the *Deuxième Bureau* of the French Secret Service in French Indo-China. He was used to living with

Marine David Ledbury from Holt. *Holt Village Hall*

Lt-Cdr 'Jack Langlais', the renegade captain of HMS *Fidelity*. *Author's collection*

danger as a constant companion and at the margins of the civilised world. He behaved like a brigand captain and ruled his crew with a rod of iron, brutally beating those who were foolish enough to step out of line. Costa had worked with a female agent named Madeleine Guesclin, who became his lover and who came with him when he handed over *le Rhin* at Gibraltar. Combining her sexual allure with a ruthless streak matched only by that of Costa, Guesclin rarely left his side and unusually was given a commission in the WRNS and the *nom de guerre*, First Officer Madeleine Barclay. *Fidelity* was probably unique in the wartime Royal Navy in having a female first officer onboard a warship.

David Rupert Nelson Ledbury was born in 1924 at Melksham, the son of Richard and Lottie Frances Ledbury (nee Tucker), of Melksham. David joined the Royal Marines and underwent combat training with 40 (RM) Commando on the Isle of Wight in 1942 in preparation for special service duties. Formed on 14 February 1942, 40 Commando was the first all-volunteer Royal Marines Commando 'to undertake special duties of a hazardous nature'. It was involved in the disastrous landings at Dieppe in August where it took heavy casualties, but the unit was brought up to strength again and later served in Sicily, Italy and the Adriatic.

HMS *Fidelity* was an unusual looking ship that bore a resemblance to a tramp steamer. The 2,455-ton special service vessel concealed two Kingfisher seaplane aircraft with launch catapult, two landing craft – HMS LC(V) 752 and LC(V) 754, and a motor torpedo boat, as well as four 4-inch guns and four torpedo tubes. She was manned by a mixed Free French and Royal Navy crew.

The Royal Navy had decided *Fidelity* could be of more use in the Far East theatre so in December 1942, with David Ledbury and 52 other men from T Company 40 (RM) Commando embarked, she joined convoy ONS154 en route to the Far East via the Cape. It is possible that special operations (raids and commando operations) in South East Asia against the Japanese were in mind, with *Fidelity* acting as a commando carrier. By hiding her in among a merchant convoy it was hoped to conceal her true identity and purpose.

On 26 December, 600 miles due west of Brest, some twenty German U-boats of Groups *Spitz* and *Ungestum* had found ONS154. At dusk on 28 December, the senior officer of the Canadian convoy escort force gave orders for the *Fidelity* to launch one of her aircraft to cover an alteration of course, but the plane crashed on take-off. *Fidelity's* troubles had only just begun because her main engine then broke down and, falling behind the convoy, she was ordered to make for Gibraltar for repairs.

During the night of 28–29 December the U-boats attacked from all quarters and overwhelmed the escorts, sinking nine merchantmen. Five torpedoes were fired at *Fidelity*, but all missed. By 5.00am on the 29th, her main engine had been repaired but by now she was capable of only 2kts. Fidelity became a sitting target for the German U-boats. Even

HMS *Fidelity*, formerly the French vessel *Le Rhin*. *Author's collection*

This rare photograph was taken on 29 December 1942 at about 4.24pm. It shows gunners on *U-435* preparing to sink the SS *Norse King*, sailing in convoy with HMS *Fidelity*. At 3.07pm *U-435* hit the Norwegian cargo ship with one torpedo and shelled her with over 100 rounds of gunfire, but the *Norse King* stubbornly remained afloat and had to be sunk by a *coup de grâce*.
U-Boat Archive

so, she launched her two landing craft to pick up survivors from the merchantman *Empire Shackleton* that had been torpedoed, and returned them to *Fidelity*.

At 11.30am on 30 December *Fidelity* sent a routine signal reporting her position as 42°N, 28°W, but nothing more was heard from her. Between 4 and 5.00pm off the Azores, *Fidelity* was stalked and sunk by the German U-boat, *U-435* (*Kapitänleutnant* Siegfried Strelow), which came in as close as 300 metres to torpedo her. The power of the explosions as the three torpedoes struck home surprised Strelow and he crash-dived. When he surfaced again some distance away he was amazed to see hundreds of survivors in the sea and on life rafts. Some 334 men were lost, which included the entire ship's company from *Fidelity*, the commandos (including David), and survivors from the merchantman *Empire Shackleton*.

A destroyer escort was despatched to search for *Fidelity* and continued to scour the ocean for a week, but no trace of her was ever found. The Admiralty deduced that she must have been lost during the night of 31 December 1942 and 1 January 1943; so, 1 January 1943 is the presumed official date of her loss. The Commonwealth War Graves Commission gives the date of sinking as 1 January 1943, and therefore that of David's death; but German naval records show that *Fidelity* was actually sunk on 30 December 1942, which means that all the other dates are wrong.

Kapitänleutnant Siegfried Strelow (in white cap), commander of *U-435. U-Boat Archive*

Strelow did not survive the war. He was killed on his second U-boat patrol in the Atlantic on 9 July 1943 when *U-435* was sunk by a Wellington of Coastal Command, and lost with all hands.

Marine David Rupert Nelson LEDBURY

Service No: PO/X 5001; *Unit:* T Company, 40 (Royal Marines) Commando; *Died:* 1 January 1943 aged 19; *Commemorated:* Portsmouth Naval Memorial, Panel 79, Column 3; Holt WM; St Andrew's Church, Chale, Isle of Wight.

ARCTIC CARNAGE

Able Seaman Leonard Albert Taylor, RN, HMS *Mahratta* – Bradford-on-Avon

For the convoy escort destroyer HMS *Mahratta*, the end when it came in the pitch black of an Arctic winter was swift and overwhelming. 'The explosion was out of this world,' recalled 18-year-old survivor Able Seaman Jack Humble. 'The ship was shaking. People in front of me were shouting, "We can't get out".'

The door leading to the upper deck had been blocked by debris from the blast caused by a torpedo strike. Men were trapped but they cleared it aside and rushed out on to the heaving deck. The scene that greeted them was chaotic: 'People were throwing themselves overboard because the ship was sinking. They were shouting for their wives and their mothers. It was terrible.'

At 10.07pm GMT on 25 February 1944, inside the Arctic Circle to the south of Bear Island, the Type VIIC U-boat *U-956* commanded by 24-year-old *Kapitänleutnant* Hans-Dieter Mohs, struck the 1,920-ton 'M' class destroyer with two T5 homing torpedoes. They smashed into *Mahratta* in quick succession causing her to sink in the freezing waters of the western Barents Sea, 280 miles west of the North Cape at position 71°17'N, 13°30'E. The destroyer HMS *Impulsive* was sent back to pick up survivors, but the night was so black and the seas so high that any rescue attempts were practically impossible.

Able Seaman Len Taylor, RN, from Bradford-on-Avon. *Joyce Hough*

Len Taylor from Bradford-on-Avon had been on *Mahratta* for only a couple of months before she was sunk. He was one of 220 crew for whom rescue was all but impossible and he died when the ship went down.

Leonard Albert Taylor was born on 6 June 1920, one of three sons and the youngest of six children to Stanley James and Eliza Alice Taylor, of 43 Newtown, Bradford-on-Avon. His two brothers were also serving with the British armed forces: James Taylor (b.1916) was in the RAF; Gordon Taylor (b.1912) was with the Army in India. Their father, Stanley, owned an outfitters' shop at 35 Silver Street in Bradford for 30 years and was well-known in the town. Len attended Trinity Senior School and afterwards worked in the town for Mr Alex Brown the ironmonger, whose shop was just across the street from the Taylor's. Len was a very strong swimmer and a member with his brothers of Bradford Rowing club.

Len's first ship was the 27,500-ton 'Queen Elizabeth' class battleship HMS *Valiant*. He was serving on her as an able seaman when she was involved in the Battle of Matapan in March 1941, and two months later in May when she was bombed off the island of Crete. Len was still on *Valiant* when she suffered serious damage in the harbour at Alexandria on 19 December 1941, as the result of a daring Italian human torpedo raid.

When HMS *Valiant* paid off at Plymouth for refit on 10 October 1943, Len went on leave before he was drafted to HMS *Mahratta* (Lt-Cdr Eric Drought, DSC, RN) at Grimsby. *Mahratta* made three passages with the Arctic convoys before sailing on what became her last voyage with the destroyer escort for Convoy JW57.

On 20 February 1944, Convoy JW57 comprising 43 merchant ships, escorted by 35 escort vessels that included *Mahratta*, 3 cruisers and the escort carrier *Chaser*, left the naval base and anchorage at Loch Ewe on Scotland's northwest coast, bound for the north Russian port of Murmansk. When three days out from Loch Ewe, the convoy was sighted by a long-range Focke-Wulf Fw200 *Kondor* aircraft. Its crew directed U-boats from the German 11th U-Flotilla based in Norway to shadow the vessels.

The escort carrier HMS *Chaser* launched her Wildcat aircraft which drove off the *Kondor*, but in actual fact the large four-engine aircraft maintained distant contact with the convoy. The Wildcat crews reported that they had spotted several U-boats in the vicinity of the convoy which were almost immediately detected by a Swordfish patrol. Commander I.J. Tyson, RNR, in the destroyer HMS *Keppel* attacked and sunk *U-713* (*Oberleutnant* Henri Gosejacob) with depth charges. The boat was lost with all hands.

On 25 February a long-range Catalina flying boat from the RAF's 210 Squadron based at Sullom Voe in the Shetlands attacked *U-601* (*Kapitänleutnant* Otto Hansen) which was tailing the convoy, and sank her with all hands. But during the brief hours of daylight when *Chaser*'s Swordfish were still aloft the wolf pack continued to stalk JW57, either fully submerged or 'trimmed down' so that their hulls rode just below the surface, using their *Schnorkels* so their diesel engines could breathe. Then surfacing and drawing ahead, they taunted the destroyers to work up to full speed so their propellers created the underwater 'noise' that favoured the use of the German T-5 acoustic torpedoes.

In the rough seas the convoy commanders thought themselves to be even more vulnerable than usual to a stern attack by U-boats because only two Home Fleet destroyers

Len Taylor's ship, the 1,920-ton 'M' class destroyer HMS *Mahratta*, under way. *IWM FL22421*

On *Mahratta*'s Arctic convoy escort duties, Len would have been witness to frightening sights like this one. Seen from the deck of an aircraft carrier, a merchant ship is bombed in Convoy PQ18. It was the biggest allied convoy to Russia and fought through a four-day attack by enemy torpedo aircraft and U-boats to deliver its cargo at an Arctic port. *IWM A12017.*

covered this sector. One of these was *Mahratta* and the pair had been allocated arcs to sweep with their radars in the search for attackers.

There was a short sea running astern, with a stiff following breeze and the spray from the wave tops could cause 'clutter' interference on the destroyers' radar screens, making the detection of U-boats very difficult. A clever U-boat commander could take advantage of this and get in on the surface to make his attack undetected.

Lt-Cdr Drought on *Mahratta* called up the convoy commander, Vice-Admiral Irvine Glennie, in the cruiser *Black Prince,* on the R/T: 'Have been hit by torpedo aft and am stopped.' After a short pause came a further message: 'have been hit amidships by a second torpedo'. Then another pause followed by, 'Life-saving equipment is being cleared away'. Finally, 'We are abandoning ship – we are sinking – we cannot last much longer!' After that, nothing more was heard from *Mahratta*.

Ian McCunn, who was 3rd Mate on the Liberty Ship SS *John W. Powell*, was on his first convoy after graduating from maritime college in the USA:

> 'It was on my watch, 20.00 to 24.00hrs, that HMS *Mahratta* was torpedoed abreast our starboard side. It was pitch-dark, sub-zero, with on and off blowing snow. She lost steerage when a torpedo struck her stern and moments later, when a second one hit her magazine, she exploded like a rocket, lighting up much of the convoy momentarily, and then went down in minutes. We could hear her radio operator over the speaker on our flying bridge explaining what he knew of the situation right up to the moment the magazine was hit.'

When Mohs' two torpedoes found their mark, *Mahratta* was fatally damaged and began to go down. Jack Humble and others tried desperately to release some of the Carley floats that lined the deck but they were frozen fast. The men linked arms, but before they could jump a huge wave swept them over the side of the listing destroyer and carried them away into the darkness and pitched them into the oily black sea. 'I was getting sucked under with the ship. I remember getting pushed round and round under the water. But, in a little bit of luck I suppose, I came to the top and managed to swim away from the ship. Everybody around me was dead. I tried speaking to people. Nobody answered. I couldn't find anybody alive. They had been in the water longer than I had. I just thought that was the end.'

Despite the appalling weather conditions, *Impulsive* and another destroyer were quickly on the scene but were able to rescue just 16 men from *Mahratta*'s crew of 236. *Impulsive* rescued Jack from the freezing ocean. 'I was being thrown about. The next thing I knew, a wave took me up the side of the ship to the level of the deck. They grabbed me by the hair and pulled me in.'

In the extreme cold, HMS *Wanderer* was the only ship in the escort whose guns were able to illuminate the scene with star shells to aid the search for survivors. *Mahratta*'s captain, all of the officers, and more than 100 men – including Len Taylor – were either killed when the torpedoes struck, died in the freezing ocean, or went down inside the ship.

Len Taylor's niece, Joyce Hough, remembers that 'he was always anxious about the fate of all his family members; he had a profound sense of duty. He worked very hard and had fought in a lot of campaigns and wanted nothing more than to see the war won and to be back with his mother and family.'

Joyce recalls an eerie story which her Aunt Sylvia, a sister of Len, told her. 'The night the ship was lost my grandmother, Len's mother, was woken in the night and she heard him distinctly calling "Mother, help me!". My grandmother dressed and prepared to leave the house, but my grandfather persuaded her to go back to bed. About a week later they received the telegram, which I still have.'

Able Seaman Leonard Albert TAYLOR

Service No: D/JX 214748; *Ship:* HMS *Mahratta*, Royal Navy; *Died:* 25 February 1944 aged 23; *Commemorated:* Plymouth Naval Memorial, Panel 87, Column 3; BOA WM; HT.

'HER BOWS WERE BLOWN OFF'

Able Seaman Arthur William Bennett, RN, HMS *Blackwood* – Holt

In the late evening of 6 June 1944, thirty-six German U-boats sailed from their massive concrete bunkers in the French Biscay ports to intercept and destroy the Allies' D-Day invasion armada along the coast of Normandy.

At 9.00pm, the Type VIIC U-boat, *U-764*, commanded by *Oberleutnant zur See* Hans-Kurt von Bremen, slipped from her protective bunker at Brest. In company with fourteen other U-boats from the 9th U-Flotilla, she nosed into the waters of the Bay of Biscay. Thirty minutes later the 7 boats fitted with *Schnorkel* equipment (including *U-764)* began diving at 10-minute intervals and headed north, submerged, towards their Normandy hunting grounds. The 8 non-*Schnorkel* boats proceeded north on the surface in single file astern under cover of darkness, but were soon intercepted by Allied aircraft. Their troubles had only just begun. Within 4 days RAF Coastal Command aircraft had sunk 5 of the U-boats and forced 5 more to abort and return home.

On 7 June, with the D-Day landings 24 hours old, the 1,360-ton 'Captain' class frigate HMS *Blackwood* (Lt-Cdr L.T. Sly, RD, RNR), with other ships of the 3rd Escort

No photographs are known to exist of HMS *Blackwood* after she was torpedoed and her bows blown off in June 1944. This picture is of the British destroyer HMS *Eskimo* in May 1940, whose stern was blown off by a torpedo during the Norwegian campaign. It gives an idea of the likely damage sustained by *Blackwood* at the hands of *U-764* in June 1944. *IWM N233*

Group (EG), assembled at Milford Haven in South Wales to escort a convoy down the English Channel.

Able Seaman Arthur Bennett from Bradford-on-Avon was onboard *Blackwood* as one of the ship's company of 156 officers and men. Arthur William Bennett was born in 1916 at Caernarfon, the son of Alfred James and Edith Bennett (nee Williams) of Caernarfon; and the husband of Gertrude Mary Bennett of Caernarfon.

When the escort duty was completed, the 3rd EG took up its patrol area, which stretched from Portland westwards down the Channel to Cherbourg. On 14 June *Blackwood* was detached to Portland to take on oil and stores and returned to the group on the 15th, which was then in position in the Western Channel northwest of Cap de la Hague. *Blackwood* had just manoeuvred into place on the destroyer screen when she was struck at 7.11pm by an acoustic torpedo fired from the German U-boat, *U-764*.

The torpedo hit just forward of *Blackwood*'s bridge superstructure in the 'hedgehog' bomb magazine, causing a massive explosion. The forward part of the ship was blown off and sank, the mast collapsed and the bridge structure was flattened back. Amazingly what was left of the ship remained afloat and two air-sea rescue launches nearby were quickly on the scene, taking off all the survivors and wounded. Even so, 58 of her crew died in the carnage that followed the torpedo strike, including Arthur Bennett.

Blackwood was taken in tow but foundered at 4.10am on 16 June, 23 miles southeast of Portland at position 49°04'N, 02°15'W, and sank in 180ft of water.

In the ensuing counter-attack by the 3rd EG, *U-764* shot all the rest of her torpedoes with no result, but was badly damaged by 'hedgehogs' fired by the frigates HMS *Duckworth* and *Domett*. She managed to escape to St Peter Port, Jersey, with a broken snort mast and eventually made it home to Brest on 21 June.

The only U-boats that saw action from the 36 that sailed were the 15 from Brest. Of the 8 *Schnorkel*-less boats, 5 never returned to base. By 30 June, U-boat operations against the Allied invasion had been a disaster: 2 destroyers and 5 merchant ships, for the loss of 22 U-boats.

Able Seaman Arthur William BENNETT

Service No: D/JX 346912; *Ship:* HMS *Blackwood*, Royal Navy; *Died:* 15 June 1944 aged 27; *Commemorated:* Plymouth Naval Memorial, Panel 85, Column 3; BOA WM, AR; Holt WM.

Chapter Four

U-Boat Killers

RAF Coastal Command

'When proceeding to ONS 20, a U/B [U-boat] was sighted at posn 57°27'N 28°17'W. An attack was made with three DC's [depth charges] but the result was not observed. Owing to intense flak a second attack was postponed. At 19.10, when it was beginning to get dark, a second attack was made and one of the remaining 3 D/C's fell near to the hull of the U/B. Within a few minutes the bows were low in the water and puffs of black smoke were issuing from each side of the after deck. The U/B finally slithered under the waves leaving 35 survivors in dinghies and in the water.'
Report on the sinking of U-964 *by an 86 Squadron Liberator, 16 October 1943*

During the Second World War the wastes of the Atlantic Ocean became vast battlegrounds for aircraft and U-boats. It was not easy for an RAF Coastal Command aircraft to find a U-boat in the featureless expanses of water. But when found, and if the U-boat chose to remain on the surface and fight it out, a large aircraft was an easy target for determined gunners. From the seemingly endless skies above the convoys, RAF aircrews waged fierce battles against the 'grey wolves'. In the end Coastal Command aircraft and new scientific advances, like the Leigh Light and air-to-surface radar, had the U-boats on the run.

SCOURGE OF THE GREY WOLVES

Pilot Officer Nelson Henry Webb, DFM, RAF, 217 Squadron – Bradford-on-Avon

On 2 June 1940, over the Western Approaches to the English Channel, Sgt Nelson Webb was at the controls of an Avro Anson of 217 Squadron flying a routine convoy patrol. From several thousand feet above the ocean to the southwest of Land's End, Webb sighted and attacked with bombs a surfaced U-boat, which immediately crash-dived. He later spotted another fully surfaced U-boat that he attacked from 300ft with the Anson's single forward-firing machine gun. Once again, the U-boat crash-dived to safety, without suffering damage. (It later transpired that on both occasions Nelson had attacked *U-57* captained by *Oberleutnant zur See* Erich Topp, who was to survive the war as one of Germany's top U-boat aces.) For bravery in pressing home his attack on the U-boat, Nelson was awarded the Distinguished Flying Medal (DFM) and commissioned as a pilot officer.

Flg Off Nelson Webb, DFM, RAF, from Winsley. *Ruth Godfrey*

Nelson Henry Webb was born in 1917 at Bradford-on-Avon, the son of Henry and Florence Webb (nee Hart) of Bradford-on-Avon; and the husband of Hazel Joan Webb. Nelson was a pupil at Fitzmaurice Grammar School from 1927 to 1932, after which he joined the RAF in September 1932 as an aircraft apprentice at RAF Halton.

He graduated as a wireless mechanic in 1935 and he was posted first to 9 and then to 214 Squadron at Abingdon, where he volunteered as an air gunner. Eighteen months later Nelson embarked for service in Iraq, joining 70 Squadron at Hinaidi and Habbaniya flying Vickers Valentia transports. Late in 1937 he was selected for training as an airman pilot and was awarded his wings in September 1938 with promotion to sergeant.

Nelson's first operational posting was to 217 Squadron in RAF Coastal Command at St Eval, Cornwall, in May 1939, where he flew twin-engine Avro Ansons on maritime patrol duties over the Western Approaches. After he had completed thirthy-three convoy patrols the *London Gazette* announced on 20 February 1940 that he had been awarded a Mention in Despatches for 'gallantry and devotion to duty in the execution of air operations'.

On 4 June 1940 Nelson and his crew were engaged in a convoy patrol when they spotted a surfaced U-boat, *U-101*, in the Channel 40 miles southwest of Falmouth. Taken by surprise, the U-boat crash-dived just as Nelson released two 100lb anti-submarine bombs. Although slightly damaged in the attack the U-boat and its crew, commanded by *Kapitänleutnant* Fritz Frauenheim, lived to fight another day.

By now, Nelson had acquired a reputation as a pilot who sought out the enemy. On 11 July he intercepted a German Heinkel He59 seaplane about 20 miles off Start Point, which was heading for Guernsey. He attacked the seaplane with the Anson's front gun causing it to crash-land on the sea. Its crew of three escaped in a dinghy before the aircraft rolled over and sank.

When 217 Squadron traded its Ansons for the newer and more potent Bristol Beaufort in November 1940, Nelson had flown 108 operational sorties in the former. Most of the early raids by the Beauforts were bombing and mining operations against the Atlantic coastal ports in northwest France, where elements of the German Navy's U-boat and surface fleets were based for operations in the Atlantic.

On 20 December, Nelson took off at 3.25am on his 115th operational sortie, in Beaufort L4474, loaded with a TIM, to attack the military port facilities at Lorient on the Brittany coast. Three of the five aircraft that took off failed to find their target owing to bad weather and returned early. Nelson actually reached Lorient and was searching for the target when his Beaufort was hit by flak, causing his aircraft to crash at nearby Lanester. All four crewmembers died and the Germans buried them with full military honours in Lanester Cemetery.

Pilot Officer Nelson Henry WEBB, DFM

Service No: 44594, RAFVR; *Unit:* 217 Squadron, RAF Coastal Command; *Died:* 20 December 1940 aged 23; *Buried:* Lanester Communal Cemetery, Morbihan, France, Collective Grave 1-2; *Commemorated:* BOA WM; CC.

This is the actual Bristol Beaufort torpedo bomber (L4474) in which Nelson Webb was lost during a bombing raid on the Breton port of Lorient, France, on 20 December 1940. ***IWM C2058***

ABOVE THE EMPTY WASTES

Sergeant Eric John Brown, RAFVR, 86 Squadron – Bradford-on-Avon

Take-off and landing are the most critical points of flight for any aircraft, but under war conditions they can become even more dangerous. In the Second World War, when most Bomber and Coastal Command aircraft were overloaded beyond their design weights with fuel and bombs for their missions, a sudden engine failure as they struggled to take-off could easily spell disaster. It was rare for anyone to survive when a heavily laden aircraft smashed into the ground and exploded in a fireball, or crashed into the sea.

Eric John ('Jack') Brown was born in 1921 at Bradford-on-Avon, the second child and only son of Arthur F. and Ethel G. Brown (nee Mead) of 13 Trowbridge Road, Bradford-on-Avon. Jack was a pupil at Fitzmaurice Grammar School from 1933 until 1938 when he left to join the law firm of Alex Wilkins, solicitors. Soon after war broke out he volunteered for service in the RAF and was selected for aircrew training.

Jack was later posted to 86 Squadron as an observer in a nine-man Coastal Command Consolidated B-24 Liberator crew, skippered by Squadron Leader (Sqn Ldr) Leslie Frank Cooper, RAF.

Based at Ballykelly in Northern Ireland, 86 Squadron was one of many Coastal Command units involved at this time in convoy protection duties over the North Atlantic. Operating in conjunction with naval escort vessels, the RAF's long range patrol aircraft flew arduous escort sorties over the featureless wastes of the ocean, often for up to sixteen hours at a time. Their primary task was to seek out marauding German U-boat wolf packs that stalked allied merchant convoys sailing the North Atlantic between the UK and North America, and attack them with depth charges and guns.

On 8 October, Flying Officer (Flg Off) C. Burcher DFC was flying Consolidated B-24D Liberator Mk IIIA, FL954 'Z', when his crew shared in the sinking of a U-boat with a Liberator of 120 Squadron, south-west of Iceland. *U-643*, a Type VIIC boat (*Kapitänleutnant* Hans-Harald Speidel), was disabled by depth charges and machine gun attacks before her crew abandoned her and the boat blew up and sank. *U-643* was one of two U-boats sunk by 86 Squadron Liberator crews on that day.

At about 8.00am on 24 October 1943, FL954 took off from Ballykelly on an anti-submarine convoy escort patrol. The intention was to rendezvous in the mid-North Atlantic with Convoy ON207, en-route to Halifax, Nova Scotia, when it was about 600 miles SW of Iceland.

The Liberator's take-off was normal but it failed to climb as it should and a few minutes after take-off FL954 crashed into nearby Loch Foyle from a height of about 200ft. The aircraft sank without trace. With no wreckage for the RAF's accident investigators to examine, the precise cause of the crash was never established. Informed speculation was all they had to go on. The Chief Technical Officer at RAF Ballykelly suggested to the Inquiry that the constant speed unit on one of the four Twin Wasp radial engines may have failed, and that the aircraft may have lost height and crashed while the pilots were trying to trace and rectify the fault.

Armourers prepare to load 250lb Mk VIII depth charges into a Liberator GR Mk VA in preparation for an anti-submarine patrol over the North Atlantic. *IWM CH12373*

A German Type VIIC U-boat under attack from depth charges dropped by a Coastal Command aircraft. *Author's collection*

A Consolidated Liberator GR Mk V of 86 Squadron RAF, from Ballykelly, Co Londonderry, in flight. *IWM CH11800*

The aircraft captain, Leslie Cooper, was an experienced pilot with 1,134 hours solo flying time in his log book, which included 80 hours on Liberators.

All nine crew died and the only body recovered was that of the 22-year-old second pilot, Flg Off David Gwynne Evans, RAFVR, from Tenby, Pembrokeshire. The others, all NCOs, were never found and are commemorated on the Commonwealth Air Forces Memorial, Runnymede.

Lough Foyle varies in depth from 15ft to a maximum of 45ft, so it is surprising that no attempt was ever made to salvage the wreckage of FL954.

Sergeant Eric John BROWN

Service No: 1316499, RAFVR; *Unit:* 86 Squadron, RAF Coastal Command; *Died:* 24 October 1943 aged 22; *Commemorated:* Commonwealth Air Forces Memorial, Runnymede, Panel 143; BOA WM; HT.

Chapter Five

WRONG TIME, WRONG PLACE

LUCK AND FATE DECIDE

'There are three different types of luck: Constitutional luck, that is, luck with factors that cannot be changed (for example place of birth and genetic make-up); Circumstantial luck, with factors that are haphazardly brought on (accidents and epidemics are typical examples); Ignorance luck, that is, luck with factors one does not know about (for example, it can be identified only in hindsight).'

Luck and chance can both play a big part in the way our lives unfold. It could mean we feel lucky to have been in a certain place at a certain time, when events turn out to our benefit; or if, when we take a gamble and follow a different pathway to arrive somewhere that we are not expecting, the outcome is far better than we'd hoped for. But the flip side of this is when unwittingly we find ourselves in the wrong place at the wrong time, and inadvertently follow what turns out to be the wrong pathway, with catastrophic results.

ONLY A SHORT RIDE

Trooper Sidney Jack Pratten, Royal Wiltshire Yeomanry – Bradford-on-Avon

On 22 December 1939, Trooper Sidney Pratten set off from his Army billet in Nottinghamshire on a borrowed motorcycle to collect his pay packet. Later that day he was due to travel home to Bradford-on-Avon on embarkation leave; the money would ensure his family would not go short over the festive period.

Three weeks earlier, the Royal Wiltshire Yeomanry had decamped to the Southwell area of Nottingham prior to their imminent departure overseas for Palestine with the 1st Cavalry Division. They had travelled north on 2 December aboard five troop trains that left from south Somerset railway stations at Wincanton, Bruton and Castle Cary, and from Gillingham in Dorset.

It was only a quick ride to the paymaster's office on that wintry morning. With the pay packet safely tucked away inside his pocket, Sidney planned to return to his billet as quickly as possible, pick up his kit and then dash to the railway station and catch the train home.

The fog was thick and visibility poor as Sidney, who was wrapped up warm in his greatcoat, rode towards the Yeomanry's Regimental Headquarters that had been established

Tpr Sidney Pratten, from Bradford-on-Avon, pictured before the war in Royal Wiltshire Yeomanry bandsman's uniform.
Beryl Mayell

in Lowdham village. As he turned into Main Street the shape of an Army lorry, which had been parked at the roadside, loomed out of the swirling fog ahead of him. Before he knew what was happening, Sidney had crashed into the back of the stationary lorry.

Sidney Jack Pratten was born on 7 March 1915 at Bradford-on-Avon, the youngest of nine children to James (1870–1945), a quarry worker, and Rosa Pratten (1874–1956), of Wine Street, Bradford-on-Avon. He was the husband of Violet Maude Pratten (nee Bagg, 1915–86) of 5 Kingston Road, Bradford-on-Avon, and father to Beryl (b.1935, Bradford-on-Avon), their only child.

Before he joined the Army, Sidney worked for Spencer, Moulton & Co and was a member of Spencer Moulton Football Club with whom he played at full back. He was a cornet player in the Royal Wiltshire Yeomanry Band and was a familiar figure at the town's Armistice Day parades in Westbury Gardens when he played the Last Post and Reveille.

Sidney suffered serious head injuries in the collision with the Army lorry but remained conscious, although the next day he died from delayed concussion and a brain injury. A subsequent inquest returned a verdict of accidental death.

Sidney was due to travel home to Bradford-on-Avon by train within a few hours of his accident, and his wife and daughter were awaiting his arrival at the town station. The Royal Wiltshire Yeomanry left Nottinghamshire in mid-January for overseas service in Palestine.

Trooper Sidney Jack PRATTEN

Service No: 552762; *Unit:* Royal Wiltshire Yeomanry; *Died:* 23 December 1939 aged 24; *Buried:* Bradford-on-Avon Cemetery, Wiltshire, Sec S, Grave 95; *Commemorated:* BOA WM; HT; AR.

MOTORCYLE ACCIDENT

Sapper Douglas Herbert William Vincent, 260 Field Company, Royal Engineers – Bradford-on-Avon

Douglas Herbert William Vincent was born in 1917 at Bradford-on-Avon, the eldest son of Frank E. and Ethel Lilian (nee Bricker) Vincent (1890–1951) of 243 Winsley Road, Bradford-on-Avon. His brother Dennis (1919–2000) was a sergeant in the Commandos and had seen action in the raids at Dieppe, St Nazaire, and in Italy.

Douglas had been an engineer at Trowbridge Road Agricultural Works before the war and was reputed to have been an excellent blacksmith and fitter. He was one of the original members of 260 Field Company, Wessex Royal Engineers, which he joined in 1938 as a Territorial soldier. When war broke out in September 1939, being a reservist Douglas was called up straight away.

The Company was made up from new recruits and old hands who had served with the Territorials before the war. Between the outbreak of war and D-Day in June 1944, the Company was based in southern England where it trained hard for the role it would eventually play in the liberation of Europe.

260 Field Company was stationed variously at Codford (Wiltshire), Pangbourne (Berkshire), Dedham (Essex), Deal and Hawkhurst (Kent), before they sailed for Normandy on 19 June 1944. During their time in training they practiced digging trenches, bridging and watermanship, demolition and the use of explosives, mine laying and removal.

Douglas went through all this training but never made it to Normandy: he died in hospital on 3 April 1944 from injuries received in a motorcycle accident near 260 Field Company's base at Hawkhurst, Kent.

Sapper Douglas Herbert William VINCENT

Service No: 2093533; *Unit:* 260 Field Company, Royal Engineers; *Died:* 3 April 1944 aged 26; *Buried:* Christ Church churchyard, Bradford-on-Avon, Wiltshire, Grave 2; *Commemorated:* BOA WM; CC.

SHEFFIELD BLITZ

Private Reginald George Collins, Cheshire Regiment – Bradford-on-Avon

From the age of sixteen Reginald Collins had been employed by Lady Hilda Montgomerie Tothill at The Chantry, latterly as her butler-chauffeur. Lady Tothill also employed Reginald's father, Arthur. The Collins family lived close by in Chantry Lodge. 'He was of a quiet, retiring nature. He was not of an adventurous spirit, and wars and fighting had no appeal for him,' said Emily Collins in an interview with the *Wiltshire Times*, when news was received that her soldier son Reginald had been killed in the Sheffield Blitz.

Reginald George Collins was born in Penzance, Cornwall, in 1911, one of two sons and two daughters to Arthur Edward and Emily Annie Collins of Chantry Lodge, Bradford-on-Avon. Reg, who was engaged to be married, took a keen interest in the work of the Church Army and was a member of the Church of England Men's Society, as well as being a regular attendee at Holy Trinity Church in the town. He was also a keen sportsman and played cricket for the Bearfield Club.

On 10 August 1940 Reg joined the Cheshire Regiment. In December he was being schooled in the use of medium machine guns at the Army's Machine Gun Training Centre in Ladysmith Barracks, Ashton-under-Lyne. Since the day that he reported for duty, Reginald had been unable to visit his parents or fiancée, Miss I. Walker, in Bradford-on-Avon.

He died not on the field of battle manning a Bren gun, but on the streets of an English city, the victim of an enemy bomb. On the evening of Thursday 12 December 1940, the south Yorkshire steel town of Sheffield was attacked by 406 German bomber aircraft, causing extensive material damage and heavy casualties.

Reginald Collins' body was later found on Cherry Street, south of Sheffield city centre, and a stone's throw from Sheffield United's ground. We can only guess at why Reg was in Sheffield on the first night of the Blitz. The street is a 10-minute walk from the main railway station, so at a guess he may have been out with some Army pals. He would not have been at a football match because blackout regulations prohibited stadium floodlighting. Cherry Street was also the site of the old cricket pavilion that was demolished in 1973 to make way for United's South Stand, but being December there was no cricket being played. The Anchor Brewery was a prominent feature of the street and there were many pubs in the area, too, but Reg's personal background – a staunch churchman, engaged to be married – makes it less likely that he was out drinking, but the fact he was a keen sportsman (and a cricketer in particular) might explain his presence in the neighbourhood. When the raid started he may have taken shelter somewhere on

Burned-out trams on the streets of Sheffield after the Blitz of 12 December 1940. *Author's collection*

Cherry Street, Sheffield, as it was in the 1960s. The cricket pavilion is on the right behind the hoardings. It was on this street that Reg Collins died during the blitz on the city. *Sheffield City Council*

Cherry Street that was then hit by a falling bomb, which killed him and covered him with debris, his body laying undiscovered for a week. The fact that his death was not registered until 21st December might support this theory.

In the chaos that followed the raids, Sheffield's Civil Defence services were overwhelmed. Many times during the Phoney War they had rehearsed what to do in the event of an air raid, but nothing could have prepared them for the terrible reality of that Thursday night. The area around United's ground and Cherry Street were badly hit on the night of 12–13 December. Hundreds of bodies were recovered from across the city and the public mortuaries simply could not cope. Identification of individual victims was a priority for the police and Civil Defence, but this was not always so straightforward. The discovery and retrieval of Reg's body, and its subsequent identification, took the overburdened authorities some time. His death was eventually registered by his commanding officer nine days later.

After the war, Yorkshire writer and historian Joyce Holliday recorded the following interview with a Sheffield policeman, who had dealt with the huge numbers of blitz casualties:

> 'If they found a person who was dead as a result of war activity, a form called a Civilian War Death Form had to be filled in by the person who actually found the body... They wanted to know the exact place where the body was found of course, but the most important thing, if it could be established, was the time and date of death... What happened to those Civilian War Death Forms was absolute chaos. They were coming in with just names on and no other details... So the result of that was when I went on duty – we were all working twelve hours from six o'clock at night until six o'clock in the morning – the Superintendent called me in. He had a pile of these forms, incomplete. And he'd got a list of all the men who were on duty, those for whom motor cars were available, those who'd got motorcycles, those who'd got bicycles and those on foot. And we went through them, sat down there from six o'clock till one o'clock in the morning, worked straight through. And we'd get one marked out to Sergeant Smith or whoever it was. "The information I want from him is ----. I want to know the address of this person, the age of this person, where the body was found, was any property found on the body...?" All things like that, sufficient to fill it in. They were all sent out and it took us four or five days to get it in anything like order. Then the question of identifying people came up ...'

It was three months before that particular air-raid mortuary was finally cleared. More than 60 years later, 92 Sheffield blitz victims remain unidentified.

On 15 December the Luftwaffe visited death and destruction again on the city of Sheffield. The butcher's bill for both raids amounted to 668 killed and hundreds more seriously injured – nearly half as many deaths again as those in the infamous Coventry blitz one month before.

Private Reginald George COLLINS

Service No: 4132833; *Unit:* Cheshire Regiment; *Died:* 12 December 1940 aged 30; *Buried:* Bradford-on-Avon Cemetery, Wiltshire, Sec T, Grave 86; *Commemorated:* BOA WM; HT.

London under blitz on the night of 8–9 September 1940. *Author's collection*

LONDON BLITZ

Student Nurse Cynthia Graham Walker, St Thomas's Hospital, London – Winsley

During the invasion summer of 1940, 27-year-old Cynthia Walker from Winsley was a student nurse at St Thomas's Hospital in the heart of London. The big teaching hospital, strung out along the south bank of the River Thames adjacent to Westminster Bridge, looks out across the river to the Houses of Parliament.

I visited St Thomas's on a beautiful autumn day in October 2008 because I wanted to walk the same corridors that Cynthia may have walked nearly 70 years before, and to see for myself the commemorative plaque to the hospital's blitz dead in the Victorian Memorial Hall. St Thomas's Hospital of the 21st century is a very different place to look upon than the austere hospital buildings of the 1940s. Today it has shops and a bank inside the modern concrete and glass extension that leads to the older hospital building. I doubt whether staff and patients of the war years would recognise today's hospital as a place of healing.

Like other London hospitals, St Thomas's had been well prepared for the Blitz that all expected was soon to come. Disaster plans had been rehearsed and everyone knew what they had to do.

Cynthia had spent much of Sunday 8 September with her father, an Army medical officer, at his military hospital in Goodwood House, Sussex. Concerned for the safety of his daughter in London, he asked her to stay the night and go back to duty early the next morning. Cynthia insisted on returning to London that night, fearing that enemy bombing might disrupt trains into the capital and delay her return to work.

A few days before on 6 September, Hitler had given orders for the first major air raid by the Luftwaffe on London. On the afternoon of Saturday 7 September, up to 1,000 German fighters and bombers took off from airfields in France and crossed the English Channel. Herman Goering, commander of the Luftwaffe, stood gleefully on the cliff top at Cap Gris Nez with his sycophantic entourage to wave the great aerial armada on its way to destroy the English capital. This late-summer Saturday afternoon and night saw the opening salvoes in a relentless onslaught that was to last for the next 57 days and nights, and which became known as the London Blitz.

On this the first day and night of the Blitz, Goering's bombers had fixed in their sights the working class streets of East London and the Docklands. Their high explosive bombs and incendiaries killed 436 men, women and children and badly injured some 1,600 more.

By Christmas 1940, more than 13,000 Londoners had been killed and over 50,000 wounded.

Not long after 7.30pm on Sunday evening the air-raid sirens wailed out all over London and at one minute to eight, just as the blackout went up, raiders were overhead and bombs began to fall again on Docklands. The distinctive throb of German bombers was heard over London throughout the night, their crews using the still burning fires from Saturday night's raid to guide them in.

At 2.30am on Monday morning, Block 1 of St Thomas's Hospital received a direct hit from a German bomb causing extensive damage and loss of life. Cynthia was one of six hospital medical staff, all women, who were in the building and who died that night.

Cynthia Graham Walker was born in 1913, one of three daughters to Colonel Spencer Graham Walker, MD, RAMC, and Kathleen Walker, of Burghope, Winsley, Bradford-on-Avon.

All knew Cynthia's father, not unsurprisingly, as 'Johnnie'. He was an outstanding Army doctor of the old school who had seen service in the far-flung outposts of the Empire including India and Egypt, and at Gallipoli during Britain's ill-fated campaign in 1915. Johnnie had retired from the Army in 1938 aged 57 to enter general practice at Bradford-on-Avon in partnership with Dr Eamon Maloney and Dr Beale Gibson. The family moved to an old manor house in Winsley village called Burghope, where they were to stay for more than thirty years.

War broke out in the following year and Johnnie was recalled to take command of No 5 General Hospital with the BEF at Le Tréport in northern France. When it became plain that the BEF was to be evacuated to England, Johnnie led his unit on a trek westwards in front of the advancing German Army, through France to the Breton ports. He succeeded in bringing No 5 General Hospital safely home to its new base at the requisitioned stately home of Goodwood House in Sussex.

Cynthia is buried at Lambeth Metropolitan Borough Cemetery with more than 1,500 other civilian victims of the London Blitz. They include five women who died alongside

Cynthia when the bomb struck St Thomas's: Physiotherapists Miss Marguerite Doucet (29), Miss Stephanie Dunn (25), Miss Gwendolen Lockyer (39), Miss Barbara Thomas (32); and Nurse Miss Sarah Durham (28).

In some areas where experience of air raids was particularly heavy – including parts of London, Hull, Sheffield, Coventry, and Liverpool – mass public funerals for the blitz dead were arranged. The public funerals made full use of the Union flag, which was often draped over the coffins and at the grave and processions that included military and civic dignitaries. But despite the patriotic rhetoric, the burials were too reminiscent of the hated pauper funeral, with its anonymous interment in mass graves. After the war the Government was pressed to pay for memorials at the sites of massed civilian graves, and limited funds were finally made available in 1948. By this time, however, the desire to remember the war had started to wane – people's memories were surprisingly short.

Student Nurse Cynthia Graham WALKER

Unit: Hospital nurse, St Thomas's Hospital, London; *Died:* 9 September 1940 aged 27; *Buried:* Lambeth Metropolitan Borough Cemetery, London; *Commemorated:* Winsley WM; St Thomas's Hospital, London.

DEADLY CLOUDS

Sergeant Charles William Cooch, RAFVR, 7 (Pathfinder) Squadron – South Wraxall

'When Charlie was home on leave he received a telegram from the RAF saying he had to return to base early to make up numbers in a crew. He needed to catch a bus from Five Ways to get the train at Bath, so I lent him my bicycle,' remembers his younger brother John. 'Our black cat followed him up the lane. We never saw our cat again. And we never saw Charlie again either. He was killed the next day.'

Charles William Cooch was born at Monkton Farleigh on 18 October 1922, the eldest of six children to Sidney John (1901–64) and Annie Beatrice Cooch (1902–73). The Cooch family lived in a cottage next to the church, a short distance from Manor Farm where Sid Cooch worked as a cowman for farmer Charlie Tucker. Charlie Cooch attended the village school and sang in the church choir. When he left school Charlie joined his father at Manor Farm. In the summer of 1940 when invasion fever swept the country Charlie joined the Local Defence Volunteers, the forerunners of the Home Guard.

Charlie was a man of many parts. His younger brother John remembers that he 'enjoyed his cricket and singing in the church choir. He was sensible, but full of life.' He was also a great radio enthusiast who loved making wireless sets, and was well known in the surrounding villages where he offered to mend people's radios. Charlie's first success was when he built a 'cat's whisker' set. Not content with playing cricket for the village team, singing and tinkering with radios, Charlie was also a keen amateur photographer, kept racing pigeons and was a good shot with a rifle.

Soon after Charlie had celebrated his eighteenth birthday in October 1940 he was called up to join the RAFVR. He was selected for aircrew training and with his love of

Sgt Charlie Cooch, RAFVR, from South Wraxall, brought home his full flying kit to show his family and to proudly pose for a photograph. He wears a Sidcot flying suit, gauntlets and sheepskin flying boots, and holds a leather flying helmet. *John Cooch*

radios it was almost inevitable that he would become a wireless operator. In April 1943 Charlie completed his basic training and was posted to 4 Radio School at Madley near Hereford. Here he learned the basics of wireless operating and air gunnery in Dominie, Proctor and Anson aircraft. Four months later he was posted to 12 Operational Training Unit (OTU), at Edgehill and Chipping Warden, which used tour-expired Wellington bombers to prepare pupil aircrews for service in Bomber Command. A short spell of training on Short Stirlings followed at 1665 Heavy Conversion Unit, Woolfox Lodge, to accustom Charlie and crew to flying a four-engine bomber, then 15½ hours on Lancasters at 3 Lancaster Finishing School, Feltwell. With his training complete, on 3 March 1944 Charlie was posted to 7 Squadron, an operational Lancaster bomber squadron in the RAF's elite Pathfinder Force.

Charlie and his crew flew on six cross-country training exercises in the squadron's Lancasters to hone their skills as a crew, before they were deemed ready to fly operationally. But Charlie Cooch and the rest of his crew never made it as far as their first operational trip.

As if to underline the desperately short life expectancy of RAF heavy bomber crews, at least three of the five pilots with whom Charlie flew training sorties in his first month on 7 Squadron were dead within five months: 7 Squadron's commanding officer, Wg Cdr William Lockhart and his crew, were shot down and killed on 28 April; Plt Off Arthur Hookway RAAF and crew were lost without trace on 21–22 May; Flt Lt Robert Banks survived long enough to receive a commission and promotion, but he and his crew were fated to die on 12 September 1944.

On 5 May Charlie and his crew were detailed for a 'Y' Exercise – a cross-country training flight during which they would practice using their 'Y', or H2S, radar set under the tutelage of an experienced bomb aimer, Flt Sgt Adrian Carson, RNZAF. On Bomber

Command's Main Force and Pathfinder heavy bomber squadrons it was not uncommon for an extra (eighth) crewmember to be carried to operate the H2S set. He was usually a navigator, but occasionally a bomb aimer, and was known as the 'Y' operator.

Flg Off Ian Bennington, RNZAF, the crew captain, was a 34-year-old married man from the small township of Masterton on New Zealand's north island. He had 278 hours solo in his logbook, with 27 hours on Lancasters. His crew comprised: navigator Flt Sgt Doug Matthews, RAFVR, 23, from Tyseley, Birmingham; bomb aimer Flt Sgt Denis Mayhew, RAFVR, 22, from London's King's Road (his 15 year-old brother Anthony, a deck boy in the Merchant Navy, had been lost at sea in 1941 when MV *British Security* was sunk); mid-upper gunner Warrant Officer (WO) Kenneth Spencer, RAF, 23, from Halifax, Yorkshire; rear gunner Flt Lt Cecil Todd, RNZAF, 22, from Palmerston North, New Zealand; and flight engineer Sgt William Young, RAFVR, 31, from Southampton.

The eighth man onboard Lancaster ND906 with Ian Bennington and his novice crew was their 'teacher', 31-year-old Flt Sgt Adrian Carson, RNZAF, from Brunswick, New Zealand. Carson was a 'screened' (tour-expired and not required to fly again operationally) bomb aimer with 47 operational sorties under his belt – 27 on Short Stirlings with 75 (NZ) Squadron, followed by 20 as a Pathfinder with 7 Squadron on Lancasters. He was a skilled and determined target marker who had survived a gruelling first tour of operations in the summer of 1943 during the hard-fought Battles of the Ruhr and Hamburg, when Bomber Command's losses had reached unsustainable levels.

Nicknamed 'Shorty' when on 75 Squadron, because he was the least-tall member of his crew, Carson was later recommended for the Distinguished Flying Medal (DFM) on 7 Squadron for his 'admirable courage and devotion to duty under difficult circumstances'. He may have been told informally by his squadron commander in April that he had been recommended for the DFM, but official notification was not forthcoming until 27 June 1944, by which time he was dead. Adrian Carson did not live to see the DFM pinned on his chest at Buckingham Palace by the King. His senseless death only underlines the sober fact that at the end of the day it was lady luck that decided who should live and who would die. Experience was often no guarantee of survival.

The Bennington crew took off from RAF Oakington at about 10.00am on the morning of 5 May in Avro Lancaster ND906, K for King. About one hour into the training flight, Ian Bennington encountered difficulty in controlling the bomber. Witnesses on the ground saw the Lancaster emerge from cloud in a steep high-speed dive before crashing into the ground near Ashby St Ledgers, 12 miles north west of Northampton, killing all onboard.

The village of Ashby St Ledgers is largely unknown today outside Northamptonshire. Apart from being where Charlie Cooch's Lancaster fell to earth in 1944, the village also has a place in infamy as where the Gunpowder Plot was hatched more than three centuries earlier in 1605.

George Goode, a farm worker in the neighbouring village of Welton, was probably the last person to see the aircraft before it crashed. He and another man were sorting potatoes in a field at Thrupp Grounds when at about 11.00am George remarked that he could see

No 7 SQDN.

Time carried forward :— 123.20 72.25

Date	Hour	Aircraft Type and No.	Pilot	Duty	Remarks (including results of bombing, gunnery, exercises, etc.)	Flying Times Day	Flying Times Night
		LANCASTER III					
3.3.44	1145	P	F/SGT BANKS	W/OP	X-Country.	4.20	
4.3.44	1115	T	F/SGT BANKS	"	X-Country.	2.50	
28.3.44	1826	Q	F/LT EVANS	"	X-Country. (Recalled. Returned early)	1.30	
5.4.44	1945		F/LT McGILVRAY	"	X-Country. — RECALLED.		2.15
8.4.44	1445	W	W/CDR LOCKHART	"	ERIC. NTGM.	3.35	
9.4.44	1459	U JA911	F/SGT BANKS	"	AIR-TEST	0.20	
12.4.44	20.45		P/O HOOKWAY	"	X-COUNTRY. NIGHT.		3.00
18.4.44	20.55	U JA911	P/O HOOKWAY	"	X-COUNTRY.		3.05
5-5-44		K	F/O BENNINGTON	"	-Y- EX. CRASHED.		

[signature] S/L
O.C. "A" FLT.

Killed on Active Service
5. 5. 44.

TOTAL TIME ...

Charlie Cooch's flying log book with the page bearing the entry for his final flight. *John Cooch*

Excavated wreckage of Sgt Charlie Cooch's Lancaster is brought to the surface at Ashby St Ledgers in 1985. *John Cooch*

and hear an aircraft. It seemed to be following the Northampton-Rugby railway line but sounded as though it was 'struggling'. George had the impression that the engines were developing barely enough power to stop the aircraft from falling out of the sky. His view of the Lancaster from the field was like 'looking at it on its side, rather than looking at its underside', and he lost sight of the bomber when it disappeared from view behind high ground and trees to his left.

The Lancaster emerged from low cloud in a steep high-speed dive. George heard the engines 'roar out' as the aircraft flew almost vertically into the ground with the four Merlins under power. There was an explosion as the Lancaster hit the ground. The force of the impact was so great that much of the airframe, wings and engines were driven up to 30ft into the earth. Eyewitnesses said that nobody was seen to escape from the aircraft before it hit the ground.

Approaching the scene of the crash from the bottom of the field, bystander Mr K. Rushall could see 'the freshly erupted soil with remains of the aircraft forming a mound in the contrasting green of the grass field'. Before he reached the mound he noticed 'pieces of human remains among the grass scattered over the ground… There was no one else there at the time and I left the site deeply disturbed and tried to put the whole incident out of my mind.'

Local troops were quickly on the scene and took charge. An RAF salvage team arrived the next day and began the difficult tasks of recovering the remains of the aircraft and its crew, both of which were strewn over a wide area. It took the RAF team four particularly unpleasant days to clear the crash site.

The precise cause of the accident is not known, but the official RAF investigation recorded it as being a loss of control in turbulent cumulus cloud, probably due to icing of the wings and airframe. Weather forecasters had warned that there was a high risk of aircraft icing up in cloud at low level in the East Midlands area on this day. The report went on to say that Bennington was flying in cloud instead of above it and he may have got into difficulties either through the effects of icing, buffeting or bad instrument flying. The crew had not attended the Met briefing prior to their flight and took off without any definite knowledge of the weather conditions they might encounter en route. What is hard to correlate with the official facts is that several people witnessed the Lancaster on fire as it came out of the cloud and dived into a field about 1 mile north east of Ashby St Ledgers. We will probably never know the truth.

As if the deaths of eight young men were not enough, an unseemly squabble soon broke out between the vicars of South Wraxall and Monkton Farleigh, both of whom claimed Charlie Cooch for their respective villages, and for burial in their village churchyards. In the end Charlie was laid to rest at South Wraxall, his adopted home, although his brother John still believes he should have been buried at Monkton Farleigh, the village of his birth.

Sergeant Charles William COOCH

Service No: 1585116, RAFVR; *Unit:* 7 Squadron, RAF Bomber Command; *Died:* 5 May 1944 aged 21; *Buried:* South Wraxall (St James) churchyard, Wiltshire, Row C, Grave 4.

NEVER A SECOND THOUGHT

Aircraftman 1st Class Herbert Maurice Bird, RAF – Bradford-on-Avon

Friday 7 September 1945. Almost four months since the war in Europe had ended. The fighting against Japan had just been brought to a dramatic close when the Americans dropped A-bombs on two Japanese cities. Peace had finally broken out across the world. In a corner of rural England, flying activity from the RAF airfield at Hullavington in Wiltshire was now for peaceable training flights.

Soon after lunch, 32-year-old AC1 Herbert Bird from Melksham and three other RAF airmen passengers climbed the short metal crew ladder into an Avro Lancaster bomber of the Empire Central Flying School at Hullavington. 'We were all aircrew cadets, all interviewed and selected for aircrew duties,' recalled one of the four, Aircraftman Tony Allard from Bellott's Road in Bath. 'The station commander agreed we could go up for some "learning on the job".'

At 14.20 hours the Lancaster Mk I, ME584, took off on a local flying training exercise. Its two pilots were familiarising themselves with the handling characteristics of the four-engine bomber. The first pilot (and captain) was Sqn Ldr Roy Gregory, AFC, RAFVR; its second pilot was Capt Edward Larter, DFC, AFC, of the South African Air Force.

The Lancaster, ME584, was an old hand. She had originally served with 626 Squadron, a heavy night bomber squadron that had flown in the war from Wickenby in the Lincolnshire Fens. Her squadron code letters and call sign were UM-D2 – or 'Dog Squared' for short. Beginning with the gruelling Battle of Berlin in the freezing early months of 1944, Dog Squared always brought her crews safely home, defying enemy flak and night fighters. The old 'Dog' bucked the odds time and again when Bomber Command's losses were running high. It was a minor miracle that she survived more than fifteen months of hellish night operations over Germany to be 'retired' to the ECFS in May 1945.

Roy Gregory and Edward Larter were both experienced pilots, each of whom had flown extensively during the Second World War. At the time of the crash, 33-year-old Gregory from Brentford, Middlesex, was the Officer Commanding the Training Command Examining Flight of the ECFS at Hullavington, an appointment he had held since June 1944. He had accumulated 3,022 hours of solo flying in his logbook. The award of the Air Force Cross (AFC) to Gregory, in recognition of the good work he had done to improve the standard of flying training instruction at ECFS, was officially announced on the day that he died. He may never have known about the award.

Edward R. Larter, a South African from the foothills town of Stutterheim in the Eastern Cape Province, also 33, had flown de Havilland Mosquitoes with 60 Squadron SAAF from Italy in 1944 on strategic photo-reconnaissance sorties in the Mediterranean theatre and over southern Germany.

Larter's fellow squadron pilots and ground crews held him in high esteem. He had successfully completed an exacting tour of photo-recce operations in the summer of 1944 for which he was recommended the Distinguished Flying Cross (DFC) on 30 September.

His award citation describes how he often 'pressed on to the target in spite of extremely hazardous flying conditions and determined opposition from the enemy'.

On one occasion, although briefed to fly his sortie at 30,000ft over the Munich area, Larter chose to descend below cloud cover to 23,000ft in order to make sure he obtained vital photographs.

The citation concludes that Larter's 'example of outstanding keenness, magnificent airmanship and rare courage has been a rare inspiration to all the flying crews of the squadron'.

As a flight commander during the last six weeks of his tour of duty with 60 Squadron he had amassed 2,278 hours of solo flying and also held the AFC, which had been awarded to him in January 1944.

A more experienced pair of pilots in the RAF would have been difficult to find. With such expertise in the cockpit, Herbert Bird and his fellow passengers may never have given their personal safety a second thought as they boarded the Lancaster.

Gregory and Larter were practising landing the Lancaster at Hullavington on three of her four engines and then taking off again, a procedure known as 'roller landings' or 'touch and goes'. The Lancaster made a heavy landing on three engines with the fourth engine feathered (that is, stopped, with the blades turned edge-on to the airflow to stop the propeller from windmilling). It was climbing away from the runway when the pilot attempted to un-feather the dead engine while banking to go around again for another approach to the runway. The Lancaster quickly lost vital air speed and entered a dangerous

A Lancaster goes up in flames after crash-landing. The impact with the ground has broken her back behind the mid-upper turret and one of her four engine bearers lies in the foreground. The intensity of the fire will quickly reduce the airframe to a heap of ashes. *Author's collection*

AC1 Tony Allard, RAF, was the sole survivor of the crash, but he was very badly burned. *Tony Allard*

The grave of AC1 Herbert Bird, RAF, at Melksham Cemetery. *Author*

stall (which means she was flying too slowly to stay airborne) then one wing dipped and the aircraft fell out of the sky. She struck a tree in a field between Kingsway Bridge and Hullavington railway station before hitting the ground at about 2.55pm, whereupon she caught fire. A volatile cocktail of high-octane petrol, hydraulic fluid and exploding oxygen cylinders caused the Lancaster to blaze fast and furiously until she was all burned out.

Five of the six occupants, including Herbert Bird, were burned to death in the inferno. The sixth man, Aircraftman Tony Allard, had a miraculous escape from the blazing bomber.

> 'It was the first time I had flown with these two pilots and I didn't really know them. I was up in the cockpit where the flight engineer usually stood. It all happened very quickly. We were low down in any case and it was only a matter of seconds before we hit. To this day I've never found out how I got out. I suppose the aircraft must have broken its back and I was thrown clear. Then I found myself outside and on fire, but I had the presence of mind to roll over in the field to try and put it out.'

Tony staggered 200yds across two fields until he reached a Land Girl who was hurrying towards the crash, and then he collapsed. Although fully conscious, he had suffered third degree burns to his hands, face and legs, and after emergency treatment was transferred to the RAF Station Hospital at Melksham. He then lost consciousness and was out cold for a fortnight. Tony was eventually transferred to the specialist burns unit at Queen Victoria Hospital, East Grinstead, where he came under the care of the famous plastic surgeon, Sir Archibald McIndoe. He spent two years as one of McIndoe's 'guinea pigs' and underwent numerous operations and skin grafts to restore his burned hands and face.

Herbert Maurice Bird was born in 1913 at Melksham, the only son of Alfred (b.1884, Hilperton), and Ada R.S. Bird (nee Sawyer) of Bradford-on-Avon, husband of Constance L. Bird of 573 Semington Road, Melksham, and father to Penelope and Angela. Herbert joined the RAFVR on the outbreak of war, prior to which he had worked in the sales department of the Avon India Rubber Works at Melksham. He was also well known in Bradford-on-Avon.

Despite their undoubted experience as wartime fliers, second pilot Edward Larter had logged no time at all piloting Lancasters, while the aircraft captain, Roy Gregory, had logged only six hours solo on the type. The official report into the accident attributed no blame for the crash.

Besides Herbert Bird, there were two other airmen who died in the crash and ensuing fire. They were Jack Gray and Roland Meadows, both of whom were aero engine fitters and recent graduates of the RAF's premier technical apprentice school at RAF Halton in Buckinghamshire. Educated at Bath Technical College, AC2 John 'Jack' Gray, 18, from Odd Down, Bath, was one of three brothers who lost their lives serving in the British Forces. Jack's elder brother, Tom, was one of the first two RAF Victoria Cross winners of the war (awarded posthumously); brother Bob was a Wellington pilot, lost senselessly in 1946 when his aircraft ran out of fuel over the Irish Sea. A greater sacrifice by one family would be difficult to find.

AC1 Roland Meadows, also 18, of Berkeley, Gloucestershire, was the other passenger who died. Roland, who was nicknamed 'Blondie', joined the RAF direct from Lydney Grammar School in February 1943 as a technical apprentice and was trained at RAF Halton. He was a star pupil and passed out with an award for Best Sergeant Apprentice at the end of his course.

Jack and Roland both joined No 1 School of Technical Training in the same (46th) Entry in February 1943; they were in the same group (1 Wing, B Squadron); and they probably shared the same barrack block at Halton. There was a three-week age difference between them and a four-digit difference in their respective service numbers. Both were West Countrymen. The chances are they were friends, too, and by a twist of fate they were destined to die together.

The ECFS was the RAF's centre of flying training and research. It was responsible for examining and inspecting the RAF's own flying instructors; preparing Pilots' Notes for all new types of aircraft coming into service; giving advice on aircraft handling and all-weather flying; and for operating a Research Flight.

Aircraftman 1st Class Herbert Maurice BIRD

Service No: 1187049, RAFVR; *Service:* RAF; *Died:* 7 September 1945 aged 32; *Buried:* Melksham Cemetery, Wiltshire, Grave D15; *Commemorated:* BOA WM; HT; Melksham WM.

Sgt Sam Curnock, RAFVR, from Wingfield, pictured as a newly qualified sergeant pilot. *The Curnock family*

CHARLIE INDIA DOWN

Sergeant (pilot) Samuel David James Curnock, RAFVR, BOAC – Wingfield

In May 1942, fifteen Armstrong Whitworth Whitley Mk V bombers were handed over to the civil airline BOAC from Bomber Command. The twin-engine aircraft had played an important part in bombing Germany during the early stages of the RAF's strategic air offensive, but its lacklustre performance saw it removed from Bomber Command's frontline inventory in April 1942.

Stripped of their armament but with additional fuel tanks fitted in their bomb-bays, BOAC's fleet of Whitleys were used as freighters, flying regularly from the UK to Gibraltar carrying aircraft and engine spares for onward shipment to Malta and Lagos. On the Gibraltar-Malta run they flew vital supplies of ammunition and fighter aircraft spares to the beleaguered island during the siege of 1942–43.

By October 1943 BOAC had returned its Whitleys to the RAF. The aircraft had been found unsuitable for operations in the Mediterranean theatre, owing largely to engine overheating problems.

Sam Curnock had volunteered to join the RAF in October 1940 on his eighteenth birthday, just as the fortunes of the RAF seemed to be swinging in its favour after the desperate air battles of the Battle of Britain in the summer months. He learned to fly on Tiger Moths at 7 Elementary Flying Training School, Desford in Leicestershire, before sailing to Canada for further flying training at 13 Service Flying Training School, North Battleford, Saskatchewan. Sam qualified as a pilot and returned to England. With the shortage of flight crews for civil aircraft he was transferred in May 1942 to fly transport aircraft with Britain's national airline, BOAC, from Whitchurch Airport south of Bristol.

Samuel David James Curnock ('Sam') was born on 9 October 1921 at Grantham, Lincolnshire, the eldest of three sons to David John Curnock (b.1881, Wingfield) and Arabella Gertrude Curnock. In the First World War the Curnock family had lived at Shop Lane, Wingfield, in a house built by David's father.

David Curnock had seen service with the 10th Hussars in India before the First World War. He had also served as a corporal on the Western Front and suffered a shrapnel wound in his back. After the war David joined the railway police, rising to the rank of detective inspector. In 1942 the family lived at 59 Minehead Street, Leicester.

'Sam was a gentle person who had a good sense of humour,' recalls his brother Bob. 'He was a very nice brother and was generally the leader of the three of us. We were a group in ourselves.'

Dick, the third of the Curnock brothers, remembers: 'As children all three of us were interested in aircraft. We used to make flying and static models. Mum boarded across the front part of our lounge to make a small room where we could build our models.'

In September 1942, Sam Curnock was Second Officer in the four-man crew of Whitley Mk V, G-AGCI, which was operated by BOAC on its route between the UK and Gibraltar. Thirty-three year-old Capt Charles Browne, from Richmond, Surrey, was in command of 'Charlie-India'. Born in India in 1909, Charles had gained a chemistry

A BOAC Whitley of the type flown by Sam Curnock. *Author's collection*

degree from Magdalen College, Oxford, before spending four years in Germany as a research chemist. In 1935 he entered civil aviation and began his flying career with British Air Transport, joining Imperial Airways in May 1939. Charles was on the Indian, Far Eastern and trans-African routes before being posted to Home Landplane Operations.

The Second Navigating Officer was Pilot Officer (Plt Off) Philip Dean, RAFVR, 21, from Princes Risborough, Bucks. Philip had won a Kitchener Scholarship to Oriel College, Oxford, but had postponed his studies in 1940 to volunteer for aircrew duties in the RAF. He was seconded to BOAC at the same time as Sam in May 1942.

Radio Officer Ronald Mallett was born at Portmadoc in North Wales. After some time with the Marconi Company he joined Imperial Airways in 1937, serving on the European routes on ground duties at Tiberias, and on the trans-African services.

Charlie-India had flown in to Gibraltar from England on 10 September 1942 and the aircraft's Master had stated in his Voyage Report that the aircraft was tail-heavy for the landing. The aircraft left again for England on 13 September, but her Master decided to turn back after only 25 minutes, reporting that Charlie-India was now flying nose-heavy.

Dick Curnock recalls: 'I noticed that Sam had become nervous towards the end. I remember when he came home on leave from Bristol his fingers were stained yellow from smoking.'

Not long before his death, Sam was second pilot in a BOAC Whitley that crashed in England on take-off due to engine failure. He was uninjured and managed to walk away from the wreckage. In the fortnight that remained before her fatal crash, Charlie-India was the subject of several engineering inspections and three test flights after reports by several pilots of nose and tail-heaviness during flight. These problems appeared cured, but on 19 September the Master reported Charlie-India was underpowered during take-off and the initial climb, and unstable in flight. A further detailed inspection was carried out and another test flight was arranged.

To add to Charlie-India's woes, on 24 September the twin Bristol Hercules engines of an RAF Beaufighter were run up on Gibraltar's tarmac, tail-on to the BOAC Whitley. The powerful propeller wash from the two radial engines caused damage to the trailing edge of the Whitley's elevators and the rudder trim tabs. Engineers made temporary repairs to the elevators, the damaged trim tab mechanisms were replaced, and a test flight was arranged for 3.56pm on 26 September.

With Charles Browne in command, and Sam, Philip and Ronald as crew, Charlie-India took off normally from Gibraltar's east-west runway at 3.56pm and climbed out over the Bay of Gibraltar to about 300ft, whereupon Browne eased the Whitley into a left-hand turn. Then something went badly wrong because the aircraft assumed a power-glide attitude and continued in a shallow dive until it struck the sea at 3.59pm, sinking almost immediately in more than 900ft of water.

With a major military base close at hand, naval vessels were on the scene of the crash within minutes. Apart from a few small items of wreckage floating on the surface, the aircraft was not retrieved, there were no survivors from her crew of four, nor were any bodies recovered.

The fine wooden memorial to Sam Curnock in Wingfield Church. *Author*

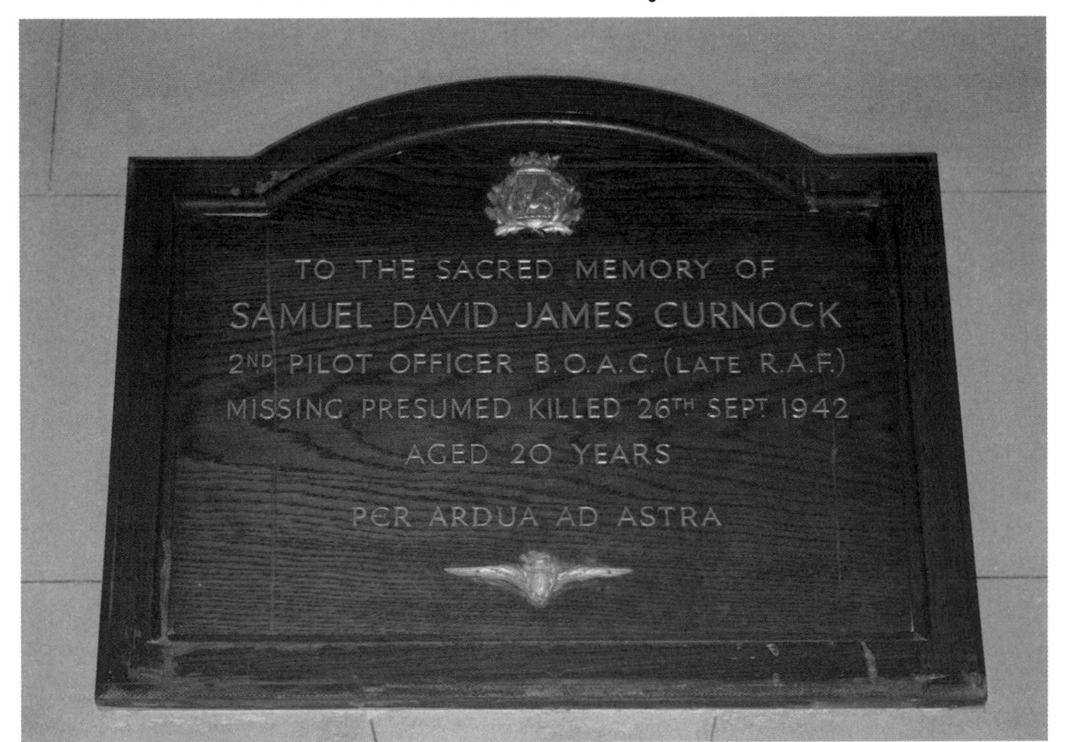

BOAC's technical investigators launched an immediate inquiry into the crash and on 19 October 1942 they made their report. Its conclusion was based more on informed speculation than hard fact, but in the absence of any wreckage or survivors this was the best that could be hoped for: 'The precise cause of the accident cannot be determined, but a possible cause was an uncontrollable elevator trimmer tab due to a fracture in some part of the actuating mechanism... There exists a possibility that subsequent to the take-off one or both of the elevator trimmer tab mechanisms fractured, with the result that the Master was unable to maintain longitudinal control of the aircraft.'

When Sam's parents retired in 1952 they returned to live at Spitalfield in Wingfield. They funded a memorial to their son on the north wall in the village church that can still be seen today.

Sergeant Samuel David James CURNOCK

Service No: 1209186 RAFVR; *Unit:* RAF, seconded to BOAC; *Died:* 26 September 1942 aged 20; *Commemorated:* Commonwealth Air Forces Memorial, Runnymede, Panel 81; St Mary's Church, Wingfield.

ON THE RUN

Sergeant Joseph Groves, 2 Regiment, Royal Horse Artillery – Bradford-on-Avon

When the Italians capitulated on 8 September 1943, thousands of Allied prisoners of war (PoW) escaped into the Italian countryside in the confusion that followed the Armistice. At Campo PG59, Servigliano, the war-weary Italian guards offered no resistance when some 3,000 PoWs poured through a hole they had punched in the perimeter wall and fled into the Tenna valley. The escapees headed into the countryside towards the Sibylline Mountains where the local population were happy to help them.

In the confusion that followed the Armistice, some 20,000 Allied former PoWs roamed aimlessly around the Italian countryside near to the camps from which they had recently escaped. Within a few days local Fascists and the German Army had regained control and combed the areas around the prison camps in search of escaped prisoners. Despite the risk of violence and death at the hands of the Fascists and Nazis, many local Italian families continued to offer help to the escaped PoWs.

The advancing Allied armies in the south of Italy had met stiff German and Fascist resistance, and a front line had more or less established itself on either side of the Po River. For most escapers this was a long and dangerous trek to freedom, although by heading south some did manage to reach the Allied lines. Going east towards the Adriatic was a shorter walk for most, in the hope that they might be taken off by an Allied ship or submarine. Some never made it to freedom and were killed fighting for their lives against Fascist and Nazi troops, who buried them where they fell in the Italian countryside as 'unknown soldiers'. Others were unidentifiable – drowned while attempting to escape, or killed wearing the uniform of another army.

In a perverse irony Joseph Groves was one of the lucky ones, but only inasmuch as he has a named grave in a war cemetery. He was born in 1908 at Bristol, and later married

Phyllis May Groves of Bradford-on-Avon. He was captured in North Africa and shipped across the Mediterranean with other PoWs to a prison camp in Italy.

Joseph died on 11 February 1944 at Pito, a small village 25 miles south of his former PoW camp, in the mountains in the eastern Italian province of Ascoli Piceno. Royal Artillery records tell us that as a PoW he was shot while escaping from the enemy on the orders of the German military authorities in Italy. In 21st century Britain, the Data Protection Act and Ministry of Defence rules governing the disclosure of personnel records mean that unless I can obtain written permission from Joseph's next of kin, I am unlikely ever to find out what actually happened to him at Pito. My guess is that he was hiding out with a family in the village, but was discovered by a German patrol and shot.

Ancona, where Joseph is buried, fell to the Allies on 11 July 1944 when Polish troops of the 8th Army took the strategic Adriatic port city.

The grave of Sgt Joseph Groves, RHA, from Bradford-on-Avon, in Ancona War Cemetery, Italy. *Jane Hutchings*

Sergeant Joseph GROVES

Service No: 777836; *Unit:* 2 Regiment, Royal Horse Artillery; *Died:* 11 February 1944 aged 36; *Buried:* Ancona War Cemetery, Italy, Grave II.H.17; *Commemorated:* BOA WM.

Chapter Six

STRIKE HARD, STRIKE SURE

THE RAF'S STRATEGIC BOMBER OFFENSIVE

'The pilot threw the aircraft into a dive to port but at the same time cannon shells started striking the aircraft. Our mid-upper and rear gunners returned the fire and it seemed to me that all hell had been turned lose. It became evident later that we had been attacked by three Ju88s.' *Lew Parsons, Stirling flight engineer, 75 (NZ) Squadron, August 1943*

RAF Bomber Command had been conceived in the 1930s as a daylight bomber force along the lines of contemporary strategic thought that 'the bomber would always get through'. After war broke out in 1939 the reality became very different. Unsustainable heavy losses in aircrew and aircraft quickly forced most of the Command's efforts into a night offensive which lasted for almost six years, and for which – initially – its crews were poorly prepared and ill-trained. In the opening few years of war, small forces of daylight bombers continued to fly dangerous missions against targets in enemy-occupied Europe, suffering dreadful losses in the process. As the night offensive got into its stride, Bomber Command adapted to the new operational requirements and became equipped with some of the finest bomber aircraft of the war – the Halifax, Lancaster and Mosquito – manned by well-trained aircrew with high morale.

The hard-fought six-year bomber offensive against Germany cost the lives of 55,000 Bomber Command aircrew and more than 8,000 of its aircraft. It had brutally remodelled the face of urban Germany and caused much material damage to the towns and cities of France and the Low Countries. Whether it hastened the end of the war in Europe remains a hotly debated issue, but the bravery of the men who flew by day and night with Bomber Command is an undisputed fact.

DEADLY 'GARDENING'

Sergeant Reginald Talbot Miller, RAF, 44 Squadron – Winsley

The attractive harbour town of Skagen lies at the northernmost tip of Denmark's Jutland peninsula, a narrow spit of land that pokes out into the North Sea. In the north the isthmus is a sparsely populated area of shifting sand dunes, grasses and pine

The crew of a Handley Page Hampden Mk I of 83 Squadron climb down from their aircraft at Scampton, Lincolnshire, on returning from a flight. The upper and lower gun positions occupied by Reggie Miller and Pop Green can be clearly seen.
IWM CH256

German investigators examine the remains of Reggie Miller's Hampden bomber, washed up on the shore at Spirbakke Mile in northern Denmark. ***Søren C. Flensted***

trees, constantly lashed by the westerly winds that reel in from the North Sea. To the west are Tannis Bay and the Skagerrak, the strait that separates Denmark from Norway. To the east is Albaeck Bay, and beyond that the waters of the Kattegat, the narrow stretch of sea that separates Denmark and Sweden. Skagen itself has a population of much the same size as Bradford-on-Avon. Today it is a popular holiday destination for Danes and has been favourably compared with Cornwall by travel writers. In 1940 its coastline was favoured by RAF Bomber Command as a place to sow sea mines.

In July 1940 the opening shots were fired in what came to be known as the Battle of Britain. All through the hot summer the Spitfires and Hurricanes of RAF Fighter Command fought pitched battles against the German Luftwaffe over southern England. The nation's survival hung in the balance. By day and by night during the same period, Bomber Command was hard at work attacking enemy airfields, ports and communications targets in France, Belgium and Germany in a bid to spoil Hitler's invasion plans for Britain. Sgt Reggie Miller from Winsley was a Bomber Command wireless operator/air gunner on Handley Page Hampden medium bombers with 44 Squadron, flying from RAF Waddington in Lincolnshire.

Born at Conkwell in 1921, Reginald Talbot Miller was the only child of Talbot William (b.1882, Castle Coombe, Wiltshire), the gardener at Burghope Manor, and Lilian Miller (nee Marrett, b.1885, St Helier, Jersey). The Millers were one of several families that lived at Richard Villa (now split into two houses and called Plum Cottage and Nightingale Cottage) in the hamlet of Conkwell. Later, they moved to a cottage in

Winsley next to Burghope. As a youngster Reggie was a great favourite in the village and was known to many as 'the boy with the sweet smile'. From 1932 to 1936 he was a pupil at Fitzmaurice Grammar School where he was a keen footballer, playing at right-half for the school XI before joining the RAF in 1936. Reggie travelled to RAF Cranwell in Lincolnshire where, as a boy entrant in Entry 8B9E, he trained as wireless operator at Cranwell's Electrical and Wireless School. In 1939 he passed out of training and was posted to 44 Squadron at RAF Waddington.

On the night of 19 July 1940, Hampden L4087, C for Charlie, with its crew of four, took off from its base at Waddington and headed east across the North Sea. Its mission was to lay sea mines in the narrow coastal waters off Fredrikshavn between Denmark and Sweden, known as the Kattegat but codenamed 'Yewtree' by Bomber Command.

When introduced into service with the RAF in September 1938, the twin-engine Hampden was faster and more agile than its two Bomber Command contemporaries the Armstrong Whitworth Whitley and the Vickers Wellington, and could carry twice the bomb-load of the Bristol Blenheim. It was regarded as a fine, modern medium bomber aircraft and made an important early contribution to the RAF's bombing activities, but its unorthodox configuration and poor defensive armament meant it was soon outclassed.

The slender Hampden, nicknamed the 'flying panhandle' and the 'flying suitcase' by its crews, was a curious looking aircraft with an 8½ foot-deep, slab-sided forward fuselage measuring just 3ft across – the width of a single bed. It was designed to carry a 2,000lb bomb-load and a crew of four – pilot, observer, wireless operator/upper rear gunner, and lower rear gunner. With such a narrow fuselage interior, the crew were not able to move about easily from one crew station to another if the need arose. The Hampden's fuselage interior was unheated which meant the crew needed to wear electrically heated flying clothing to keep warm. When compared to the next generation of RAF bombers like the Lancaster, in many ways the Hampden was a very unsatisfactory aircraft.

C for Charlie's pilot was Sgt Edward Farrands from Hove in Sussex, who had celebrated his twenty-third birthday only a few weeks earlier. Edward had studied for a Bachelor of Science degree in engineering before joining the RAF in November 1937 to train as a pilot. (On 21 December 1939 the Hampden in which he was the second pilot had been shot down into the sea in a case of mistaken identity. Returning from a long range reconnaissance mission to Norway, the Hampden was attacked by two Spitfires of 602 Squadron which had mistaken the RAF bomber for a German Dornier 17. The Hampden crashed into the Firth of Forth, but luck was with the crew when they were pulled from the water by a fishing boat just as the daylight began to fade.)

The pilot's cramped compartment had more the feel of a fighter aircraft than the twin-engine bomber that the Hampden was. Once he had strapped into his seat at the front of the aircraft the pilot could not see or speak directly to his crew, except via the intercom. That said, he would have enjoyed a superb field of view through the large sliding canopy and three-piece windscreen.

The crew's observer (or navigator) was Sgt Percy Nixon, 24, from Sheffield. In 'civvie street' he had been an articled chartered accountant in the City before choosing to join the

RAF in March 1939. A keen Scout, Percy also gave generously of his time to the Sheffield Borstal Committee on which he was a representative. Percy sat in the glazed nose section beneath the pilot's compartment. His small navigation table was stowable when the aircraft neared its target and he was required for bomb-aiming.

Manning the twin Vickers gas-operated (GO) guns in the cramped ventral cupola was Plt Off Bernard 'Pop' Green, from Bourne End, Buckinghamshire. He fired his gun through an opening window to the rear, either prone or kneeling. At 52 years old he was by far the oldest member of the crew as his nickname implied, and had fought in the First World War when he won the Military Cross for bravery. In mid-1940 there had been an influx into Bomber Command of air gunner officers – some of whom were medically not fit enough, and others who were too old, to become pilots or observers. Several, like Pop Green, were veterans of the First World War.

At 19 years of age, wireless operator/air gunner Sgt Reggie Miller was the youngest crewmember. He shared his compartment in the narrow upper rear fuselage with a pair of Vickers 'K' guns and bulky wireless transmitter and receiver sets. Due to a lack of space the receiver had to be installed on its side. A hinged Perspex cupola could be lowered when the gun was not in use to protect Reggie from the airstream and the elements.

Minelaying – or 'gardening' as RAF bomber crews knew it – was not a popular pastime. Its main purpose was to disrupt enemy sea traffic by laying sea mines. Sea mining by RAF aircraft had begun in April 1940 and at first involved a relatively low dropping height of 1,000-1,500ft – and sometimes even lower – at which aircraft were particularly vulnerable to light flak, notably from flak ships in the vicinity of the mining areas. A long timed run-in from a visual pinpoint on the enemy coastline was also necessary, together with the need for the pilot to hold a steady course for two or three minutes after releasing the mines.

Therefore it was not hard for German anti-aircraft (flak) gunners to get Edward Farrands' slow-flying Hampden in their sights. Flying a straight and level course to drop its cargo of mines, the bomber was hit by flak at 00.50am from *4. Res. Flakabteilung 615*, which caused it to ditch five minutes later into Tannis Bay, some 300yds off Kandestederne on the western coastline of the Jutland peninsula. As it hit the surface of the sea the Hampden flipped over onto its back, broke up and sank in shallow water.

Several hours later, at 8.00am, peat cutters in the neighbouring village of Hulsig informed the local police they had found a British airman wandering in the dunes. It was the rear gunner, 'Pop' Green, who told the police that his aircraft had crashed into the sea a few hundred yards off the west coast and that he had swum to the shore. He had then walked east for a couple of miles in the direction of smoke coming from the village. The Germans in nearby Skagen were alerted to his presence and arrived soon after to take him into custody.

It was not long before the police received a further report of another British airman at large. The pilot, Sgt Edward Farrands, had been found sheltering inside a summer cottage in Kandestederne. Although he had injured a leg in the ditching, Farrands had still managed to struggle ashore but was soon rounded up by the Germans.

On 21 July the body of Sgt Reggie Miller was found washed up on the beach near Spirbakke Mile, close to where the bomber had crashed into the sea, and was taken to

Skagen Cemetery. The graves of Reggie Miller and Percy Nixon are among the group of five beside the aircraft propeller.
Søren C. Flensted

Skagen mortuary. On the 24th he was laid to rest in Skagen cemetery, the same day that the body of Sgt Percy Nixon was found further away on Nordstrand (North Beach) at the northern tip of the peninsula. The day after he, too, was buried in Skagen cemetery.

Sgt Pilot Edward Farrands and air gunner Plt Off Bernard 'Pop' Green, MC, survived their ordeal to become prisoners of war. In March 1944, 'Pop' Green broke out of Stalag Luft 3 prison camp in the 'Great Escape', but he was soon recaptured and returned to captivity with 22 other escapees. They were the lucky ones: 50 of their fellow escapers were murdered by the Gestapo in one of the worst atrocities of the Second World War against unarmed prisoners of war. Three men eventually made it to freedom.

After the war, Reggie's parents Talbot and Lily travelled to Denmark to visit their son's grave, staying with a family at Skagen. Queen Alexandrine, the consort of King Christian X of Denmark (whose lady in waiting, by coincidence, had some personal interest in Winsley and Limpley Stoke), heard of their presence in the town and invited them to come and see her informally. Sadly, the Millers were unable to accept this honour because their homeward flight was due to leave almost immediately.

Lily Miller kept every letter that Reggie wrote home from the RAF. When she died they went into her coffin as a pillow.

Sergeant Reginald Talbot MILLER

Service No: 551536, RAF; *Unit:* 44 Squadron, RAF Bomber Command; *Died:* 20 July 1940 aged 19; *Buried:* Skagen Cemetery, Denmark, Coll Grave M.2; *Commemorated:* Winsley WM; Battle of Britain Chapel, Westminster Abbey.

Sgt Deryck Fletcher, RAFVR, from Holt.
Holt Village Hall

LOST WITHOUT TRACE

Sergeant Deryck Fletcher, RAFVR, 40 Squadron – Holt

The ancient Hanseatic port city of Hamburg on Germany's Baltic coast, home to more than 2 million inhabitants, was a favourite target for the RAF's night bombers in the Second World War. In six years of war the RAF and US 8th Air Force mounted seventeen major attacks on the city, not to mention dozens of smaller attacks, reducing three-quarters of Hamburg to rubble. During three muggy nights in late July 1943, RAF heavy bombers set the city ablaze, causing a cataclysmic firestorm that largely destroyed Hamburg and incinerated 42,000 of its inhabitants.

Hamburg had been struck three times in four nights between 8 and 11 May 1941, when the shipyards and the city were targets for Bomber Command. On 11 May, 92 aircraft were despatched. Among

This Wellington Mk II bomber of 40 Squadron is similar to that flown by Deryck Fletcher when he went missing over Hamburg on 12 May 1941. *Andy Thomas collection*

their number was Wellington bomber navigator Sergeant Deryck Fletcher from Holt. For Deryck and his 40 Squadron crew it would prove to be their final trip.

Deryck Fletcher was born in 1920, the son of Albert and Elizabeth Fletcher, latterly of High Heaton, Newcastle-upon-Tyne. Deryck taught commerce at the Gregg School in Ilford, Essex. The school specialised in business education and was a branch of the de Bear Schools group, which at the time was one of the largest chains of commercial schools in the world.

Deryck volunteered for the RAF in 1939 and was selected for aircrew training. He trained as a navigator and was posted to 40 Squadron flying Wellington bombers from RAF Alconbury in Suffolk. On the night of 11 May 1941 at 10.25pm, Vickers Wellington Mk Ic, R1330, H for How, took off from Alconbury to bomb Hamburg. In command of the six-man crew was 24-year-old Sgt Pilot Roderick Finlayson, RNZAF, from Dunedin, New Zealand. Deryck Fletcher was the navigator. The other crew members were second pilot Sgt James Murray, RAFVR, (23) of Silecroft, Cumberland; Flt Sgt Harold Tuckwell, RAFVR, aged 20, wireless operator/air gunner, of New Brighton, Cheshire; and air gunners Flt Sgt Percy Beckett, RAFVR, (25), married, from Taunton, Somerset, and Flt Sgt J. Shaw.

Nothing further was heard from the aircraft after take-off and it later transpired that H for How had been lost with all her crew, except one. The front gunner, Flt Sgt J. Shaw, had survived whatever fate had befallen the bomber, to become a prisoner of war at Stalag Luft 1, Barth Vogelsang, east of the Baltic port city of Lübeck. The other crewmembers are buried at Kiel War Cemetery in northern Germany.

It is almost impossible to say what caused Deryck's Wellington to disappear without trace, and the likely causes are many. Was H for How lost on the way to Hamburg, over the target, or on its return flight? The bomber's loss could have been due to a single factor, or may have been down to an unlucky comination of several, like enemy action (fighters and flak), mechanical failure (such as an engine fault), running out of fuel, a mid-air collision with another aircraft, or falling victim to bad weather.

Of the three bombers that failed to return, two were from 40 Squadron. The other squadron Wellington lost that night was R1461, Z for Zebra, skippered by 21-year-old Midlander Sgt Fred Luscombe, RAFVR, which crashed into the sea killing all its crew.

Sergeant Deryck FLETCHER

Service No: 902403; *Unit:* RAFVR, 40 Squadron; *Died:* 12 May 1941 aged 21; *Buried:* Kiel War Cemetery, Germany, Grave 4.C.2; *Commemorated:* Holt WM.

VANISHED OVER THE SEA

Sergeant Jeffcote Louvain Angell, RAFVR, 405 (RCAF) Squadron – Bradford-on-Avon

More than 22,000 Allied airmen disappeared without trace on operations during the Second World War and have no known graves. Gloved hands waving from a darkened cockpit to a huddle of ground crew beside the runway may have been the last anyone saw of them – in this world at least. Their names are commemorated on the Commonwealth Air Forces Memorial at Runnymede in Surrey, overlooking the River Thames and the historic water meadows where Magna Carta was signed in 1215.

A five-man bomber crew gather around the rear turret of a Wellington. *Author's collection*

Jeffcote Louvain Angell was born in 1916 at Nuneaton, Warwickshire, one of six children to Frank and Frances Angell (nee Gorton). On 5 October 1916 Jeffcote's father, Frank, was killed in action on the Somme while serving as a lance-corporal with the 1st Battalion Wiltshire Regiment. In 1927 aged 11, Jeffcote went to Fitzmaurice Grammar School where he was a pupil until 1933.

When war broke out in 1939, the Angell family were right behind the nation's call to arms. Five of the children joined the armed forces; the sixth was in a reserved occupation as a railway guard on the GWR at Swindon. Jeffcote volunteered for service in the RAF and was selected for aircrew training. He later joined 405 (RCAF) Squadron, a Wellington bomber squadron based at RAF Pocklington in Yorkshire.

On 16 June 1941, Jeffcote was one of a six-man crew captained by 29-year-old Sgt William MacGregor, RAFVR, from Rochdale, Lancashire. They took off from Pocklington at 11.03pm in Vickers Wellington Mk II, W5522, Q for Queenie, and climbed away over the Vale of York. Queenie crossed the Yorkshire coast and headed east across the North Sea as part of a 105-strong Bomber Command force that had been briefed to attack the Rhineland cathedral city of Cologne in western Germany, the third consecutive raid on the city in as many nights.

The MacGregor crew would have been unaware of other bombers in the night sky around them. The only indication of another aircraft nearby would have been if they were bumped around in its slipstream. If it was a clear night one of the gunners might have spotted the tell-tale fiery glow from engine exhausts, or moonlight glinting on polished Perspex.

Queenie's crew had probably reached Cologne, dropped their bombs and were heading towards home, when a distant radio station in England picked up a transmission from their wireless operator. He may have been transmitting a distress call in plain language which located their position as somewhere over the North Sea. Q for Queenie was heard briefly on the W/T at 3.03am before the airwaves went dead. She is then presumed to have crashed into the sea midway between the Dutch coast and Orfordness, Suffolk.

What caused the bomber to crash is not known. The aircraft and all six crew were lost without trace and their names are commemorated on the Commonwealth Air Forces Memorial, Runnymede. They were the Wellington's second pilot, Plt Off Geoffrey Pullen, RAFVR, 25, from Ealing, West London, who had worked as a solicitor before joining the RAF; Sgt Robert Martin, RAFVR (23), of Heaton, Northumberland; Sgt Sidney Harvey, a regular RAF serviceman, age 21, from Bishopstoke, Hampshire; and Sgt Lewis Goode, RAFVR, (20), from Nottingham. They had the sad distinction of being the first aircrew in the Second World War to be lost on operations with a RCAF bomber squadron. Two other bombers failed to return that night.

The Commonwealth War Graves Commission records Jeffcote's age at death as 27 years old. His birth was registered in the first quarter of 1916, which made him at least 25 when he died.

Sergeant Jeffcote Louvain ANGELL

Service No: 924774, RAFVR; *Unit:* 405 (RCAF) Squadron, RAF Bomber Command; *Died:* 17 June 1941 aged 27; *Commemorated:* Commonwealth Air Forces Memorial, Runnymede, Panel 38; BOA WM, HT.

Sgt Bunny Willmer, RAFVR, from Bradford-on-Avon. *Yvonne Gosselin*

CONFRONTING THE PAST

Sergeant Bernard Kenneth George Willmer, RAFVR, 104 Squadron – Bradford-on-Avon

In the early hours of 5 July 1941 a Wellington bomber from 104 Squadron made an emergency landing at RAF Exeter, a Fighter Command airfield in south Devon. It had been so badly damaged by flak during a night raid on the French port of Brest that its pilot was not able to fly the bomber home to its base in Yorkshire. The Wellington, a Rolls-Royce Merlin engined Mk II, was repaired at Exeter. Several months later on 27 September another crew from 104 Squadron at RAF Driffield, which included Sgt Bernard Willmer from Bradford-on-Avon, was sent to collect the aircraft.

Bernard Kenneth George Willmer, known to his family and friends as 'Bunny' (apparently, because of his great speed as a footballer), was born in 1920 at Chippenham, the only son and second child of George Willmer, latterly of 101 Trowbridge Road, Bradford-on-Avon. George worked at the mushroom farm on Frome Road, which was a feature of Bradford life until well into the 1980s.

In 1938 Bunny married Joan Patricia Varnam (1920–2004), whose family had recently moved to Bradford-on-Avon from Nottingham when Joan's father took over the management of the Coop on Silver Street. The newly-weds set up home at Southville Gardens where they raised two children, Yvonne and Tony.

Bunny was a pupil at Fitzmaurice Grammar School from 1931 to 1936 where he was a keen footballer, playing outside right for the school XI. When he left school he went to work for Wiltshire County Council before joining the staff of the Urban District Council as a plumber. In the autumn of 1940 Bunny volunteered for aircrew duties in the RAF, eventually joining 104 Squadron in 1941 at RAF Driffield, Yorkshire, as a wireless operator/air gunner.

With 126 hours solo flying under his belt, but only 23 hours on Wellingtons, 26-year-old crew captain Plt Off John Robertson, RCAF, a farmer's son from Iroquois, Ontario, was not an experienced pilot. But his meagre level of flying experience was not unusual among newly qualified RAF bomber pilots at this time in the war. He had certainly impressed the

Sgt Jim Wright, RAFVR, was married three months before the fatal crash that claimed his life and those of his crew. *Duncan March*

panel at his enlistment interview in Kingston, Ontario, as robust and healthy-looking, quick-witted, dependable and suitable for commissioned rank. In civilian life John Robertston had worked as a crane operator with a coal company for several years before volunteering for the RCAF in June 1940. He completed his flying training in December when he passed out as a sergeant pilot, and continued his training in the UK at 19 OTU in March 1941 before posting to 104 Squadron on 6 May. John was finally commissioned in August 1941.

Robertson's all-sergeant crew was sent to collect the Wellington from RAF Exeter. In its number it included 20-year-old wireless operator/air gunner 'Bunny' Willmer from Bradford-on-Avon; second pilot Leslie Rhodes (21) from Flixton, Suffolk; 23-year-old observer Matthew 'Jim' Wright, a married man from Hampton, Middlesex; and air gunners Victor Riddiford aged 21 from Southampton, and Gordon Dundas (24, and married) from Dundee.

Before Robertson could fly the Wellington back to Driffield it was necessary for him to carry out an air test. With all six crew on board, Wellington Mk II, W5432, H for Harry, took off from Exeter in the mid-Saturday afternoon of 27 September. Minutes after take-off Robertson flew a circuit to bring the Wellington back in towards the airfield from the direction of Poltimore village, to the northwest, but it was then that he ran into low cloud, mist and rain. Crash investigators presumed that he had been startled to see the flank of Pinn Hill rising in front of him through the murk and, banking hard to avoid striking the hillside, the Wellington had clipped trees with a wing before crashing into a field at 4.45pm. H for Harry ploughed through a hedge on Old Park Farm between West Clyst and Pinhoe and burst into flames when escaping fuel ignited. The Wellington's point of impact was less than a minute's flying time and no more than a mile away from a safe touchdown at Exeter.

First to reach the crash site was the local ARP warden Ernest Oddy, who found John Robertson still alive but fatally injured. The rest of his crew had died on impact. On striking the ground the tail section of the bomber had broken off and was found virtually intact in the centre of the field. At the time, there was speculation that if the rear gunner had stayed in his turret he might well have survived the crash.

There are two especially sad postscripts to this tragedy: the first is that Bunny had celebrated his 21st birthday only a few days earlier; and the second concerns the Wellington's navigator, Jim Wright, who had married just three months before. Six weeks after the crash Jim's widowed bride, Mollie, made a pilgrimage with her sister, Beryl, to lay flowers on her husband's grave in Exeter Higher Cemetery. In her wartime diary, Beryl Phippen wrote:

> 'November 15, 1941. Mollie and I caught the 2.50pm train from Waterloo to Exeter. We arrived about 7pm and took a bus to Pinhoe.
>
> 'Arrived at Mr and Mrs Potter's house about 8pm. They made us very welcome. We sat and talked to the family and to bed about 11 o'clock. The Potters have four daughters and one son. Mr Potter is the village policeman.
>
> 'November 16. Up about 9am. Raining hard. Mr Potter got a lift for us to the cemetery in Exeter and we put flowers on Jim's grave. We had to inquire which one it was as we had no number. It was still pouring with rain and we were soaked. Back to Mr Potter's house where they gave us tea and dried our coats in front of the fire. Left the house at 4.30pm and caught the 5pm train to Waterloo. Arrived home at Hampton at 10pm.'

The human kindness shown to a pair of total strangers by the Potter family probably made their painful graveside homage, on such a bleak day, only just bearable.

'I couldn't have known it at the time,' remembers Bunny's daughter Yvonne Gosselin, 'but when my father died they didn't have time to bring him home to be buried near us. When men like my father were killed in service, they just buried them where they died.' Thus, over time, Bunny Willmer's burial site was lost to his two children who were too young to have known him. All that Yvonne had to remind her of her father was a studio portrait photograph of him in uniform. It had been taken shortly before Bunny's death at the age of 20.

Yvonne: 'Right after my father died my mother joined the WAAFs and became a wireless operator. When the war ended she met an American GI named Andrew Foley. They married and we moved to the States.' In turn, Yvonne married an American and raised her own family. Her youngest daughter, Bonnie, a school teacher in Nottingham,

New Hampshire, inadvertently stumbled on the key that would let her mother unlock the answer to a lifelong question.

Working on an Internet project with her students in 2003, Bonnie discovered the Commonwealth War Graves Commission website. Out of curiosity she entered her grandfather's name in the search engine, and within moments she had the answer to the question that had evaded her mother for more than half a century.

'Basically, it was 62 years of wondering,' said Yvonne. 'I'd been back to England many times and I never would have known where to look for my father's grave in a million years. Now I knew where he was buried and I soon discovered much more besides – like where he died and how he died.'

Knowing all this, Yvonne returned to England in November 2003 when she was invited by the Royal Marines to place a wreath on her father's grave during the Remembrance Day ceremony at Exeter Higher Cemetery. After the wreath laying Yvonne reflected on the occasion: 'It still boggles my mind,' she says. 'Obviously you go on and you live your life, but as I've gotten older you can't help but wonder: I had a father; where is he buried? What happened to his family? Now this. You just never know when you'll come face to face with your past.'

Sergeant Bernard Kenneth George WILLMER

Service No: 1183439, RAFVR; *Unit:* 104 Squadron, RAF Bomber Command; *Died:* 27 September 1941 aged 20; *Buried:* Exeter Higher Cemetery, Devon, Section Z.K. Grave 47; *Commemorated:* BOA WM; HT.

Wellington Mk II aircraft of 104 Squadron. W5461 R-EP in the foreground, sister aircraft of W5432, failed to return from Berlin on 12–13 August 1941. *Author's collection*

THE HUNTER AND THE HUNTED

Flying Officer Ronald Percy David Perkins, RAFVR, 83 (Pathfinder) Squadron – Bradford-on-Avon
Flying Officer Ralph Leonard Reeves, RAFVR, 156 (Pathfinder) Squadron – South Wraxall

Late evening on 19 February 1944. Chill winds curl in from the North Sea bringing snow to the low-lying bomber airfields of eastern England. Despite the awful weather forecast, tonight is a 'maximum effort' for Bomber Command. Its squadrons will despatch 832 heavy bombers and more than 5,800 aircrew against the far-distant city of Leipzig in eastern Germany. At 530 miles, Leipzig is at the extreme range of both the Lancaster and Halifax. The 7½-hour round trip will be made in total darkness and freezing temperatures.

The so-called Bomber Battle of Berlin has been raging throughout the bitter winter months of 1943–44 and Air Chief Marshal Sir Arthur 'Bomber' Harris, the Commander-in-Chief of RAF Bomber Command, has now realised that the 'Big City' (as the German capital is known to RAF bomber crews) is not going to crack under bombs alone. With losses running high on his bomber squadrons and morale among the crews at low ebb, Harris has decided to switch his attention away from the Reich capital to other German cities.

On that Sunday night, the names of two Wiltshire men were among the hundreds of aircrew rostered to fly with the RAF's elite Pathfinder Force. The task of the Pathfinder squadrons was to fly ahead of the Main Force bombers and mark the target with brightly coloured pyrotechnics to ensure those following dropped their bombs in the right place.

Flg Off Ronald Perkins, from Bradford-on-Avon, was the bomb-aimer in an 83 Squadron Lancaster crew flying from RAF Wyton in Huntingdonshire, skippered by 20-year-old Plt Off Victor Langford, from Leigh-on-Sea in Essex. With him were Flt Sgt William Lindley Lloyd, navigator, 23, from Walton-on-Thames, Surrey; Sgt Ernest Curzon, flight engineer; Sgt William Crockford, wireless operator; and the two air gunners – 19-year-old Sgt Thomas Davies from Westcliff-on-Sea, Essex, and Australian Flt Sgt William Sutton, RAAF, aged 23, from Ryde, New South Wales.

From the village of South Wraxall, Flg Off Ralph Reeves was an air gunner with 156 Squadron – also a Lancaster unit – based at RAF Warboys in Cambridgeshire. As tail gunner he had the loneliest position in the aircraft, but he was often the bomber's first line of defence – and vulnerable to injury or death in an enemy night fighter attack. Ralph's crew was captained by 25 year-old Acting Sqn Ldr Anthony Saunders from Forest Gate in Essex. Saunders was an experienced Pathfinder skipper who had already flown at least 48 operational sorties and had with him an equally experienced crew, most of whom had already flown a complete 30-op tour of bomber operations.

Up at the front in the Lanc's cockpit with the pilot was the 22-year-old flight engineer, Plt Off John Taylor, from Finchley in Middlesex – Saunders' right-hand man when it came to flying the big bomber. Beneath the pilot and engineer's positions in the glazed nose section was the bomb-aimer's compartment, where Flg Off Cedric Gough could be found with his bomb sight and array of bomb selector switches. Only a few weeks before, he had learned of the award of his DFC. In the curtained off compartment behind the pilot, ensconced at his dimly-lit chart table, was the navigator Flt Lt William

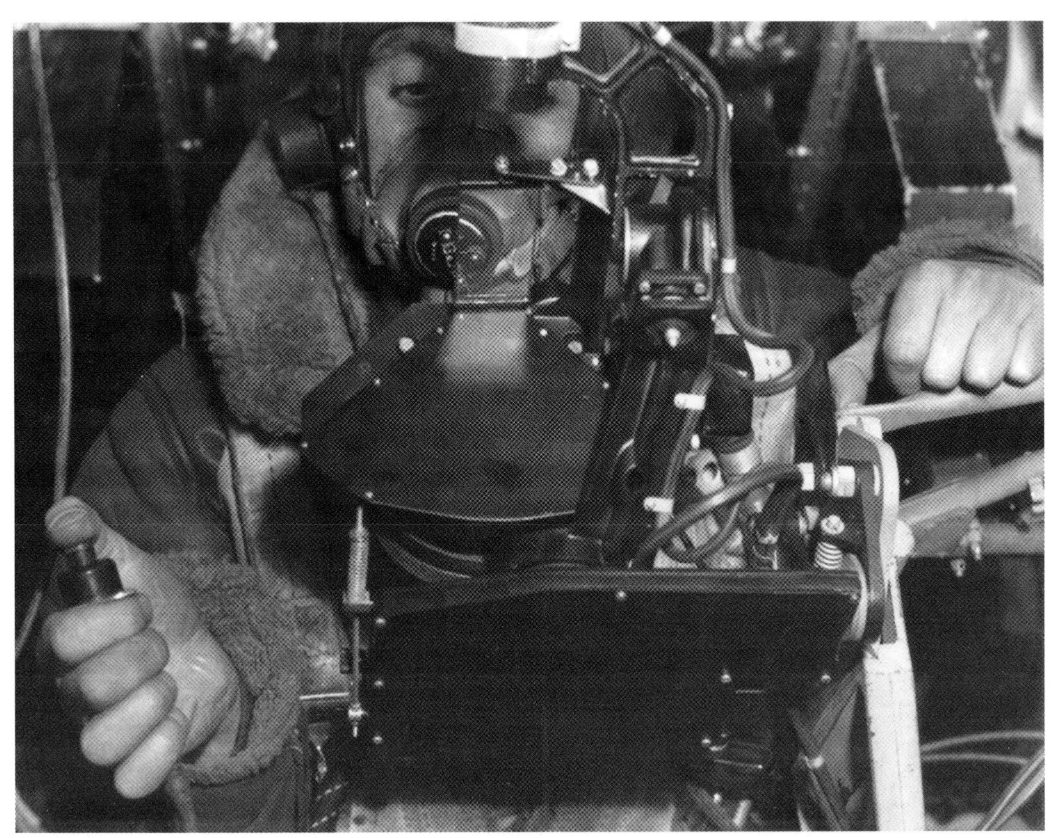

The bomb-aimer in an Avro Lancaster operating a Mk XIV Stabilised Vector Bombsight at his position in the nose of the aircraft. *IWM CH12283*

Sterns, DFC, a 26-year-old Canadian from Ottawa, Ontario. Sterns, a graduate of McGill University in Montreal, had won his DFC in 1942 serving with 148 Squadron, a Wellington bomber squadron flying from Malta and Egypt against Axis targets in Italy and Libya. Behind the bulkhead wall and forward of the front wing spar sat the wireless operator, WO John Webster, tuning in to his TR1154/1155 radio set. Midway along the fuselage was the mid-upper gun turret where Flt Lt William Donner, DFM, 25, an Aussie from Woodford, Blue Mountains, New South Wales, sat in a sling-like canvas seat suspended beneath the turret mechanism. Donner, a married warehouseman in civilian life, had received his DFM in the summer of 1943 while flying with 50 Squadron, another Lancaster unit.

Born on 18 April 1922, Ronald Percy David Perkins was the eldest son of Mr and Mrs Perkins, and lived with his family at one of the lodges on the Moulton family's Hall estate at Bradford-on-Avon. Alex Moulton was a contemporary of Ronald. At the time of writing he is now in his eighties and still lives at the family home, an imposing Elizabethan pile a short walk from the town centre. Alex clearly remembers the Perkins family:

'After the First World War, Perkins became the chauffeur to our family at the Hall. The Perkins family lived in one of the three lodges by the gate. In the first lodge lived the head gardener called Keen; the middle lodge was used as a schoolroom for the Moulton grandchildren; and in the far lodge was the Perkins family. Mrs Perkins was responsible for the Hall's dairy. We kept a herd of Jersey cows and a man called Bodman brought down the milk in pails from the Tump [above St Margaret's Place]. The Perkins had two children – Ronnie and Gordon [b.1926]. Ronnie was a contemporary of my brother, John. Ronnie was two years younger than me. He was very bright. Not everybody went to the Grammar school, but Ronnie got there on merit.'

Alex recalls how the children of the Hall household played with their contemporaries from the families of those employed on the estate. He recalls one particular incident in the garden: 'We had one of those water tanks in the garden flush with the ground for the gardeners to water the grounds. We were playing about in the garden one day when Ronnie fell into this thing and I pulled him out!'

(Alex, now Dr Alex Moulton, achieved fame as the engineer who invented the hydrolastic suspension system for the Mini car, and the small-wheeled Moulton bicycle.)

In 1933 at the age of 11, Ronald became a pupil at Fitzmaurice Grammar School. When he left in 1939 he went to work for Spencer, Moulton & Co before volunteering in 1942 for RAF aircrew training. In July 1943 Ronald married Josie Morris at Holy Trinity parish church. (She gave birth to their only child and daughter, Judith, soon after receiving a telegram from the Commanding Officer of 83 Squadron telling her Ronald was missing on operations.) On completion of his training, Ronald was posted as a bomb aimer to 83 Squadron, a Lancaster squadron in the elite 8 (Pathfinder) Group, stationed at RAF Wyton in Huntingdonshire.

Little is known of Ralph Reeves' background, other than that he may have been born at Long Ashton in Somerset in 1920, and that his mother's maiden name may have been Phelps. The Reeves family lived at South Wraxall in the Second World War.

Against the background of mounting losses, the Saunders crew had been posted in to 156 Squadron from neighbouring 7 Squadron at RAF Oakington on 5 January 1944. They were a hurried response to help plug gaps left by the loss of so many experienced 7 Squadron crews during December 1943.

No 156 Squadron had lost 8 Lancasters and 54 aircrew in December, but worse was to come in the first three days of January 1944 when 9 more Lancasters and their crews failed to return. By the end of January the squadron's losses in that month alone had climbed to the unsustainable total of 17 Lancasters and crews – equivalent to the strength of nearly a whole squadron. In human terms this equated to 98 aircrew killed and 21 taken prisoners-of-war. They were tough times in which Ralph Reeves joined 156 Squadron during the long hard winter of 1943–44 – and the blood-letting showed no sign of abating.

The Saunders crew, with Ralph Reeves as their tail gunner, took off at 11.51pm from RAF Warboys in Lancaster Mk III, ND358, T for Tommy, carrying bombs and red pyrotechnic target indicators (TIs). Seven minutes later at Wyton, as snow showers slashed through the darkness, Langford's 83 Squadron Lancaster Mk III, ND505, coincidentally also coded T for Tommy, thundered off the end of the main runway and climbed away into the night towards Germany.

The Met men had said they expected Leipzig to be cloud-covered by the time the bombers reached the city, so the Pathfinder crews of 83 and 156 Squadrons were ordered to act as Primary Blind Markers. This meant that their H2S ground mapping radar and Gee radiolocation apparatus would be used to identify the aiming point beneath the cloud, enabling them to drop their red TIs blindly (that is by radar, without actually seeing the ground below them) to mark the spot for the Main Force bombers.

Over England the weather was bad, too. Thanks to this and an incorrect forecast of winds issued to crews at their pre-op briefing, the bomber stream became spread out along its route. Many bombers found themselves arriving over Leipzig too early, which meant they had to circle the target area waiting for the Pathfinders to arrive. Some of the more experienced navigators soon realised that the wind speeds were different to those forecast, and deduced that they would need to insert a series of 'dog legs' into their flight plans to make sure they arrived over the target on time.

To make matters worse the Luftwaffe fighter controllers on the ground had directed

The result of a German night fighter attack over Berlin – but unlike the aircraft of Ronald Perkins and Ralph Reeves, this Lancaster of 550 Squadron made it home to the Emergency Landing Ground at RAF Woodbridge in Suffolk. In the course of the attack both the rear gunner and the mid-upper gunner were killed, and the bomb-aimer bailed out having misunderstood orders. The pilot managed to bring the crippled aircraft back without any navigation aids. ***IWM CE121***

their night fighters into the bomber stream early on in their flight to the target. A stiff fight ensued from the moment the bombers made landfall over the Dutch coast and all the way across Germany to Leipzig. Then they harried them all the way back to the coast.

A German night fighter intercepted and shot down the Saunders crew, in all probability on their way to the target. Huddled in his rear turret, did Ralph Reeves see the attacker closing in for the kill – probably a twin-engine Messerschmitt Bf110 – and did he manage to get in a few bursts from his four .303-inch Browning machine guns before the Lanc went down? Or did a night fighter fitted with *schräge musik* upward-firing cannon attack them from directly beneath, in the crew's blind spot? Loaded with bombs, petrol and pyrotechnic target markers the Lanc would have caught fire quickly and lit up the night sky like at massive firework. With the speed of the attack and the ferocity of the resulting explosion the crew may not have known what had hit them.

Luftwaffe combat records list two possible interceptions and shoot-downs of four-engine bombers by Messerschmitt Bf110 night fighter crews of *NJG5* at 3.12am in the vicinity of Zasenbeck, one of which may have been Ron Perkins' ND505. Both bombers mentioned in the records were attacked at about 19,000ft, one over Tangerhutte (40 miles from Zasenbeck) by Oblt Werner Hopf of *Stab V./NJG5*, and the other over Gardelegen (20 miles from Zasenbeck) by Lt Otto Keller of *7./NJG5*. Each location lay in a straight line NW-SE along the bombers' probable flight path.

What was left of Lancaster ND505 and her crew crashed to earth in Germany at 3.10am on 20 February, about ½ mile south of the small village of Zasenbeck in Lower Saxony, 100 miles west of Berlin. Ralph Reeves and his crew were all killed.

The Langford crew had dropped their bombs and were on their way home. To avoid giving a stalking night fighter an easy shot, Vic Langford needed to keep up a gently weaving flight path so as to avoid flying straight and level for too long. The gunners still needed to keep alert, peering into the darkness for any sign of an attacker closing in for the kill. With their mission accomplished and thoughts of a bacon and egg breakfast and blissful sleep between cotton sheets filling their minds, the crew may have momentarily dropped their guard.

It was 5.45am on 20 February when the Langford crew were shot down by a Messerschmitt Bf110G night fighter flown by *Leutnant* Heinz Oloff, of *I./Nachtjagdgeschwader 1* (*I./NJG1*). We will probably never know whether Oloff bagged them in a short sharp engagement, or in a running fight of several hundred miles across Germany and the Dutch flatlands towards the North Sea coast. The Lancaster crashed in Holland at 5.45am on 20 February near the village of Wolphaartsdijk in southwest Holland, 3 miles north west of Goes on Zuid Beveland. All the crew were killed and are buried in nearby Vlissingen (Flushing) Northern Cemetery.

ND505 was virtually a brand new Lancaster that had only been delivered to 83 Squadron in January. When it was shot down it had flown just three ops and logged 27 hours, underlining the painfully short life expectancy of an RAF heavy bomber and its crew.

Squadron records show that Reeves was on only his second op with the Saunders crew when he was killed. Their first trip had been to Berlin on 15–16 January 1944. It is not certain whether Reeves was already part of this crew and had been posted in from 7 Squadron with them; or if he had joined 156 Squadron from another unit and had ended up flying with Saunders as a stand-in gunner. Saunders and wireless operator John Webster had each been awarded the DFC, but in both cases it was not gazetted (announced) until several months after their deaths.

The grave of Flg Off Ralph Reeves, RAFVR, from South Wraxall, at Hanover War Cemetery in Germany. *Author's collection*

Leutnant Oloff, the Luftwaffe night fighter pilot who had shot down Victor Langford and his crew, later rose to the rank of *Oberleutnant* with the German night fighter unit *NJG1* and claimed at least ten bomber 'kills' by the war's end. He survived the war and died in 1999.

The Leipzig raid was not a success from Bomber Command's perspective: the attack was scattered and 78 bomber aircraft were lost from the 832-strong force. German night fighters relentlessly pursued the bombers back to the North Sea coast and succeeded in shooting down at least thirty of them. Ronald Perkins and Ralph Reeves were two of more than 500 RAF and Commonwealth bomber aircrew who died that night. Nos 83 and 156 Squadrons each lost 2 Lancasters and their crews – 28 men.

Thus far it was easily Bomber Command's worst night of the war, but much worse was to come less than a month later on 30–31 March when the Bavarian city of Nuremberg was raided. The RAF was set to lose 95 bombers from a force of 795 despatched – an unsustainable loss rate of 11.9 per cent that was to make the Nuremberg raid Bomber Command's Second World War equivalent of the Somme, and its single greatest loss.

Flying Officer Ronald Percy David PERKINS

Service No: 137552, RAFVR; *Unit:* 83 Squadron, RAF Bomber Command; *Died:* 20 February 1944 aged 21; *Buried:* Flushing Northern Cemetery, Netherlands, Row H, Grave 1; *Commemorated:* BOA WM; HT; AR.

Flying Officer Ralph Leonard REEVES

Service No: 146103, RAFVR; *Unit:* 156 Squadron, RAF Bomber Command; *Died:* 20 February 1944; *Buried:* Hanover War Cemetery, Germany, Grave 8.B.8; *Commemorated:* St Peter's Church, South Wraxall.

MOSSIE PILOT

Flying Officer Kenneth Henry King, DFC, RAFVR, 128 (Pathfinder) Squadron – Bradford-on-Avon

Fitzmaurice Grammar School boy Kenneth 'Peter' King was desperate to join the RAF. By running away from home and lying about his age he thought he could improve his chances. In January 1941, perhaps with this in mind, he and another Bradford-on-Avon youth named Eric Vennell left their homes and caught a train to Salisbury where they stole a car, drove it back to Bath and dumped it. Then they stole another car and drove it to Trowbridge, but this time they were caught by the police and arrested on 24 January. Both youths were charged and appeared before the courts where they were bound over for 12 months and ordered to pay costs of 15 shillings. It was probably due to the facts that neither boy had come before the courts before and each was of 'very respectable parentage' (as the *Wiltshire Times* reported) that they escaped custodial sentences.

This Halifax B Mk II Series 1A, LW235 'EY-B', of 78 Squadron RAF, was based at Breighton in North Yorkshire and is pictured on 25 September 1943. It was in a Halifax like this that Kenneth 'Peter' King won his DFC on 9 August 1943. ***IWM CH11328***

Kenneth Henry ('Peter') King was born in 1923 at Malmesbury, the eldest son of Stuart Henry and Winifred Carolyn (nee Salter) King of 39 Southville Gardens, Bradford-on-Avon. Peter was a bright boy and won a scholarship to Fitzmaurice Grammar School. In July 1941 he joined the RAF and was sent overseas to Canada where he trained as a pilot.

Peter passed out from training with above average marks and was commissioned as a pilot officer, returning to England for further training at an operational training unit. In May 1943 he joined 78 Squadron, a heavy bomber squadron operating Handley Page Halifaxes from RAF Linton-on-Ouse in Yorkshire. Later the squadron moved to nearby RAF Breighton.

As a captain of aircraft, Peter went on to complete a tour of thirty operational sorties at a very dangerous time in the Allied Strategic Bomber Offensive when Bomber Command aircrew casualties were running at an all time high. Between 23 May and 27 August 1943 he flew on twenty-three trips that included the Battle of the Ruhr, the Hamburg fire raids and the attack against the German secret V-weapons development site at Peenemünde on the Baltic coast.

During a raid on Mannheim on 9 August he saved his aircraft and crew, for which he was awarded the Distinguished Flying Cross (DFC). The events of that night are described in the official award citation:

> '... the port inner engine gave trouble and it was necessary to feather it immediately. As the aircraft would not maintain height the bombs were jettisoned and shortly afterwards the starboard inner engine over-revved and it also had to be feathered. As the aircraft was still heavily laden with petrol the pilot was unable to maintain height on two engines, but in spite of this he was able to reach an aerodrome on the south coast, where he landed without further incident.
>
> 'In view of his consistently good work and outstanding skill on this occasion he is strongly recommended for the award of the DFC.'

Peter was 'screened' from operations in September 1943 and went to instruct pupil bomber pilots at an operational training unit in England. As a bomber pilot with operational experience his skills were soon in demand again and he was picked to join the elite 8 (Pathfinder) Group. On 29 October 1944 Peter left 1655 Mosquito Training Unit to join 128 Squadron at RAF Wyton in Huntingdonshire, which was a Mosquito bomber squadron in 8 Group's Light Night Striking Force.

Peter and his navigator, 36-year-old Flg Off Cecil Meigel Arrieta DFM (who had flown his first tour of operations with 10 Squadron on Halifaxes), went missing on the first trip of their second tour raiding Berlin. Cologne was the main target for Bomber Command that night against which 905 aircraft were despatched; the raid on Berlin was a relatively minor affair with 62 Mosquitoes briefed for the operation.

As a sergeant navigator, Arrieta had been known by his oppoes on 10 Squadron as outstandingly efficient, which is why he was awarded the Distinguished Flying Medal at the end of his tour and was later selected for the Pathfinders. His first tour of operations, which was on Halifaxes with skipper Flt Lt Ken Munro, RAAF, was certainly eventful: at the end of their first trip the aircraft crashed returning from Genoa; on his fifth sortie Arrieta was forced to 'hit the silk' and bale out; and on 20 December 1942 two enemy night fighters subjected his Halifax to a 10-minute attack during which time the gunners downed one of their assailants.

At 7.49pm on 30 October, King and Arrieta took off in Mosquito Mk XX, KB199:A, carrying three 500lb HC and one 500 GP bomb. As pathfinders, they were equipped with the latest navigational aids of Gee and Loran. What caused the aircraft to be lost is not known, but Cecil Arrieta survived to become a prisoner of war; Peter died and is buried in the Reichswald Forest War Cemetery in Germany. He was 21 years-old.

The Luftwaffe claimed no British bombers shot down that night, so it may have been flak that was responsible for downing Peter's Mossie. Surprisingly, no aircraft were lost from the main operation, and Peter's Mosquito was the only aircraft to be lost on the Berlin raid.

Between its formation on 15 September 1944 and the end of the war, 128 Squadron flew 1,531 sorties and lost only two aircraft in 157 bombing raids – an incredibly small loss rate of just 0.1 per cent. After all that Peter King had been through since his first operational sortie in May 1943, it was sheer bad luck that he should lose his life when he did.

Flying Officer Kenneth Henry KING, DFC

Service No: 149202, RAFVR; *Unit:* 128 Squadron, RAF Bomber Command; *Died:* 31 October 1944 aged 21; *Buried:* Reichswald Forest War Cemetery, Germany, Grave 31.F.7; *Commemorated:* BOA WM; HT.

(Note: Ken Munro, 28, from Burnie,Tasmania, was awarded two DFCs in the space of six months for 'displaying exceptional operational courage whilst flying'. Had he lived he would probably have joined Cecil Arrieta in the Pathfinders, but Munro was fated to die in a flying accident on 1 July 1943. Ken Munro, who had been an accountant on 'civvie street', was posted to 3 Flying Instructors School at Babdown Farm near Tetbury, Gloucestershire, where he was being taught how to instruct pupil pilots. Less than one hour into a training flight with another instructor [Flt Lt William Colledge, DFC, RCAF], their Airspeed Oxford struck trees in a low flying area near Ross-on-Wye. The aircraft was damaged and the pilot lost control of the twin-engine trainer, which crashed at Bishopswood, killing Munro and Colledge. The cause of the crash was attributed to flying below the safety height of 250ft.

Both men were highly experienced pilots and their loss in such a senseless accident deprived the RAF of two irreplaceable talents. In February 1943, while flying an anti-submarine patrol with 405 Squadron, William Colledge's Halifax had been attacked by four Junkers 88s and a running fight ensued. During the encounter one enemy aircraft was destroyed and two damaged. Colledge was finally able to gain cloud cover and return to base 'after a brilliant duel with superior numbers'. He was awarded an immediate DFC and his mid-upper gunner the DFM. Munro and Colledge are both buried at Haycombe Cemetery in Bath.)

Chapter Seven

D-DAY DODGERS

The Italian and Sicilian Campaigns

'We're the D-Day dodgers here in Italy
Drinking all the vino, always on the spree
We didn't land with Eisenhower
So they think that we're just a shower.
For we're the D-Day dodgers out here in Italy.'
First verse of a song sung by Allied troops in Italy to the tune of 'Lili Marlene'.

The Italian Campaign lasted from July 1943 until the surrender of German forces in Italy in May 1945. Britain and the USA planned to knock Italy out of the war (she capitulated in September 1943), achieving a major propaganda victory, re-establishing Royal Navy dominance in the Mediterranean and forcing Germany to transfer troops from the Eastern Front to defend Italy. Allied forces in Italy encountered challenging terrain, demanding weather conditions and an enemy whose fighting retreat contested every last inch of ground. More troops were killed or injured in Italy than in any other campaign in Western Europe: over 320,000 Allied and 658,000 Axis soldiers became casualties.

TANK COMMANDER

Sergeant Norman Brian Darch, 3rd County of London Yeomanry – Bradford-on-Avon

On the night of 9–10 July 1943, an Allied armada of more than 2,500 landing craft and ships crossed the Mediterranean in the greatest combined operation of the Second World War – the invasion of Sicily. The British assault force led by General Sir Bernard Montgomery sailed from ports in Libya and Egypt; the Americans under Lt-Gen George Patton embarked from harbours in French North Africa.

Sgt Brian Darch's squadron of Sherman tanks from 3rd County of London Yeomanry (3rd CLY) landed along the south-east coast of Sicily on the night of 10–11 July 1943. They came ashore at 7.30am on 'How' Beach at Cassibile, as part of General Leese's XXX Corps in support of the British 5th and 50th Divisions. Brian's 4 Troop, under the command of Lt W.H.J. 'Jimmy' Sale, MC, joined the rest of A Squadron at 9.30am. All of the squadron was ashore by nightfall and remained in the Syracuse area for the night.

Sgt Brian Darch, from Bradford-on-Avon, (centre), with fellow tank crews in North Africa, 1942. *Brian Darch*

Libya, 1942: 'our bivvy and the raw material for our cooking. Not "battle" rations and not even all issued stuff.' Brian is on the left. *Brian Darch*

Norman Brian Darch, who was known by his family as Brian, was born in 1918 at Bradford-on-Avon, the younger son of Albert James Darch (1885–1922) and Alice Doreen Darch (nee Rich, 1887–1962). From 1928 to 1934 Brian was a pupil at Fitzmaurice Grammar School, which was a few minutes walk from his home at 76a Trowbridge Road. When he left school at sixteen, Brian joined the Civil Service and moved to Surrey where he worked for the Inland Revenue at Kingston-on-Thames.

When the Second World War broke out in September 1939, Brian volunteered for the RAF hoping to become a pilot, but his enlistment was deferred and in December he was called up for the Army. He joined the 3rd Battalion County of London Yeomanry and trained as a tank driver before sailing to the Middle East in a troop convoy in the autumn of 1941, where immediately he went into action. Brian was promoted to sergeant in the summer of 1942 and his unit fought intermittently against the Axis forces in North Africa up to the end of the year. There followed a spell of training before the invasion of Sicily in July 1943.

Brian was an avid letter writer home and kept up a detailed correspondence with his nephew. The following letter was written on 6 June 1943, more than six months after the events he describes of the Allied withdrawal to El Alamein and the siege of the 'Knightsbridge Box':

Brian Darch and his Sherman tank crew came ashore in Sicily at Cassibile, on 'How' Beach, on the morning of 11 July 1943.
Author's collection

'Dear Richard
Since you wanted the story continued and as I've managed to finish the winter 41–42 business I'll start now on the bigger and better story of the withdrawal to Alamein and events preceding it.

'The last part ended with Rommel coming out from Agheila, strengthened and all according to [his] plan, and pushing us back until things became static along a line roughly from Gazala southish to Bir Hacheim. When I say "us" I mean the 8th Army, the unit having been taken right out after it had been reduced almost to nothing around Jedabya. We went on leave, spent some time near Alex and some near Cairo, refitting, reforming, training and good-timing.

'By the middle of April we were ready to go back up to Libya which we did by rail and road either on "flats" or transporters. The journey took about a week and was very enjoyable. We lazed and read in the sun on the tanks during the day and the route wasn't altogether without interest – Mersa Matruh, Sidi Barrani, Sollum, Capuzzo, Bardia. When we stopped in the evening we usually managed a swim in the sea and I remember one very fine swim one morning in Sollum Bay – beautiful blue sea, sky and bay with Halfaya and Sollum passes and scenes of battle behind us. Jerry had used Matilda turrets in underground concrete emplacements to defend the road underneath the passes. I didn't see them but I'm told he had naval guns further up Halfaya pass and on top. Sollum was a wreck, Sollum Pass a hair-pin bending road which took us some time to climb, Capuzzo a lot of neat graves with no sign of a fort, Bardia in the distance looked very pretty.

'We left the coast road beyond Bardia and pushed south into the desert not far from Gambut where we spent a very pleasant month living by our tanks doing exercises etc. Our rations were quite good – we got bread and fresh meat which made all the difference – and we became expert cooks with our petrol tin ovens etc. Beer was rationed to about a tin a week (¾ pint, circa) but we weren't badly off for canteen comforts as the railhead was at Capuzzo and not very far away. We erected "bivies" by the sides of our tanks and fitted them with electric light and so in the evenings we could read or write or play cards. As regards water we usually got the gallon per man per day, sometimes more, and we could often supplement that by drawing from "bins" (rock wells) which provided water for washing etc. and sometimes for drinking and cooking. We had to do our own laundering so the little extra was essential. Life was very pleasant then – glorified Boy Scouting.

'On 27 May we were up and breakfasted as usual. Soon came orders of a move – a practice of our "plan such and such" we were told – but the sound of firing to the south and a feeling in the air soon told us it was the real thing. We dropped our sunshades and moved off and were soon engaged with Jerry tanks. The Grants did terrific work as they had a respectable thickness of armour and a big gun and Jerry was undoubtedly shaken to come across a tank which could stand up to him. It's thought he had no idea we had such stuff with us. About midday we had a breather behind a ridge while both sides sorted themselves out. On looking at the tank I found that an AP shot had passed within a few inches of my head and chewed up my greatcoat, blankets, spare tobacco, passed through a tool locker and scattered many of those, and then sped on. Ignorance is bliss! Our Squadron Leader had been hit in the neck by a chunk of shell and had to be evacuated so the 2i/c took over. We joined battle again in the afternoon and did a few uncomfortable reccés. At last the sun sank and about 12.30am we crawled between the blankets with the usual jobs of refuelling, rations, guards etc. At 3am a solitary plane dropped a bomb on us and another did at 5am – the latter serving for reveillé – no damage being done by either.

'On 4 June we went back and rejoined the rest of the regiment which had re-equipped and we got news of our counter-attack starting the next day. We were to go forward the next morning after a 25-pdr barrage and after infantry and "I" tanks had done their stuff in the early morning and dawn hours. The guns started their noise around 3 or 4am and we moved forward soon after, and by daylight were passing through the area where the "I" tanks and infantry had done their stuff. Soon after that we bumped into trouble – firing from all angles and too much dust and mist to make sense of it. As far as our tank was concerned we made an inglorious exit early in the proceedings and through trying to tow out another tank ended by being towed ourselves.

'The next day we sorted out our repaired and broken down tanks. The good ones went off to rejoin the remnants of the regiment while the duds went back for repair. Mine had developed other troubles so I said goodbye to it and got on another. The regiment was in a sorry state – the previous day had knocked it about badly. We went off on a patrol that morning and then in the afternoon were included in a particularly unpleasant little affair.

'During the doings of the day before, the artillery etc attached to the Brigade (called a "Box") had become isolated and was now in the position of having to have more ammunition or to surrender. The Divisional General had some trucks of ammunition and we had to supply some tanks to escort them on a gauntlet running trip to this isolated "Box". We were one, and we didn't know at the time (Praise be!) but it wasn't expected that much would survive the trip. We moved off, entered the famous Knightsbridge "Guards Box", were held up, sniped at, and then eventually the rush to make the 2 or 3 miles to the other box began. We had not gone more than about ½ mile when I noticed the tank wouldn't steer and then the Commander told me we had left a track behind which puzzled me – but not for long. There was a nasty thud which I guessed to be AP hitting us and then came orders to bale out, which I carried out with the usual alacrity in such circumstances, though there was a temporary hold-up owing to the turret having to be traversed to let me out. We poured out and lay behind a wheel each as the best cover we had from machine-gunning. We could see why the track had gone – part of the driving sprocket on one side had been shot away. The other shot(s) had gone right through water and petrol tanks into the engine and both those fluids were pouring out. By some miracle the thing wasn't in flames.

'About 50 yards in front of us one of the ammunition trucks had been hit and was blazing, the shells exploding all the time and occasionally showering us. There was no cover but the tank – it was flat desert – so we had to stay. We looked around but could see little – the rest of the column had passed us when our track went. Then we noticed tanks approaching from the side opposite to where we had been hit; then came salvation – from the direction in which we had been heading raced an American light tank. It stopped for us and raced off again with us hanging on it, being fired at the while, just made the gap through the minefield surrounding the "Box" of the imperturbable Guards and then halted. The driver of it happened to be one of our chaps on loan to the Artillery who were using the tank as an OP. The tank had been hit and on fire for a time and one chap in it was wounded. How it made the trip amazes me. We got a lift in an ambulance back to the regiment a sadder and a "wiser" bunch – and once again without anything but what we were wearing – in my case torn PT shorts and a shirt.

'Later on we pieced together the story of the affair. Very few lorries got through, ours was the only tank crew to escape, the "Box" was taken shortly after and several of our chaps were taken POW in it.

'The next day, 13 June, we did a recce in the morning and spent nearly all the rest of the day gazing through the heat haze at Jerry, or where he was, "brewing up" (we had no appetites), being shelled (not very heavily), swotting flies and trying to read and write, and wondering what was up. It was the day which marked the turning point of the campaign, the day when our tank fell foul of an ambush, and of 88mm's, and 230 were lost out of 300 – or so I read in the papers.

'In the evening the bangs got louder and nearer on our left and we were suddenly rushed off to Brigade. We found our way back to the few tanks of the regiment (about six by now) in the dark and once again I tried to sleep in my seat. I went on guard soon after midnight and just before my hour was up the lights, bangs, noises to the left came to a head and hell was let loose amongst the people on our left and ourselves. Everyone dived into their tanks, started up, and moved slowly off to dodge the rain of fire around them. We moved all night and the morning brew of tea was cut short by a short tank battle. Still we had done our job – the Guards in the Knightsbridge Box had been evacuated while we had kept Jerry occupied.

'During that morning we got back towards Acroma and the few tanks left reformed into a squadron under our 2i/c and we went out again to find Jerry and engage in some form of battle which seemed to me to be the worst organised scrap I've ever seen. That night we moved eastwards through minefields, continually stopping and perhaps trying to sleep only to have to move again. We moved all the next morning across the southern perimeter of Tobruk until we finally halted where a multitude of lorries were gathered together somewhere east of El Adem. I don't think I've ever been more tired than during that drive. At the end of it we broke down and that evening were taken back into Tobruk. We spent the night there and in the morning were taken out and left near the perimeter defences again for picking up and taking on eastwards. Everything was by now streaming back along the coast road, the South Africans had left Gazala and been badly bombed on the way, and everything else was going east. Nothing was definite – one couldn't tell whether it was the intention to hold Tobruk or evacuate it.

'What follows until we finally stabilized things behind the Alamein defence will not make much sense but it was even less intelligible then. We had heard rumours of the fall of Tobruk long before and since then we had heard the news confirmed. Spirits were low and no wonder!

'The next day the regiment reformed by taking tanks from another unit and then followed days of moving to and fro while tanks broke down and once again we were reduced to a squadron with hardly any action. We hung around south of Mersa Matruh for a couple of days watching Jerry pour into the coastal plain. At the end of the second day it must have proved impossible to attempt to hold Jerry there or the C-in-C must have decided on his final stand at Alamein. We started moving that night eastwards along with other columns – at times I dozed while I drove and woke once to find myself tagging behind another column altogether. We got back to divisional HQ and then the usable tanks numbered about a squadron. The crocks carried on back whilst the "goers" carried out patrols to keep in touch with the enemy and slow his advance without engaging them. We joined in a little scrap against 14 "ITI" [Italian] tanks one morning – seven were KO'd and seven gave in. After a few days of that we started the final trip back to the Alamein line of which we had heard. By then just over half of the tanks were runners and all were very low in petrol. Nevertheless despite increasing break-downs, acute fuel shortages and a dust storm we drove and towed the whole lot back over rotten country.

'We expected this Alamein line to be a pretty solid line of defence but must have passed through it without noticing it. It was just then in the process of making but I was greatly surprised by the thinness of it. By the time we got there only three tanks were OK to carry on and the three of us joined another squadron but did little. The next day our troop of three went along to yet another squadron of yet another regiment and soon we were off on a 15-mile trip to contact a pretty strong force of Jerry tanks which had been reported. We had only to go about 3 miles to encounter shelling and contact the force. Then followed an afternoon of action, mainly by the heavier tanks and A/Tk guns. We got a few hours sleep that night and did little the next day until the evening when a little cavalry dash was executed with dire result. Our three tanks were on the right flank – the extreme right one was hit a few times and one of the crew wounded; we in the middle were hit twice but miraculously no-one was hurt (you've got the snap of the AP shell poking thru); the third was OK.

'The most amazing thing to me was how that tank, which was in poor condition when we took it over, managed to last so long, cover such a distance, survive shells in side and turret, and still keep going when there was no time to do much work on it. One could never tell how they'd go.

'Eventually the whole regiment was taken out but after a few days two squadrons re-equipped and went back up – we were lucky and stayed behind. Those two squadrons did great work when Rommel made his "Reccé in force" on 31 August – an encounter which contributed greatly to the success of the Battle of Alamein in October.

All the best, Brian.'

At 1.30pm on 12 July 1943, the Shermans of A Squadron 3rd CLY moved to the harbour area of Syracuse, west of the railway station, where they remained for the night. On the 13th Capt Hargreaves and Brian's 4 Troop (less its commander Lt Jimmy Sale), and 1 Troop (Sgt Charles Harris), moved out to join Maj Chris Wrey in support of the 15th Infantry Brigade who were held up by gunfire from enemy blockhouses at a crossroads. Sgt Harris's Shermans of 1 Troop shelled these blockhouses, which were evacuated by the enemy and then occupied by British infantry.

The Shermans of Maj Wrey and half of A Squadron moved forward at 3.00pm to a farm at Tentella. A couple of hours later they advanced to support the 15th Infantry Brigade in its attack across the ravine north of Tentella. The King's Own Yorkshire Light Infantry (KOYLI) were strongly counter-attacked in the right flank, and then German anti-tank guns and mortars heavily engaged the half-squadron of Shermans on both flanks. Six out of seven tanks were knocked out; the Sherman commanded by Brian Darch was one of four that were brewed up and left as blazing wrecks on the battlefield. Seven men were killed, including Brian, and 23-year-old Sgt Charles Harris of 1 Troop; one man died later from his wounds. Two of the Shermans were subsequently recovered.

Brian had just passed the War Office Selection Board and was about to be commissioned as an officer.

Sergeant Norman Brian DARCH

Service No: 7906125; *Unit:* A Squadron, 3rd County of London Yeomanry (Sharpshooters), Royal Armoured Corps; *Died:* 13 July 1943 aged 25; *Buried:* Syracuse War Cemetery, Sicily, Grave VIII, G.3; *Commemorated:* BOA WM; HT; BOA C.

MOUNTAIN SKIRMISH

Private Ernest John Pearce, 2nd Battalion Wiltshire Regiment – Bradford-on-Avon

Although very little is known about Ernest John Pearce, other than he was born in 1917 at Mere, Wiltshire, we do know about the circumstances surrounding his death.

By 25 October 1943 the British 8th Army was ready to resume its advance in Italy, with plans to cross two major rivers that lay in its path. The 8th Army's objective was the Pescara-Avezzano lateral road that crossed the Apennine Mountains to Rome.

The German High Command was not prepared to give ground easily and was committed to digging in and fighting along the historic defence line across the narrow western part of Italy. This was the Sangro River, through the mountains to the formidable country around Cassino, and thence to the Aurunci Mountains on the west coast.

The Allied crossing of the first river obstacle – the Trigno – was resisted by the Germans with the greatest determination, and when the bridgehead was finally secured the enemy fell back step-by-step to the Sangro.

As part of Field Marshal Albert Kesselring's German 10th Army in retreat in the face of the steady Allied advance, elements of the 26th Panzer Division fought delaying actions in terrain and weather that gave them a considerable defensive advantage.

At 4.00pm on 31 October the Germans brought down heavy shellfire with 150mm self-propelled (SP) guns along the ridge in the Appenine Mountains where the 2nd Wiltshires were dug-in. At last light, which was at about 5.30pm, two enemy fighting patrols broke into the Wiltshires' positions, killing three men, wounding seven, and taking five prisoners. The shelling ceased by 6.00pm, but the battalion spent a cold and wet night on Point 762 without blankets or greatcoats.

Ernest Pearce was probably injured on the 31st – Halloween – in a skirmish with troops of the 9th Panzergrenadier Regiment in the mountains about 20 miles north-east of Cassino. He died of his wounds on 2 November. Two Germans were found dead on the morning of 1 November, All Saints' Day – in front of the Wiltshires' positions; four prisoners were taken, including the commander of the self-propelled gun company that had shelled them the day before.

Private Ernest John PEARCE

Service No: 5572121; *Unit:* 2nd Battalion Wiltshire Regiment; *Died:* 2 November 1943 aged 25; *Buried:* Cassino War Cemetery, Italy, Grave VII.J.18; *Commemorated:* BOA WM; HT.

JOURNEY'S END

Lieutenant-Colonel Iain O'Brien MacGregor, 154 (The Leicestershire Yeomanry) Field Regiment, RA (TA) – Winsley

Iain MacGregor had a passion for foreign adventure. In the 1920s and 30s he travelled widely on the continent of Europe, and in India, North Africa and the West Indies, feeding a desire to seek out new horizons. His thirst for adventure reached new heights in 1933 when he piloted a light aircraft from England to India via Egypt and Persia, a distance of some 4,000 miles. As a member of the Royal Geographical Society, Iain's love of geographical science led to his election as a Fellow (FRGS) on 11 June 1934.

Born at Yarmouth, Norfolk, on 4 February 1901, Iain O'Brien MacGregor was the younger son of Colonel John MacGregor, MD, Indian Army, and Mabel MacGregor. He was educated at the Imperial Service College, Windsor (September 1915–December 1918), where he was school captain and house captain (Camperdown). Iain excelled at sports and played for the first XV in 1916 and 1917, and was captain of boats in 1918. He was also a sergeant in the school's Officer Training Corps. He went up to the Royal Military Academy Woolwich in 1919 as an officer cadet where he gained distinction in boxing, winning the Welter Weight Army Officers' Boxing Challenge.

Iain passed out from Woolwich and was commissioned into the Royal Artillery as a 2nd lieutenant on 23 December 1920. Promoted to lieutenant on 23 December 1922, he was seconded to the Air Ministry for four years from 1923 to 1927. From 1929 to 1931 he was made *aide de campe* to the divisional commander of Aldershot Command. Iain was promoted to captain on 23 December 1933 and in the following October he was attached again to the Air Ministry, where he remained until September 1936. On 1 August 1938 he was promoted to major.

In June 1944, Iain was commanding 154 (Leicestershire Yeomanry) Field Regiment, Royal Artillery (TA), one of three divisional artillery field regiments in the British Army's

Lt-Col Iain MacGregor's 154 Field Regiment used the Sexton 25pdr self-propelled gun. *IWM NA20334*

50th Division. The division had fought in Persia and North Africa in 1942–43, and with the 8th Army it had crossed into Italy late in 1943 where it was involved in the hard fighting as the Allies pushed north.

On 16 June, when 154 Field Regiment's Sherman Sexton 25-pdr self-propelled artillery was on the move heading north, Iain died as the result of a motorcycle accident outside the southern Italian medieval town of Venafro, 10 miles east of Cassino.

In 1944, Iain's family lived at Winsley House, Winsley. He was married to Diana Evelyn MacGregor (nee Uniacke, 1910–96), of Whitegates, Camberley, Surrey, and was father to Sandy (b.1936) and Robert (b.1939).

Lieutenant-Colonel Iain O'Brien MACGREGOR

Service No: 18220; *Unit:* 154 (The Leicestershire Yeomanry) Field Regiment RA (TA); *Died:* 16 June 1944 aged 43; *Buried:* Cassino War Cemetery, Italy, Grave XVIII.D.10; *Commemorated:* Winsley WM.

NIGHT-FLIGHT TO SAN BENEDETTO

Flight Sergeant Ronald Cecil Bray, RAFVR, 178 Squadron – Bradford-on-Avon

As dusk fell on 4 October 1944, seven drab-painted Consolidated B-24J Liberator heavy bombers of the RAF's 178 Squadron prepared to take off from Amendola airfield in southern Italy for a target up in the north of the country. At 7.40pm Liberator Mk VI, KG942, climbed away from the end of the runway with its seven-man crew skippered by 22-year-old Warrant Officer (WO) Richard Gregory, RCAF, a farmer's son from the tiny settlement of Bents on the rolling prairies of Saskatchewan in Canada.

Sgt Ronald Bray from Bradford-on-Avon wears the white flash in his side cap denoting 'aircrew under training'. *Golda Bray*

In the bomb-aimer's compartment was Flt Sgt Ronald Bray from Bradford-on-Avon, also 22-years-of-age. The navigator was another Canadian, Flg Off Burnie Thorp, aged 24, from Sault St Marie, Ontario. Sgt Ronald Parsons (21), from Exeter, was the flight engineer, and Flt Sgt Colin Wilshaw (22), from Stoke on Trent, the wireless operator. The mid-upper and tail gunners were Sgt Ernest Finney (24), from Oldham, and WO Louis Irving.

Born in 1922 at Bradford-on-Avon, Ronald Cecil Bray was the second of five children to Cecil and Annie Bray. Of the five children – Joan, Ronald, Golda, Jerry and Cyril – four of them went into the Forces in the Second World War: Ronald volunteered for RAF aircrew duties, Golda went into the WRNS, Jerry into the Wiltshire Regiment, and Cyril joined the RAF Regiment. Their father, Cecil, worked at the Spencer, Moulton & Co rubber factory in the town. Golda Sheppard (nee Bray) clearly remembers her older brother Ronald:

> 'He moved out of home not long after leaving Fitzmaurice Grammar School – he was there from 1934 to 1938 – and went to work as a projectionist at the Kinema and Gaumont cinemas in Trowbridge. He then moved over to Chippenham to work at the Gaumont.
>
> 'Ronald was a brilliant harmonica player and a good artist – he used to sketch funny little drawings at the bottom of his letters home from the RAF, and when we ran a dance in the town he did the posters for it. He had been in the choir at Holy Trinity and after he joined the RAF he would carry the cross in church when he was home on leave.'

In 1940 Ronald volunteered for aircrew duties in the RAF. After his basic training in England he was selected for flying training and went overseas in 1941 for 18 months further training in Canada and the USA. Frustratingly for Ronald he quickly discovered that he suffered badly from airsickness, which saw him 'washed out' as a trainee pilot, but instead he was re-mustered as a trainee bomb-aimer.

During his time in Canada as an airman under training, Ronald met and fell in love with a girl named Amy Crawford. Their romance blossomed and they became engaged, but when the time came for Ronald to return home to England in March 1943 they had to make their tearful farewells.

The final phase of his training was in Scotland at 20 Operational Training Unit, Lossiemouth, where Ronald met and 'crewed up' with Richard Gregory and the five others with whom he would soon go to war. They spent all their time together, in the air and on the ground, and learned to work as a team. On 1 May 1944 the crew was posted overseas to the Mediterranean theatre where they joined 614 Squadron in Italy at Stornara airfield, near Cerignola. With its four-engine Handley Page Halifax Mk III bombers, the squadron was engaged in bombing raids over Italy and the Balkans, as well as making supply drops to partisans. On 14 July they were posted to 1675 Heavy Conversion Unit at Lydda in Palestine (now Ben Gurion Airport in Israel) to convert onto the Consolidated

Ronald Bray with his Liberator bomber crew in 1944. From left: Richard Gregory (pilot), Burnie Thorp (navigator), Ernest Finney and Louis Irving (air gunners), and Ronald Bray (bomb-aimer). The flight engineer and wireless operator are not present in the picture. *Golda Bray*

Liberator, and on 15 September the Gregory crew flew across to Italy where they joined 178 Squadron at Amendola.

Ahead of Gregory and his crew lay an arduous night flight up the length of Italy in almost total darkness. A typical bombing sortie would normally take around five hours, which usually meant taking off late in the evening and returning in the small hours. Most ops flown from the RAF's bomber airfields in Italy were made at night and were mainly to targets in northern Italy, over the Alps to Austria or across the Adriatic into Yugoslavia.

Gregory retracted the Lib's undercarriage and with the aid of the flight engineer, Sgt Ronald Parsons, the engine settings were adjusted and control surfaces trimmed as KG942 climbed away from Amendola. The Canadian navigator, Flg Off Burnie Thorp – in 'civvie street' a newly-qualified PT teacher and the only officer in the crew – gave Gregory a course to steer for the target in the northern Italian province of Lombardy, some 330 miles distant. Ronald may have assisted him with map reading in their flight north, since his bomb-aiming skills were not really needed until they neared the target. Not long after take-off the weather began to deteriorate.

Gregory's crew was one of 55 bomber crews from the RAF's 205 Group that had been briefed to attack the pontoon bridge at San Benedetto Po, nine miles southeast of the

No.178 Squadron,
Royal Air Force,
Central Mediterranean Forces.

1st.November,1944.

Dear Mrs Bray,

By the time you receive this letter you will have been informed by telegram that your son Sergeant Ronald Cecil Bray has been reported missing from operations against the enemy.

Your son's aircraft took-off from this airfield at 19.54 hours on the 4th.of October,1944 to carry out a bombing attack against the pontoon bridge at San Benedette from which he failed to return. I have no indication as to what may have happened to him. There is of course always the possibility that he may be a Prisoner of War;in which case the International Red Cross will inform you immediately they have any news of him.

May I now express the deep sympathy which I and my entire Squadron feel with you at this anxious time. Although your son had not been long with this Squadron he had shown great promise as a Bomb Aimer and his loss so early in his operational career is tragic. He was very popular with his comrades,and is greatly missed in his Mess.

All his kit and belongings have been collected and packed,and an inventory made of them. They have been forwarded to the R.A.F. Standing Committee of Adjustment who will communicate with you to ascertain your wishes as to their disposal.

If there is any way in which I can help you do not hesitate to let me know.

Yours sincerely

J.C. Millar

J.C. MILLAR,
WING COMMANDER.

Mrs. C.L. Bray,
99,Southville Gardens,
Bradford-on-Avon,
Wilts.

A letter that was difficult to write but painful to receive: the official notification to Ronald Bray's mother from the commanding officer of 178 Squadron, informing her that her son was missing in action. *Golda Bray*

ancient cultural city of Mantua in Lombardy. Most of the road bridges across the River Po had been destroyed in ground fighting, so the Germans had been using pontoon bridges to restore crucial communication links with their forces holding the Gothic Line. Now that the Adriatic port city of Rimini was in Allied hands, it was believed that enemy troops and equipment were crossing the River Po using the pontoon bridge at San Benedetto Po.

Lancasters and most Halifaxes could not be spared from the night offensive against Germany, so instead the RAF decided to equip 205 Group with the B-24 Liberator. Some 2,500 of these slab-sided American-built four-engine heavies were supplied to the RAF and Commonwealth Air Forces under the Lend-Lease arrangement with the US. Until October 1944, 178 Squadron was the only RAF Liberator unit in 205 Group operating in the Mediterranean.

The Gregory crew would have found the Liberator a modern, comfortable aircraft in which to fly, particularly when compared to British-built bombers of the period and in particular the venerable Vickers Wellington on which they had trained, and the Halifaxes on 614 Squadron. The Lib was stable in flight, roomy inside and the cockpit was even carpeted – a far cry from the cramped but functional 'Wimpy', and the narrow cockpit of the Halifax.

A large number of the Mediterranean Allied Air Force's (MAAF) bomber squadrons were stationed at a network of basic airfields hewn out of the olive groves and fields on the Foggia Plain in southern Italy. Foggia Main airfield was at the hub of a system of twelve satellite bases, each the home to several squadrons. Amendola airfield's 3,600ft strip of mud, pierced steel planking (PSP) and aircraft hard stands was situated just off the end of Foggia Main. It was home to USAAF bombers as well as those of the RAF's 205 Group, which flew Halifaxes and B-24s on night operations, making it one of the busier airfields in Italy.

Facilities at Amendola were very rudimentary and offered personnel little in the way of creature comforts. Conditions were widely described as primitive, with air and ground crews sleeping in tents. When it rained the dusty ground was quickly turned into a sea of oozing mud, which clung to everyone and everything. Even so, Ronald Bray and his oppoes would have grudgingly admitted that they had a slightly better deal than the troops on the frontline.

The operation against the pontoon bridge at San Benedetto Po on 4 October was the fourth in a series of attacks against this recalcitrant target. Allied photo-reconnaissance sorties had shown that three previous attacks by the RAF had been unsuccessful, the bridge was still intact and it remained in use by the Germans. Clearly, another raid on the bridge was needed to knock it out once and for all.

As the bombers drew closer to the target area the weather became progressively worse and visibility poorer. All eyes in KG942 would have been straining for any visual cues that might help them to identify the target. When they finally arrived over San Benedetto, the River Po and the pontoon bridge were obscured by thick cloud, but when dropping down below the 2,500ft cloud base some crews thought that the bridge itself was no longer in position, and had probably been removed by the Germans in anticipation of their attack.

Bombing raids by 205 Group were usually flown at heights of between 12 and 15,000ft. To prevent the German flak gunners on the ground from singling out individual aircraft, it was essential that the bombers were streamed over the target in the short space of three minutes. To achieve this it meant accurate navigation was vital.

By now the enemy ground defences in the vicinity of San Benedetto had been roused. The flak barrage was much heavier than on previous raids, with very accurate light and medium flak hosing up to greet the attackers.

Even so, the first bombs went down at 10.06pm. Lying flat on his belly on the bomb aimer's couch in the nose of KG942, Ronald Bray would have squinted through the bombsight and pressed the tit to release his 8,000lb load of high explosive bombs and incendiaries. Whether or not he got to drop his bombs will never be known.

Nothing more was heard from KG942 and her crew. It was the only squadron Liberator that failed to return to Amendola in the early hours of the 5th. In the post-raid debriefings of the two other 178 Squadron crews that had bombed, they described seeing an aircraft going down in flames over the target area at 10.30pm, probably a victim of the accurate flak. It was the only RAF aircraft to be lost on this operation.

After the war a British Graves Registration Unit in Italy investigated the fate of the Gregory crew. They discovered from local reports that KG942 had been hit by anti-aircraft fire from an enemy flak battery at Ostiglia, 10 miles east of the target. The Liberator was set on fire and dived out of control to crash on the small industrial town of Saletto, 31 miles northeast of San Benedetto. KG942 had been flying relatively low when it was hit and the fire would have spread quickly inside the damaged bomber – it may even have lost a wing to the flak, sending the aircraft into a spin – but whatever the chain of events, the crew probably had little chance to save themselves.

'We got a telegram from the RAF on a Sunday morning and mum knew what it was about,' recalls Ronald's sister Golda. 'I can remember her saying "that's the last we'll ever see of him".'

Next day the people of Saletto pulled charred bodies from what was left of the Liberator and buried them in individual coffins at the town cemetery, in a single grave. The bodies of the crew had been badly burned in the crash and only those of Ronald Bray and Burnie Thorp were identifiable. In February 1946, the Gregory crew were exhumed and re-interred at Padua War Cemetery in accordance with the Commonwealth War Graves Commission's policy to bring together burials from isolated locations into special military cemeteries.

Four other 178 Squadron aircraft never made it to the target that night. Two failed to take off from Amendola owing to mechanical difficulties, one suffered an engine fire en-route which caused it to turn back, and a fourth was unable to identify the target and jettisoned half its bomb load over the Italian countryside, but with the fuses made safe.

The pontoon bridge at San Benedetto Po was fated not to last much longer. It was visited again a few weeks later by fifteen bombers of 205 Group on the night of 21–22 October, whose bombs reduced it to a tangle of useless metal in the River Po.

Flight Sergeant Ronald Cecil BRAY

Service No: 1315659, RAFVR; *Unit:* 178 Squadron RAF, Middle East Air Force; *Died:* 4 October 1944 aged 22; *Buried:* Padua War Cemetery, Italy, Grave IV.C.8; *Commemorated:* BOA WM; HT.

Chapter Eight

THE GREAT CRUSADE

D-DAY AND THE BATTLE OF NORMANDY

'Just before HQ reached Eterville a hell of a barrage came down upon us, several were wounded... After some terrible minutes dodging shells and mortars, the odd few of us decided to remain until the barrage eased up and then move on. Shells were still raining down like hailstones. The battalion's casualties poured into the village church, besides many Germans lying around wounded. Everyone was told to dig in for their dear lives' sakes.' *Sgt Wally Caines, 4th Dorsets, near Eterville, Normandy, 10 July 1944*

Operation 'Overlord' – the Allied invasion of France in 1944 – was the largest single-day amphibious invasion of all time. Aircraft and glider-borne troops landed in Normandy soon after midnight on 6 June. At 6.30am, over 5,000 vessels began landing 160,000 troops onto the beaches. These amphibious landings took place along a 50-mile stretch of coastline that was divided into five beaches or sectors: Utah and Omaha (USA), Gold (British), Juno (Canadian), Sword (British), plus the airborne bridgeheads at St Mère Eglise (US) and the Orne – Ranville and Pegasus Bridge (British). The desperate battle of Normandy that ensued continued until 19 August when Allied forces finally won through and crossed the River Seine – it was also a time that was more dangerous for British soldiers than on the Somme in 1916.

BLOODY MALTOT

Private Herbert Llewellyn Aland, 5th Battalion Wiltshire Regiment – Holt

Herbert Llewellyn Aland was born in 1923 at Bradford-on-Avon, but very little is known about him other than his family lived at 170 Highfield, Holt, and that he had a sister, Florence. Before he was called up in 1941 for Army service, Herbert had worked as a gardener for Lady Cecilie Goff and her husband at The Courts in Holt. From 1920 Lady Cecilie Goff, influenced by the English garden designers Gertrude Jekyll and Lawrence Johnston, created beautiful vibrant formal gardens at The Courts, divided by yew hedges, shrub borders and raised terraces. As one of Lady Goff's team of gardeners, Herbert Aland was involved in the realisation of her vision for the gardens, which were

Pte Herbert Aland, Wiltshire Regiment, from Holt.
Holt Village Hall

completed in 1943. The contrast between the tranquility of The Courts and the bloody battlefield at Maltot could not have been more pronounced.

The Allies had landed on the beaches of Normandy on D-Day, 6 June. Once they had fought their way out of the beachhead the armies pushed inland. In the coming weeks reinforcements of men and equipment were sent from England and landed in Normandy to bolster the allied effort. As a private soldier in the 5th Battalion Wiltshire Regiment, Herbert sailed from Tilbury docks for Normandy on 18 June 1944.

Herbert arrived at Mulberry Harbour off Arromanches on 19 June where the battalion disembarked. The 5th Wiltshires advanced to la Gaule on the 26th before reaching the Baron area towards the end of the month. For much of July they occupied a defensive position near Baron from where they were involved in the assault on Hill 112 (Operation 'Jupiter') on the 10th when they sustained heavy casualties. The battalion deepened and strengthened their positions at Baron on the 11th before the 1st Worcesters relieved them on the 17th. On 19 July the battalion moved to a new position east of Verson in preparation for an attack on Maltot.

Supported by Churchill tanks of 7th Battalion Royal Tank Regiment (7RTR) and a strong artillery presence, the 4th and 5th Wiltshires were tasked with re-taking the village of Maltot in Operation 'Express'. In reserve were 4th Battalion Somerset Light Infantry and mortars of 8th Middlesex.

At 6.30pm on 22 July the 5th Wiltshires began their attack on Maltot. The men's faces were daubed with green camouflage cream and foliage was attached to the web netting on their helmets. The sun was shining but almost immediately enemy shells and mortar bombs began falling among the Wiltshires as they advanced across the cornfields in open order. The 5th Wiltshires reached the outskirts of Maltot, despite being sniped by enemy tanks dug in on Hill 112. Close-quarter fighting ensued among the houses and orchards; Maltot was a shocking sight with dozens of German dead lying where they had fallen, bloated and unburied.

Thirty-six hours after the battalion first reached Maltot, hungry shell-shocked German troops began to emerge from their hiding places in cellars and trenches. Eventually 400

British infantry advance through wheat fields in Normandy. *IWM B6618*

were taken into captivity; 600 British rifles that had been captured in the first battle of Maltot on 10 July were also retrieved.

The 5th Wiltshires had lost a lot of men, but had won Maltot. By 10.30pm they had achieved their objectives and were making good their position. During this attack it was very likely that Herbert Aland was killed.

Private Herbert Llewellyn ALAND

Service No: 5577008; *Unit:* 5th Battalion Wiltshire Regiment; *Died:* 22 July 1944 aged 21; *Buried:* Banneville-la-Campagne War Cemetery, Normandy, France, Grave II.B.22; *Commemorated:* Holt WM.

FIGHT FOR THE CHATEAU

Private Graham Ronald Britten, 5th Battalion Dorsetshire Regiment – Bradford-on-Avon

Private (Pte) Ronald Britten was one of an estimated 16,000 British and Canadian soldiers who died in the fight for Normandy between the initial landings on 6 June and 31 August when the allies crossed the River Seine. The carnage did not stop there, for some 67,000 more British and Canadian troops were also wounded or posted missing during this time. Losses were worse still for American and German forces in Normandy.

Ronald and his battalion of the Dorsets were involved in a bitterly contested assault on the Chateau de Fontaine, near Eterville – headquarters of the German 22nd

Panzergrenadier Regiment – as part of a greater British plan to advance to the River Orne in Operation 'Jupiter'.

Graham Ronald Britten ('Ronald') was born at Bradford-on-Avon in 1925, one of five children to Ronald Thomas and Lucy May Britten (nee Mitchell) of Bradford-on-Avon. In 1944 the family was living at Avonfield Avenue. Ronald worked for Spencer, Moulton & Co and served in the Bradford-on-Avon Home Guard before he was called up for service in the Army.

By 9 July 1944, the battle for Caen had momentarily died down and Montgomery needed to maintain pressure along the British front. Operation 'Jupiter' had as its strategic objective the River Orne south of Caen. The specific objectives were Hill 112 on the right flank of the advance; and on the left flank Chateau de Fontaine, Eterville and Maltot; and then a push through to the River Orne at Feuguerolles.

In the early morning of 10 July, Ronald was with the 5th Dorsets and 7th Hampshires of 130 Brigade, supported by Churchill tanks of B Squadron 9RTR, when they advanced to seize the high ground around the Chateau de Fontaine in conjunction with an attack by 129 Brigade on the right of Hill 112. Opposition from the German defenders was ferocious. The Dorsets and Hampshires came up against the very best the German Army and the SS could throw at them: the 10th SS Panzer Division, 22nd Panzergrenadier Regiment, Hitler Youth troops, and dug-in Tiger tanks, exacted a massive toll in dead and wounded from the British force.

A Churchill tank of 7th Royal Tank Regiment supports infantry during operations in Normandy. ***IWM B6123***

Even so, the day had been a success of sorts for the 5th Dorsets, which had beaten off several determined enemy counter-attacks yet managed to hold and consolidate their position. By the end of the day C Company 5th Dorsets had captured the Chateau and 7th Battalion Somerset Light Infantry had taken over an area close by. Now, with two infantry battalions firmly established and backed up by forty anti-tank guns (17pdrs and 6pdrs), one squadron of Churchill tanks from 9RTR, and the unstinting support of the artillery, the chateau was truly a fortress, but not without cost. The 5th Dorsets suffered heavily: 2 officers missing, 9 wounded; 39 other ranks killed, 2 died of wounds, 43 missing, and 113 wounded. Ronald Britten was among these casualties.

The occupying units continued to suffer from enemy shelling, dug-in Tiger tanks, mortars and snipers. For the next eight days the battalion maintained its position against further counter-attacks, with C Company in what came to be known as the 'Fortress', and A and B Companies nearby in, and west of, 'Triangle Orchard'.

The planned Allied breakthrough to the River Orne was abandoned, but the city of Caen was eventually captured by British and Canadian troops on 22 July. The cost in Allied lives had been high: when Maltot was finally captured by the British on 29 July, the dead of the 5th Dorsets and 7th Hampshires still lay in heaps around partly dug slit trenches, and in the streets and fields.

Private Graham Ronald BRITTEN

Service No: 14610186; *Unit:* 5th Battalion Dorsetshire Regiment; *Died:* 10 July 1944 aged 19; *Buried:* St Manvieu War Cemetery, Cheux, France, Grave I.D.4; *Commemorated:* BOA WM; HT; AR.

HILL 112

Private Frederick George Chivers, 5th Battalion Wiltshire Regiment – Bradford-on-Avon

Born in Plymouth in 1909, Frederick George Chivers was one of four sons to Frederick and Beatrice Ellen Chivers, and the husband of Ethel Chivers of 30 Wine Street, Bradford-on-Avon. Fred worked for Spencer, Moulton & Co before joining the Wiltshire Regiment.

At the beginning of July 1944, Frederick Chivers was with the 5th Battalion Wiltshire Regiment that was occupying a defensive position in the Baron area of Normandy. Their position was subjected to heavy mortaring and shelling in the early hours of the 1st, which injured the commanding officer and 1 other officer, killed 17 other ranks and injured 50 more.

In the late afternoon of the 2nd, a carrier patrol investigated Hill 112 and found the enemy in occupation. During the night of 2-3 July the battalion sent out a fighting patrol to find any enemy troops who might have crept up near them in the darkness, and silence them, but none were seen and no enemy fire was drawn. During the night of 3rd–4th, standing patrols were mounted for local protection against enemy incursions.

During the day of the 4th it was fairly quiet except for some harassing fire by the enemy. There were reports of sniper activity and a patrol was sent out to deal with it, although none were found and the snipers cleared off.

The enemy: camouflaged German troops in the close countryside of the Normandy *bocage* during the summer of 1944. *Bundesarchiv*

At 5.00am on 10 July, the 4th and 5th Battalions of the Wiltshire Regiment moved forward from Baron, having suffered severe casualties from artillery fire while forming up. D and B Companies crossed the start line and attacked forward up the slopes of Hill 112. Both gained their objectives on the reverse slope of the hill without too much difficulty.

For C Company it was anything but straightforward. Their objective was the top of the hill where they were to destroy the enemy and then fall back into positions prepared for them by A Company on the reverse slope, just below the summit. C Company moved forward but when they reached the Caen-Esquay road they were pinned down by intense fire from dug-in Tiger tanks and heavy machine gun fire. The company was pinned down on the forward slope, unable to move forward or retire, with ammunition supplies running low. Heavy casualties were sustained. At about 5.00pm C Company was withdrawn under cover of a diversionary attack prepared by the Brigade HQ, to the position held by A Company, and thence back to Baron.

Casualties from the day's fighting were heavy: the 5th Battalion suffered 26 other ranks killed and 21 missing, 5 officers and 68 other ranks wounded. Frederick Chivers was one of the many who died in the bitterly contested assaults on Hill 112, a strategic vantage point that was to claim many more lives before the month was out.

Private Frederick George CHIVERS

Service No: 5570148; *Unit:* 5th Battalion Wiltshire Regiment; *Died:* 10 July 1944 aged 35; *Buried:* Banneville-la-Campagne War Cemetery, Normandy, France, Grave X.E.9; *Commemorated:* BOA WM; HT; AR.

THE BATTLE FOR HOTTOT

Private Roy Henry Llewellyn Heavyside, 2nd Battalion Devonshire Regiment – Holt

Pte Roy Heavyside, Devonshire Regiment, from Holt.
Pamela Joyce

Pte Roy Heavyside landed with the 2nd Battalion the Devonshire Regiment on Gold Beach at 8.10am on D-Day, and by late morning the battalion had advanced down the La Gronde Ruisseau valley. The 2nd Devons took Ryes as their first objective at 4.30pm on the 6th, and Chateau Maisons on the 8th. On 15 June elements of 231 Infantry Brigade launched an attack on the village of Hottot les Bagues, 8½ miles south west of Bayeux, as part of a plan to take the village and surrounding high ground. Later that day the 2nd Devons fought their way into the village and despite several enemy counter attacks they held Hottot, until the brigade commander ordered a withdrawal, as their position was so tenuous. Over the next few weeks further attempts were made to take Hottot, but the Germans maintained their vice-like grip on the village.

Roy Heavyside was born at Holt in 1917, one of three sons to Frederick and Winifred Heavyside. Upon leaving school Roy worked as a fellmonger at the tannery in Holt before the family moved to Bradford-on-Avon. In 1938 he married Joan (Rogers) and their first child, Pamela, was born in 1940.

Before he was called up, Roy worked in the canteen at the Army's vast underground ammunition dump at Monkton Farleigh. In 1940 he joined the Devonshire Regiment and trained at Paignton in Devon before he was posted overseas to Gibraltar with the 4th Battalion in 1941, where they were on garrison duty on 'the Rock'. The battalion returned home in 1943 in preparation for the impending invasion of France, and trained in southern England. When his second child Gary was born in May 1944, Roy was allowed to return to the family home at 5 St Margaret's Steps for 24 hours' compassionate leave, but that was the last time his family saw him alive.

On 11 July 1944, the three battalions of 231 Infantry Brigade (including 2nd Devons) supported by tanks of the Nottinghamshire Yeomanry, tried once again to take Hottot-les-Bagues. At 4.30am, the 2nd Devons rose for an early breakfast and then prepared for battle. By 6.45am the battalion had moved up to its start line, with A Company in reserve.

A massive rolling artillery barrage preceded the attack, moving forward at the rate of 50 metres every 2 minutes. At 8.35am under the supporting barrage, C and D Companies moved towards their first objective in Hammer Orchard. By 9.30am they were well inside the orchard, but resistance from enemy tanks and a small party of infantry led to intense fighting and the loss of a whole platoon of Devons.

Enemy shells and mortars were now raining down on the area that so far had been covered by the Devons. By 1.15pm, four enemy tanks were reported knocked out in the Hammer Orchard area and by 5.45pm it was decided to reorganise and dig-in in the area forward of the Lone House. The Devons' casualties for the day had been heavy – 1 officer killed and 4 wounded, 9 other ranks killed and 52 wounded. Roy was fatally wounded in the head and both legs and died the next day from his injuries.

Roy's daughter Pamela remembers: 'the whole platoon was wiped out. Dad was taken to hospital and died the next day. Mum was told in a letter from the War Office, and later with letters from his commanding officer and a Sister in the hospital.'

By nightfall, 231 Infantry Brigade had reached a line just north of Hottot-les-Bagues, but the Germans still held the village. It was not until the night of 18–19 July that they finally withdrew.

Private Roy Henry Llewellyn HEAVYSIDE

Service No: 5626156; *Unit:* 2nd Battalion Devonshire Regiment; *Died:* 12 July 1944 aged 27; *Buried:* Ryes War Cemetery, Bazenville, France, Grave IV.B.5; *Commemorated:* Holt WM; Melksham WM.

Roy Heavyside landed on Gold Beach on 6 June 1944. *IWM CL56*

THE ROAD TO FALAISE

Trooper Albert Edward Jones, 3rd/4th County of London Yeomanry – Westwood

Recognising that the German army in Normandy was all but beaten, General Montgomery and US General Bradley planned a short 'hook' to create a pocket and achieve an encirclement of German forces near the Norman town of Falaise. On 16 August Falaise fell to Canadian troops, and the British, Canadian and Polish armies accelerated their advance, seeking to meet American forces moving northwards in a pincer movement.

Generalfeldmarschall von Kluge, Commander in Chief West, with Hitler's approval, ordered a withdrawal eastwards out of the pocket by the German Seventh Army, Fifth Panzer Army, and Panzer Group *Eberbach*. The closure of the Falaise Pocket by the Allies and the destruction of the retreating German forces within it took place between 16 and 21 August.

Trooper (Tpr) Albert Jones from Westwood was the driver in a British Sherman tank crew involved in the pursuit of the German Army as it fled south. Under the combined pressure of the Americans and French to the south, the Americans and British to the west, and the Canadians and Poles to the north, the Germans became hemmed into the Falaise

A wrecked Sherman tank in Normandy. The Sherman was nicknamed the 'Tommy cooker' by the Germans because of its tendency to burst into flames and burn when hit. *Bundesarchiv*

Tpr Albert Jones, 3rd/4th County of London Yeomanry, from Westwood. *Pamela Ward*

Pocket. In a series of ferocious actions backed by Allied artillery and airpower, by 21 August the pocket was all but shut, sealing the defeat of the German Army in Normandy.

Albert Edward Jones was born in 1920, the twin of Ernest Leonard, and one of seven children to Ernest (1890–1943) and Florence Edith Jones (1892–1971) of 1 Staples Hill, Freshford. When he left school Albert was apprenticed to J. Alex Brown, the ironmonger, in Bradford-on-Avon, and later joined the Trowbridge engineering firm of Messrs G.N. Haden & Sons Ltd.

In October 1942 Albert married Barbara Martin, of the Gate House, Iford. Her father, known as 'Doc' Martin, was butler and chauffeur to Sir Michael Peto of Iford Manor. A few hours after his marriage to Barbara, Albert answered his call-up for the Army and reported for training. Barbara moved to Trowbridge to lodge with her cousins in Hilperton Road, where she worked nearby at the Spitfire factory opposite the top of Victoria Road (now Kenton Drive).

'He was crazy about driving,' recalls his sister Pamela. 'When he was called up he told the Army he'd drive the biggest vehicle they could give him, so they put him in the Tank Regiment and trained him as a tank driver.'

Albert served with the 8th Army in the Middle East, Sicily and Italy before returning to England in preparation for Operation 'Overlord', the Allied invasion of France, in June 1944. Albert landed in Normandy with the 3rd/4th County of London Yeomanry (3rd/4th CLY) on D-Day +1 (7 June 1944).

The 3rd/4th CLY was an armoured regiment in General Miles Dempsey's Second (British) Army, equipped with Sherman tanks. The regiment was involved in the Allies' northern element of the Allied encirclement of German forces, south from Falaise. On 18 August its task was to cut the Germans' escape route, which led them through the village of Pierrepont, 2½ miles west of Falaise. The 3rd/4th CLY's war diary records the tough fighting of that day which was to cost the regiment dearly in men and tanks:

> 'B Squadron led the advance and found the enemy mining the road. These were quickly dispersed. The leading troop was then fired on by anti-tank guns, but no hits were scored. Another troop was sent round to the east but was also held up by anti-tank guns. The country was too close for deployment so smoke was put down and the leading tanks moved forward and fired HE [high explosive shells]. This was successful – one gun knocked out and one abandoned – and the advance continued. A Mark IV special [German tank] was seen and knocked out, but shortly afterwards the two leading tanks were hit by anti-tank fire. The driver of one tank succeeded in driving his badly damaged vehicle back out of range and was able to rescue his wounded crew. Artillery fire was brought down on the suspected gun positions and another attempt was made to go forward, but the leading tank was immediately hit.
>
> 'Many attempts were made to find a way round, and A Company 2/60th King's Royal Rifles was sent into the village ahead to try and locate the anti-tank guns and clear the area of the enemy.
>
> 'At 18.00hrs, A Squadron succeeded in finding a way round and took up position

south of the village of Roufigny [3 miles south of Falaise]. B Squadron was then able to go forward and send a troop into the village to assist the 2/60th, while the remainder of the regiment were together further north. During the day, C Squadron had taken up a commanding position on high ground and accounted for several enemy vehicles attempting to escape.'

Tpr Albert Jones was one of the casualties suffered by the regiment that day, which numbered 2 officers and 8 other ranks killed, 4 other ranks missing and 7 wounded.

Albert's twin brother, Ernest, who was in the REME, had also seen service with the 8th Army in North Africa and Italy. He had somehow managed to arrange a transfer for Albert to the REME, but with the mounting casualties after D-Day the Army needed tank crews, so Albert was not transferred and remained with his regiment.

Trooper Albert Edward JONES

Service No: 7957044; *Unit:* B Squadron, 3rd/4th County of London Yeomanry (Sharpshooters); *Died:* 18 August 1944 aged 24; *Buried:* Bayeux War Cemetery, Normandy, France, Grave XIX.E.1; *Commemorated:* St Mary's Church, Westwood; Freshford Cemetery.

THE GREAT STORM

Corporal William Jesse Moore, 43rd Reconnaissance Regiment – Wingfield

Starting in the early hours of 6 June 1944 and continuing over a period of 24 hours, 156,000 Allied troops were landed by sea and air on the shores of Northern France in the greatest amphibious invasion in history. In the days and weeks that followed, more troops and materiel were poured in to secure the Normandy beachhead and prepare for the planned breakout. Included in these reinforcements were Corporal (Cpl) Billy Moore from Wingfield and 600 men of the 43rd Reconnaissance Regiment. William Jesse Moore, who was known to his family and friends as Billy, was born at Bradford-on-Avon in 1920, the second son of Jim and Elsie Moore of Magdalene Lane, Wingfield.

Once ashore in Normandy the regiment's task was to reconnoitre forward of the Allied frontline, make contact with the enemy and engage him, then report back with details of the enemy's position and strength. The 43rd were not expected to become involved in close quarters fighting with enemy tanks or infantry, but occasionally this was difficult to avoid. The regiment's equipment comprised of Humber armoured cars, light reconnaissance cars and Bren carriers, which together packed a significant punch in terms of fire power.

In the most awful weather conditions the regiment found themselves crammed into the SS *Derrycunihy*, a 10,200-ton cargo ship requisitioned by the Ministry of War Transport, anchored off Sword Beach awaiting the improvement in the weather which would allow them to be landed safely.

On 19 June, the generally poor weather that had followed D-Day turned into a severe gale in the English Channel that raged and blew for four days. 'The Great Storm', as it became called by the British, seriously damaged the two artificial Mulberry Harbours off the Normandy coast and ran at least 700 ships and smaller craft aground. The American Mulberry Harbour at St Laurent, near Omaha Beach, was completely wrecked by the driving winds and mountainous waves and was abandoned altogether. At Arromanches, the British Mulberry was also damaged but was still able to offer a reduced service. Due to the ravages of the Great Storm the Allied timetable for landing additional troops, equipment and supplies in Normandy was delayed by about a week.

By the morning of 24 June the storm had blown itself out and the dawn brought with it a flat calm sea. It promised to be a fine day and things looked good. Capt Richardson ordered the *Derrycunihy*'s engines to be started and then he weighed anchor, preparing to head for the landing point. Within seconds disaster struck – the ship's movement triggered a German acoustic mine, which split the *Derrycunihy* in two. The forward section remained afloat, but the stern section, although still attached by the keel plates, sank quickly. An ammunition truck on the ship's well deck exploded, setting fire to the spilled fuel oil on the surface of the sea.

Of the 600 men of the regiment, 179 died and 150 were injured. Of those who died, 166 men were listed as missing, their bodies never found. Their names are recorded on

The 'Great Storm' of 20 June dashed hundreds of vessels to pieces on the shores of Normandy. ***US National Archives***

the Bayeux Memorial in Normandy. Twenty-five of the ship's crew, including a number of Army gunners, also lost their lives. Most of the men who died had been trapped in the sunken stern section. It was the heaviest single British loss of life off the invasion beaches. (In 2009 the wreck stands proud, orientation NW–SE. At low tide, the aft part and a piece of a mast are visible. The front part was recovered and towed back to England.)

Lt Desmond Scarr, Commanding 'A' Squadron, 43rd Reconnaissance Regiment, was onboard the *Derrycunihy*. After the war he wrote about the awful events of 24 June in his autobiography, *Recollections,* reproduced on 'WW2 People's War', the BBC online archive of wartime memories:

> 'We arrived off the coast of Normandy on 20 June and were kept waiting due to bad weather. During the next few days our ship played a deadly game with the German shore batteries at Le Havre (we were at the extreme end of the bridgehead). Then, before dawn on 24 June, orders came for our ship to move inshore preparatory to disembarkation. The troops were still below and most of us were in bed when a violent shudder shook the ship. I saw the washbasin on the wall of my cabin fly off its brackets and end up on the floor. I had no idea what had happened but presumed we had had a direct hit from one of the coastal guns. As I started to throw on my clothes my cabin mate, who had been on duty, rushed in saying "Quick – you have no time to dress. Get out!" However, I completed dressing, which took a few seconds and went out onto the deck. I quickly came to a yawning gap of several yards and in front of me was a scene from *Dante's Inferno*, which I simply could not grasp. The stern part of the ship had fallen away and was low in the water. On the as yet un-submerged deck, part of which was in flames, lay several bodies. An ammunition truck near me was on fire and, feeling rather useless in that there was no way I could reach the stricken part of the ship, I turned a water hose on to the vehicle. Some small arms ammunition started to explode, adding to the general mayhem. Shortly after, we were told to get aboard a small craft which had come alongside.
>
> 'In this boat I found several injured men and I could not help feeling some shame that I was fully clothed and unharmed whilst others were in such dire straits. Our rescue boat was a launch of some kind and on a raised bridge two naval officers stood at the helm. As we moved off we passed within feet of the blazing ammunition truck and those of us who were standing sank to the deck instinctively.
>
> 'As we moved towards a large ship a mile or so away I spent my time comforting the injured. Our objective turned out to be a depot ship, the *Cap Tourain*, equipped with extensive hospital facilities. This was as well, as soon after we boarded the ship received a hit from the shore batteries and two of our officers were wounded, among others. There was little I could do on this ship, where I found other survivors from the *Derrycunihy*. We still had no idea of the extent of the losses suffered by the regiment and this became apparent only later in the day when the roll was called. It then became clear that a great many men, especially from "A" Squadron, had been killed or drowned immediately when our ship struck what I later learned was a mine. This

was the so-called "oyster" mine, which German aircraft parachuted down at night among the ships offshore. They were very powerful and activated acoustically when a ship passed overhead. At much the same time as the *Derrycunihy* was sunk so also, by another oyster mine, was the destroyer HMS *Swift* with the loss of most of its crew of 150. The few survivors from that ship were also on the *Cap Tourain*.

'That afternoon some of us returned to the *Derrycunihy*. The ship had settled on the bottom with the front half still above the water. The rear part was submerged. After a short service conducted on the bridge by the Padre, the Rev Gethyn-Jones, we went down to the forward holds and started to unload the armoured vehicles (which were largely undamaged). These were lifted out by cranes onto rafts manned by sappers. This work went on for 24 hours and finally, late on the evening of the 25th, I found myself landing on the continent of Europe for the first time.'

Corporal William Jesse MOORE

Service No: 6028643; *Unit:* 43rd (Wessex) Reconnaissance Regiment (2nd/5th Battalion Gloucestershire Regiment), Royal Armoured Corps; *Died:* 24 June 1944 aged 24; *Commemorated:* Bayeux Memorial, Normandy, France, Panel 3.

AMBUSH AT ETOUVY

Trooper Raymond Dudley Sutton, 2nd Household Cavalry – Bradford-on-Avon

On 28 July 1944, General 'Pip' Roberts, commanding 11th Armoured Division, received orders from Monty that VIII Corps and XXX Corps with their six divisions would launch a major offensive south from Caumont in Normandy. Codenamed Operation 'Bluecoat', their objective was the town of Vire. The 11th Armoured Division was part of this operation and its armoured cars of the 2nd Household Cavalry (2HC) were VIII Corps' reconnaissance regiment. Tpr Raymond Sutton from Bradford-on-Avon was a Daimler Dingo scout car driver with 2HC.

British armoured cars in Normandy operated at the very edge of the frontline and often probed beyond into enemy held territory. It was a dangerous and at times suicidal job. Their main task was to gain information about enemy strengths and positions, and radio this intelligence back to headquarters. Armed with only a 2pdr gun that was virtually useless against German tanks, the radio set was really the armoured car's most potent weapon – and the vehicle's speed in making a hasty getaway from trouble.

A typical reconnaissance regiment comprised of a headquarters squadron and four armoured car squadrons. Each armoured car squadron was made up of a HQ troop with four Staghound armoured cars; five troops, each equipped with two Daimler armoured cars and two Daimler scout cars; a heavy troop with two AEC armoured cars; and a support troop of riflemen riding in armoured half-tracks.

Raymond Dudley Sutton was born in 1921 at Dudley, Warwickshire, the son of Albert and Elsie Sutton (nee Thomas). In the summer of 1943 Raymond married Peggy Winona Clifford (b.1925) of Whitehill, Bradford-on-Avon.

In the early hours of 2 August the assembled troop leaders of D Squadron 2HC were briefed by their squadron commander, Major (Maj) E.J.S. Ward, who told them that the regiment was to probe south-westwards towards the village of Etouvy and the town of Vire, the latter an important communications centre. Having already endured three nights without sleep, the men resigned themselves to more fatigue and life running on adrenaline.

Just before 3.00am the main body of the regiment moved off in their vehicles towards Le Reculey and the Vire–Caen road that lay beyond, while Lt Metcalfe's Support Troop (that included the scout car of 30-year-old Cpl of Horse Frank Allenby and Tpr Raymond Sutton, aged 22) was to turn off at the village of Romesnil. They had been given the task of seizing the bridge over the River Vire at Etouvy.

Driving along the back roads and lanes in pitch darkness they at first met with no opposition, but near the village of La Bistiere the scout car of L/Cpl Jones and Tpr Lee ran into an enemy self-propelled gun which opened fire at close range, knocking out their vehicle and seriously wounding both men. They were rescued by the prompt action of D Squadron Reconnaissance Troop Leader, Lt Buchanan-Jardine, and the second-in-command Capt Waterhouse, who engaged the enemy SP gun in a fire-fight and forced it to withdraw.

As dawn was breaking, Maj Ward received a wireless message from Lt Metcalfe informing him that his Support Troop had run into trouble on the outskirts of Etouvy.

An armoured car crew camouflage their Daimler Dingo, the same type of vehicle driven by Raymond Sutton from Bradford-on-Avon. ***IWM B5969***

They had travelled by side roads with the hope of avoiding the enemy, which they had largely succeeded in doing. Even so they still found themselves driving past sizeable groups of Germans, mercifully without being challenged, but their luck was beginning to wear thin.

Allenby and Sutton were leading the column when rounding a sharp bend just as they entered Etouvy their scout car suddenly stopped dead in its tracks. Lt Metcalfe went forward on foot to find out what was wrong, only to discover Allenby's car had actually driven up beneath the gun muzzle of a German tank which was about to move off. There were more tanks guarding the approach to the river bridge. Luckily, at this moment the Germans were not on their toes so Sutton switched off the engine of his scout car which he then pushed quietly to safety around the corner, with the help of Metcalfe and Allenby. The enemy then woke up to what had happened and started firing their weapons wildly into the dawn.

It was time to take stock so the Support Troop retired about a quarter of a mile out of Etouvy, setting up a road block to control the entrance to the village from the north. There it remained until there was sufficient daylight for Metcalfe to estimate the German opposition in the village.

Half an hour later Allenby and Sutton again approached the village, but from a different direction, to see if the bridge was still held. But instead of taking a previously reconnoitred track they missed the turning completely and swung straight into the village. This time the Germans were ready and waiting for them. Metcalfe, who was approaching Etouvy on foot down another track, heard the sounds of gunfire, followed by a burst of Bren and then the explosion of grenades – then silence.

Realising that something was badly wrong, Metcalfe took a patrol across some fields towards the village to find out what had happened. They ran into a sizeable party of enemy mechanised infantry and three tanks, so they beat a hasty retreat. The enemy were heard moving off but the village was still held in some strength. Metcalfe was ordered to maintain observation and await the arrival of Sherman tanks of the Northamptonshire Yeomanry. Soon after daybreak they arrived and began shelling the village.

Sometime later Metcalfe took a further patrol towards the village, supported by tanks. The northern outskirts of Etouvy were found to be clear, but in the village several houses were burning and the Support Troop scout car of Allenby and Sutton was discovered in flames opposite the village church. Later on, the bodies of the two men were found lying in a shop window. 'We covered them up', wrote Metcalfe later, 'feeling very sad at losing two of the very best of men, and returned past the tanks on being ordered back to rejoin the squadron.'

The Etouvy flank remained troublesome for several more days, with German infantry penetrating the Northamptonshire Yeomanry positions after dark on the 2nd, knocking out several Shermans with their *Panzerfausts*.

Trooper Raymond Dudley SUTTON

Service No: 5347386; *Unit:* 2nd Battalion The Life Guards; *Died:* 2 August 1944 aged 22; *Buried:* Bayeux War Cemetery, Grave II.M.14; *Memorial:* No.

Chapter Nine

FORGOTTEN ARMY

THE WAR IN THE FAR EAST

O, dying soldier, what web are you weaving,
Waste with disease of these unfriendly climes?
Is your tired mind th' remembered things perceiving,
Straining your fading ear for Tom Tower's chimes?

Fragment of poetry written by Lieutenant-Colonel 'Joe' Hazel, 6th HAA Regiment, aboard the hell ship ***Singapore Maru.***

General Slim's 14th Army in Burma was called the 'Forgotten Army', thanks to Allied preoccupations with defeating Nazi Germany. Japan's invasion of Malaya in 1941 rudely expelled Britain from her colonial possessions. From then until 1945 the British fought to defeat Japanese forces and re-establish control in the Far East. The campaign was dominated by extreme weather, tropical diseases and difficult terrain, which all had major effects on men and operations. Campaigning against a fanatical enemy was prolonged and costly. It was not until the failed Japanese invasion of India in 1944 that the Allies went on the offensive and finally reoccupied Burma and Malaya by mid-1945.

RETREAT FROM BURMA

Private Ivor Norman Long, 1st Battalion Gloucestershire Regiment – Bradford-on-Avon

Throughout the long retreat north through Burman, the 1st Battalion Gloucestershire Regiment, was almost continuously in contact with the enemy as rear guard. Along the only available road north from Taukkyan to Prome, they prevented the Japs from harrying the tired and ill-equipped column of the withdrawing army.

Ivor Long was born in 1921 at Melksham, the only son of Alfred William and May Long (nee Powell) of 7 Whitehead's Lane, Bradford-on-Avon. Ivor worked for Spencer, Moulton & Co before joining the Territorial Force in 1938 and served abroad for several years.

Headquarters 1st Battalion Gloucestershire Regiment was at Mingaladon when

British troops wade through an infested swamp in Burma. *Author's collection*

the Japanese entered the war on 7 December 1941. It was mobilised on 17 December when the families were hurriedly evacuated north to the relative safety of Maymyo, east of Mandalay. By March the Japanese had penetrated from Siam (now Thailand) across the eastern borders into Burma. General Alexander, who was Commander-in-Chief in Burma, quickly ordered an evacuation of Rangoon and on 7 March a general retreat to the north began. The 1st Gloucesters were chosen as rearguard to the Burma Army. Ill-suited to jungle warfare the Burma Army was forced to withdraw to the Indian frontier.

Ivor Long was injured during the retreat and died in India of his wounds and diphtheria on 30 May 1942, a few days short of his 21st birthday.

Private Ivor Norman LONG

Service No: 5570145; *Unit:* 1st Battalion Gloucestershire Regiment; *Died:* 30 May 1942 aged 20; *Buried:* Delhi War Cemetery, India, Grave 6.G.13; *Commemorated:* BOA WM; HT; AR.

SHIP OF LOST SOULS

Gunner Leslie Henry Davis, 6th Heavy Anti-Aircraft Regiment, Royal Artillery – Bradford-on-Avon

Thanks to the help I received from a man in Taiwan that I've not yet met, I have been able to piece together what I believe is the most likely chain of events that led to the death of Bradford-on-Avon man Leslie Davis at the hands of the Japanese in 1942.

Leslie Davis from Southville Gardens in Bradford-on-Avon was a Royal Artillery gunner who became caught up in the fight for Singapore, and the fighting retreat into Sumatra and Java. The irony was that he should never have been out in the Far East in the first place – his regiment had been sailing to join the British 8th Army in North Africa when it received orders to head for Singapore instead.

Michael Hurst is a middle-aged Canadian ex-pat who owns and runs a factory on the island of Taiwan. His other persona is as the founder and director of the Taiwan POW Camps Memorial Society. I've never spoken to him in person – all our communication has been by email – but if email correspondence can give you even the slightest insight into someone's personality, then I'd say Michael is a good man. In fact in 2002 he was awarded the MBE for his work in bringing recognition to the sufferings of the former Commonwealth and Allied prisoners of war at the hands of the Japanese in Taiwan (formerly Formosa) during the Second World War.

I had drawn a complete blank trying to discover what had happened to Gunner Leslie Davis. Some basic research told me that his unit, the 6th Heavy Anti Aircraft Regiment, had been diverted to Singapore in early 1942 en route to North Africa, in order to reinforce the British presence on the island. When Singapore fell to the Japanese in February, Leslie's 15 Battery went on the run across the Malaysian archipelago in a vain attempt to escape from the advancing Japanese. They were forced to surrender in Jakarta on 9 March – and this is where my research trail ran cold.

The Commonwealth War Graves Commission website revealed that Leslie was buried in a communal grave in Hong Kong, but this fact did not sit comfortably with what little I already knew about him. I made further inquiries with the CWGC that revealed Leslie had been re-buried in Hong Kong after the war, but they could not tell me from where.

This is where Michael Hurst's detailed knowledge came in to play. I had discovered Michael and his Memorial Society quite by accident as I trawled the Internet for any references to British prisoners of war in Singapore. It was only logical that I should start with contacts in Hong Kong, since that is where Leslie is buried. Tony Banham of the Hong Kong War Diary – a project that documents the 1941 defence of Hong Kong, the British garrison, and their fates until liberation – very kindly referred me to Michael when he was not able to help with my enquiry himself.

One of Michael's first suggestions was that I should try and find out the names and unit details of the nine others who shared the communal grave with Leslie in Hong Kong, as this might provide some clues. As it transpired, eight of the ten men were from the same unit as Leslie, and the other was from the RAF. They had all died on or about the same date, in late October and mid-November 1942.

Leslie Davis from Bradford-on-Avon, pictured shortly before his departure for the Middle East. Unbeknown to him the final destination was to be Singapore. *Marilyn Schofield*

Copies of PoW records in Michael's possession told us that these men were almost certainly among several groups of servicemen crammed onto the so-called Japanese 'Hell Ships' and destined for forced labour in Taiwan and Japan. The dates of death that we had discovered for the other men in the collective grave lent credence to this. Based on our detailed correspondence and my own independent research this is what I believe happened to Leslie Davis.

From the moment that Japanese troops landed in Thailand on 8 December 1941, their invasion of Malaya and Singapore was swift and decisive. British forces on the Malay Peninsula fell back in the face of the relentless Japanese advance. The Japanese bombed the British colonies of Singapore and Hong Kong, and the US Navy Base at Pearl Harbor in the Philippines, and by 31 January 1942 they had reached the Johore Straits separating mainland Malaya from Singapore. Only Singapore remained in British hands.

When the colony fell to the Japanese invaders, there began one of the cruellest occupations of modern times. Allied officers were summarily executed by beheading and prisoners were forced to work on the infamous Burma Railway, or as slave labourers. The inhuman conditions they had to endure meant that many Allied soldiers died from disease, starvation and overwork.

Leslie Henry Davis was born at Bradford-on-Avon in 1916, the son of Henry and Mary Ann Davis (nee Coleman), and husband of Margaret Marie E. Davis (1915–90) of Bradford-on-Avon. Leslie lived with his wife Margaret at Southville Gardens (now called Culver Road), and worked for Spencer, Moulton & Co before joining the Royal Artillery.

On 12 November 1941 Leslie sailed for the Middle East from the Clydeside port of Gourock, with the British 18th Division. Leslie and his unit, the 15th Battery, 6th Heavy Anti-aircraft Regiment, Royal Artillery (15 Battery, 6th HAA Regiment), were embarked on the converted liner *Empress of Japan*. They sailed in convoy to Freetown, Sierra Leone, on the West African coast, where they arrived on 25 November and departed three days later for the South African Cape. As the convoy approached Cape Town, news was received that the Japanese had attacked Pearl Harbor and had landed troops in Malaya. On 18 December the *Empress of Japan* docked at Durban where Leslie and the other troops disembarked to spend several days on shore leave, a welcome break after almost five weeks at sea. For the next leg of their journey, Leslie and his regiment were transferred to the SS *Narkunda*, an ex-P&O liner that had been converted for use as a troop ship, before sailing from Durban on Christmas Eve 1941 as part of Convoy WS12Z.

Prime Minister Winston Churchill had decided that with Japan's aggressive moves in the Far East, the 18th Division was needed to reinforce the British garrison in Singapore.

The convoy split and the part that was renamed Convoy DM1 was diverted across the Indian Ocean towards Singapore, where it arrived on 13 January 1942.

Leslie's regiment disembarked in Singapore without equipment because it had all gone to the Middle East. Fortunately they were re-equipped with guns, ammunition and vehicles from Singapore's arsenal and were deployed to gun positions around the town, including the Jap Golf Course overlooking Keppel Harbour.

Pte William Cruickshank was one of the thousands of British soldiers who left England for the Middle East at the same time as Leslie. He remembers: 'We weren't actually meant for Singapore or that area at all; we were meant for the Middle East. We were trained for the Middle East, and when we were thrown into the jungle without proper equipment, without the proper arms as well, that came as a shock.'

With the situation in Singapore growing more hopeless by the hour, the decision was taken by British commanders to pull back some of its fighting units to defend the neighbouring island of Sumatra. On 30 January a convoy of small ships left Singapore for Sumatra, carrying 6th HAA Regiment (less 3 Battery). Sailing south, it arrived at Palembang on 2 February. The regiment's anti-aircraft guns were deployed to the two airfields, known as P1 and P2. P1 airfield was defended by one troop from 15 Battery (Leslie's battery) while its other troop was deployed in the large oil refineries just outside Palembang.

On 7 February the Japanese began their assault on Singapore and after a brave but futile resistance the British surrendered on the 15th.

Japanese paratroopers attacked P1 airfield on 14 February. They quickly seized the airfield and pressed on to Palembang and the oil refineries. In the face of the seemingly unstoppable Japanese advance, the British Army decided to abandon South Sumatra and survivors of the three remaining anti-aircraft batteries (including Leslie and 15 Battery) retreated to Java. They made the short sea crossing minus their guns and all but their light vehicles, arriving in Batavia (now called Jakarta) on 18 February. By 25 February, 6th HAA Regiment was reduced to 12 and 15 Batteries only. By noon on 9 March their position had become untenable and all British personnel laid down their arms and surrendered to the Japanese forces.

Pte Cruickshank again: '... when we found that we were absolutely cut off, there was no method of fighting back at the end, there was no method of evacuation; it was a terrible shock. I, personally, when we were told to lay our arms down, I just cried like a baby, I think more with temper than anything else, to think there was nothing we could do.'

Gradually, over the next few weeks, Leslie and the other British prisoners of war (POWs) were concentrated in large camps, mainly in the Batavia area, where from about August 1942 regular drafts of slave labour were sent via Singapore either to Japan to toil in the coalmines, or to Thailand to be worked to death on the infamous Burma Railway.

It is likely that first of all Leslie was moved by sea from Java with other British and Dutch POWs to Singapore, on one of two freighters – the *Dainichi Maru* or *Yoshida Maru*. He then sailed again for Japan on 28 October on one of the hell ships – the cargo vessels *Dainachi Maru*, *Singapore Maru* or *Tofuku Maru*. From the limited information available today, Leslie was probably on the *Tofuku Maru* because it carried 1,200 POWs, mainly

Dutch and British, who had been captured on Java. Also on board were some American and Australian POWs, and about 600 Japanese soldiers returning to Japan.

POWs destined for work as slave labourers were transported by sea in ferries, small cargo ships and freighters, and on larger military or merchant ships on the longer sea routes to Japan. The Japanese saw the POWs as men who had lost all right to respect – to start with they were Western and white, which meant they were considered to be racially inferior by the Japanese; and worse still they were soldiers who had surrendered, which meant they had no honour left. As such they were treated just like any other freight commodity and were transported in the cargo holds.

On *Tofuku Maru*, the POWs were accommodated in the two rear holds, which were seriously overcrowded. It was oppressively hot in the dimly lit bowels of the freighter, fetid with the smell of sweating bodies, and filthy with the residue of whatever had been carried before – like dusty coal or sticky sugar. To compound the misery and discomfort of the POWs, the holds were also infested with cockroaches and rats.

To enable the ship to carry more human cargo, the Japanese had split each hold into two with a makeshift wooden shelf about 3ft up from the floor. Those men on the shelf were more fortunate than their comrades below because they could at least stand up to ease their cramp, and perhaps get a breath of air from the deck hatch. But those below, with just 3ft of headroom, could only sit, lie, or crawl about on all fours like animals. The cramped conditions also meant the men were unable to lie down properly and had no bedding other than perhaps their own greatcoats or a few blankets.

Food was also scarce and of poor quality, and drinking water was in short supply. Needless to say, the Japanese crew and soldiers had ample rations, which were not shared with the POWs. On a voyage that was expected to last some thirty days, such conditions were quite simply inhumane.

An epidemic of dysentery soon broke out among the POWs and with little in the way of medical supplies it soon took a grip and spread quickly through their number. The stench in the hold was foul as the epidemic ran its course, and the decks ran deep with vomit and faeces. Many died.

For the POWs, the journey on these three hell ships was truly terrible. Hundreds of men died from disease brought on by the cramped and unsanitary conditions below decks, with those who died during the voyage buried at sea. An unscheduled stop was made at Takao, Formosa, on 14 November, to offload dead and sick POWs.

From a complement of 1,080 POWs onboard the *Singapore Maru,* soon after docking at Takao, 29 men disembarked sick; 62 had died onboard and were buried at sea; 280 were left sick on the vessel; and 709 were mustered on deck as able bodied. Eighty POW deaths were recorded at Formosa on the *Dainachi Maru*, and twenty-seven on the *Tofuku Maru.*

As the hell ship convoy approached Formosa, Leslie may have been one of a number of men who had already died onboard the *Tofuku Maru*, or was part of the group of 100 very sick POWs who were offloaded in Takao and then taken to hospital, where many died. He may then have been buried in the Takao Foreigners' Cemetery on the island.

In 1946 Leslie's remains were exhumed and taken to Hong Kong where they were

Newly liberated survivors of the Japanese prisoner of war camps. The 'five-mile stare' in the eyes of some of these men betrays damaged minds as well as broken bodies. *Author's collection*

re-interred at Sai Wan War Cemetery. He is buried in a collective grave with nine other British servicemen – eight from his own regiment, and one RAF airman. All these men had probably been captured on Java and had died in November 1942, probably on the hell ship convoy en route to Japan, or soon after their unscheduled stop on Formosa.

After the war, Leslie's wife and family tried to find out what had happened to him. They contacted his regiment, but the Army could tell them nothing as Leslie's cousin, Bill Rogers, recalls: 'A lot was done at the end of the war to find out what had happened to him. A man from up north came down to see Mar. He had served with Leslie and had been released from POW camp, but he couldn't tell her anything. We never did find out in the end, nothing definite that is. Aunty Mar remarried in 1947 or 1948.'

It was not until January 2008 that Leslie's family learned for the first time about what actually happened to him as a prisoner of the Japanese.

Gunner Leslie Henry DAVIS

Service No: 1714915; *Unit:* 15 Battery, 6th Heavy Anti Aircraft Regiment, Royal Artillery; *Died:* 14 November 1942 aged 26; *Buried:* Sai Wan War Cemetery, Hong Kong, Collective Grave IV.A.9-11; *Commemorated:* BOA WM; HT; AR.

Chapter Ten

THE LONG, LONG ROAD

THE BATTLE FOR EUROPE 1944–45

'It was nasty, cold, eerie and wet in the middle of those woods, trees dripping with rain in that windy forest. I lost a good friend killed by an airburst to which there seemed no protection. Sounds seemed magnified, many a rifle was fired at an imaginary enemy or a flitting "ghost" that seemed to dodge among the trees. It would have taken a group of top comedians and indeed dancing girls to have lifted our morale any higher than two degrees above rock bottom.' *Pte O'Connell, 7th Somerset Light Infantry, Eastern Holland, November 1944.*

The eleven months that elapsed between the Allied landings in Normandy on 6 June 1944 and VE-Day on 8 May 1945, saw British troops involved in some of the fiercest fighting of the Second World War. This epic campaign to defeat the Nazi armies in Europe included many of the most famous battles of the war –the breakout from the Normandy battle area and the race for Brussels, the ill-fated Operation 'Market Garden' at Arnhem and the bloody battles to clear the west bank of the River Rhine. Men from Bradford-on-Avon and district were there and in the thick of the action.

LIBERATORS FROM THE NAZI YOKE

Private Frederick Percy John Veater, 1st Battalion Dorsetshire Regiment – Bradford-on-Avon

Fred Veater came from a long line of Somerset farmers. Percy John Veater, known to all as Jack, was born in 1922 at Axbridge in Somerset, one of three children to Joseph Percy William (b.1887, Clutton, Somerset) and Annie May Veater (b.1888, Norton St Philip, nee Orchard). The Veaters owned Church Street Dairy in Bradford-on-Avon where Fred worked for his father before joining the Army in the autumn of 1941. Before they came to Bradford-on-Avon, the Veaters farmed at Leigh Farm in the village of Standerwick, near Frome. Fred's brother, Len, also helped with the family dairy business.

The 1st Battalion Dorsetshire Regiment had landed on Gold Beach on D-Day, 6 June 1944. It had been involved in the fighting to break out of the beachhead and the ensuing Battle of Normandy.

On 1 September the battalion moved to Le Bosquel, south of Amiens, before passing through the latter town amid scenes of great rejoicing from the newly liberated population. The Dorsets were part of a motorised infantry column following in the wake of British armour as it swept through large areas of liberated France and Belgium. Its task was to destroy the remaining German forces in the Low Countries and over-run the V1 flying bomb sites. Morale was high among the British troops.

The battalion's next move was to Arras on 2 September, to hold the town as a firm base while the Guards Armoured Division continued their advance on Brussels. In the absence of any other evidence, it is likely that Pte Veater was killed in an accident in the early hours of the 2nd when one of the battalion's troop carriers caught fire and exploded, causing some casualties.

Private Frederick Percy John VEATER

Service No: 5734949; *Unit:* 1st Battalion Dorsetshire Regiment; *Died:* 2 September 1944 aged 22; *Buried:* London Cemetery and Extension, Longueval, Somme, France, Plot 13, Row G, Grave 24; *Commemorated:* BOA WM; HT.

Sherman tanks of the Guards Armoured Division enter the outskirts of Arras on 1 September 1944. *IWM BU266*

Major Walter Long, Coldstream Guards, from South Wraxall.
The Hon Sara Morrison

IN THE SHADOW OF ARNHEM

Major Walter Francis David Long, 5th Battalion Coldstream Guards – South Wraxall

Major Viscount David Long had recently taken command of 1st Company, 5th Battalion Coldstream Guards, at Arnhem in September 1944 when he was killed, shot dead by an enemy sniper. Fighting alongside the 1st Squadron of 1st Coldstream Guards, his Company had just captured the village of Vokel in the early afternoon of 23 September. Another officer of David's battalion was wounded in the action.

Major Walter Francis David Long, the Lord Long, 2nd Viscount Long of Wraxall, was born at Hanover Square, London, on 14 September 1911. He was the only son of Brigadier General Walter 'Toby' Long, CMG, DSO, Royal Scots Greys, who was killed in action in France on 28 January 1917 commanding the 56th Infantry Brigade; and the Hon. Mrs Sibell Long (nee Bempde-Johnstone) latterly of Ardington, Wantage, Berkshire – but who was tremendously proud of her Yorkshire roots.

Educated at Eton College and the Royal Military Academy, Sandhurst, David Long (as he was known) was commissioned into the Coldstream Guards in 1929. In 1934 he was appointed aide-de-campe to the Governor-General of New Zealand, Charles Bathurst, 1st Viscount Bledisloe. He married in 1933, Frances Laura, second daughter of the Hon Guy Lawrence Charteris, second son of the 11th Earl of Wemyss. For some years they lived at the Long family's ancestral home of South Wraxall Manor in the village. David left the Army soon after his marriage and went to work in the City, but remained on the reserve of officers. David and Frances had a daughter, Sara, in 1934, but their marriage was dissolved in 1943.

On the outbreak of war David was recalled to his regiment, but much to his annoyance he was posted to the Royal Military Academy at Sandhurst, where he was responsible for schooling new officer cadets. He remained at Sandhurst for some time, 'coming home on leave in a bad temper because he was not allowed to rejoin his regiment,' recalls his daughter, the Hon Sara Morrison. 'He was a good teacher but a hell of a martinet and was kept at Sandhurst to knock into shape the new officer cadets. He remained there for several years.'

David eventually made good his escape from Sandhurst, thanks to none other than General Sir Bernard Montgomery who recognised qualities in him that were being wasted

Cromwell tanks of the Guards Armoured Division drive along 'Hell's Highway' towards Nijmegen during Operation 'Market Garden', 20 September 1944. *IWM B10131*

at the Academy. Monty appointed him to his headquarters staff at 21st Army Group.

Major Lord David Long was later moved from his staff job to command the 1st Company, 5th Battalion Coldstream Guards. (In September 1944 the 5th Coldstreams was part of the Coldstream Guards Group with 1st (Armoured) Coldstream, in 32nd Guards Brigade, Guards Armoured Division.)

On 22 September the German counter-attack that followed the Allies' airborne landings at Arnhem cut 'Hell's Highway' north of Veghel. General Brian Horrocks, commanding XXX Corps, was forced to turn the 32nd Guards Brigade around and drive south at Nijmegen to counter-attack back down the highway, clearing the road of Germans who had managed to effectively block the road at Veghel and put the bridge under fire. For most of that day supplies and equipment could not travel beyond Veghel, but the road was cleared and opened again by the end of 23 September, in collaboration with paratroops of the US 101st Airborne Division attacking from the south.

David, in the uniform of a staff officer and not the more usual battledress worn by frontline troops, was last seen alive in the village of Vokel between 1.10 and 2.00pm on 23 September, striding along with his batman by his side. At 6ft 3in tall, and wearing his distinctive uniform, he was easily picked out by an eagle-eyed German sniper and shot dead.

Major Walter Francis David LONG

Service No: 50864; *Unit:* 1st Company, 5th Battalion Coldstream Guards; *Died:* 23 September 1944 aged 33; *Buried:* Uden War Cemetery, Holland, Grave 3.G.13; *Commemorated:* St Peter's Church, South Wraxall.

TOWARDS THE MAAS

Fusilier Ernest Raymond Dainton, 4th Battalion Royal Welch Fusiliers – Bradford-on-Avon

With the failure of the Allied airborne operation to capture the lower Rhine bridges at Arnhem in September 1944, attention was switched to the importance of Antwerp as a supply port for the allied armies. The main winter task of 21st Army Group was the clearance of the enemy salient west of the Rhine, but the ability to use the port of Antwerp was an essential preliminary. It was therefore necessary to free the Dutch coast and clear south Holland as far as the River Maas, an operation that was to provide the next task for the 53rd Welsh Division and the Royal Welch Fusiliers (RWF). This involved the capture of the important communications centre of 's-Hertogenbosch – a city the size of Bath, and capital of the province of North Brabant in the south of Holland.

For Fusilier Ernest Dainton and the British troops advancing through the dense countryside of south Holland, progress was slow and dangerous. The enemy made good use of the terrain, with their well concealed dug-in positions taking full tactical advantage of the deep drainage ditches that criss-crossed the dead flat landscape, and the small clumps of woodland.

Infantry of the 53rd Division advance along a railway embankment during the capture of 's-Hertogenbosch, on 25 October 1944. *IWM B11257*

Ernest Raymond Dainton was born in 1922 at Bradford-on-Avon, the son of George (b.1897, Rodbourne Cheney, d.1947) and Mabel Kate Dainton (nee Coward, b.1892, Bradford-on-Avon, d.1957) of 14 Barton Orchard, Bradford-on-Avon, and the husband of Annie Jane Dainton, of Churchstanton, Somerset, with whom he had a son. Ernest had served originally with the Wiltshire Regiment before being transferred to the 4th Battalion Royal Welch Fusiliers.

On 21 October, 71 Brigade had moved to Vinkel, due south of Geffen, and at 6.30am on the 22nd their attack against the German defenders went in. The axis of 71 Brigade lay due west though Maleskamp and Varkenshoek to Hintham. The 4th RWF was on the right, with A and D Companies in the lead, and their task was to attack the western edge of the wood on the main 's-Hertogenbosch road which formed a convenient boundary between 71 and 160 Brigades, and then to clear the woods northwards.

It took until 5.45pm for the objective to be reached and the woods cleared up to the main road. It was a hard-fought battle that cost the 4th RWF 15 men killed on that day, one of whom was Fusilier Ernest Dainton who died of his wounds.

Fusilier Ernest Raymond DAINTON

Service No: 5570208; *Unit:* 4th Battalion The Royal Welch Fusiliers; *Died:* 22 October 1944 aged 22; *Buried:* Eindhoven (Woensel) General Cemetery, Holland, Plot KK, Grave 170; *Commemorated:* BOA WM; HT; AR; BOA C.

DEATH OF THE CORNWALLS

Private Albert Mark Roper, 5th Battalion Duke of Cornwall's Light Infantry – Bradford-on-Avon

From more than 150 officers and men of the 5th Battalion Duke of Cornwall's Light Infantry (DCLI), only Major Michael Lonsdale, the commander of D Company, and nine men, were all that came out of the hell they called Hoven – the only survivors of an attack against fanatical Nazi SS troops and tanks. Pte Albert Roper from Bradford-on-Avon died in the fight, his body lost forever in the quagmire that engulfed the battleground.

Albert Mark Roper was born in 1926, the fifth child of Mark and Elsie Kate Roper (nee Adams) of Bradford-on-Avon. The family lived in the small tollhouse bungalow at the junction of Frome Road and Westwood Road.

Albert died in the Allied assault on the German West Wall in Operation 'Clipper', and the bloody battle through Hochheid wood to take the hill village of Hoven, north of Geilenkirchen, on 23 November 1944. Hoven was a strategic point from which the Germans could overlook elements of the US 84th Infantry Division deployed nearby.

The Cornwalls were ordered to capture Hoven. The aim of their attack was to threaten the Germans opposing the Americans on the other side of the valley by turning their flank, and that their entry into Hoven would cause the Germans to pull back. The Cornwalls got into Hoven alright, but once there the odds against them were too great. Counter-attacked and besieged, they were surrounded almost from the start. It was a desperate fight in conditions of torrential rain and knee-deep mud, against fierce resistance

A Sherman tank carrying infantry of the 43rd (Wessex) Division advances through the rain and mud towards Geilenkirchen on 18 November 1944. *IWM B11917*

from regular German infantry and SS troops and tanks of 22nd SS Panzergrenadier Division and 10th SS Panzer Division.

Early next morning the remnants of the gallant Company, some ten men all told, returned to the battalion lines in the rear.

The 5th Battalion Duke of Cornwall's Light Infantry had been defeated. It was the only battalion on the British side of the battlefield at Geilenkirchen that had tried to advance since 20 November, but had been stopped dead in its tracks and forced to withdraw right back to its start line, having suffered dreadful casualties.

Private Albert Mark ROPER

Service No: 14736748; *Unit:* 5th Battalion Duke of Cornwall's Light Infantry; *Died:* 23 November 1944 aged 18; *Commemorated:* Groesbeek Memorial, Netherlands, Panel 4; BOA WM; HT; St Mary's Church, Westwood.

MINED IN THE CHANNEL

Private William Edgar Staite, Corps of Military Police – Bradford-on-Avon

Little is known of William Edgar Staite, except that he was born in Gloucester in 1904, the son of William Gilbert (b.1877, Gloucester), a furniture and removals dealer, and Kate Elizabeth Staite. The family clearly had links to Bradford-on-Avon towards the end of the Second World War because William is commemorated on a memorial inside Christ Church to the war dead of the parish. He had served originally with his local county regiment, the Glosters, before transferring to the Corps of Military Police and was living in Bristol at the time of his death at sea on 7 November 1944. He has no known grave.

Landing Ship Tank (LST) 420, commanded by 30-year-old Lt-Cdr Douglas Everett, RNR, was in a trooping and supply convoy with four other LSTs that sailed in the early hours of 7 November 1944 from Southend for the Belgian port of Ostend. She was packed with officers and men of the RAF's 1 Base Signals and Radar Unit (1BSRU), personnel from a number of British Army regiments and corps, Army trucks, tanks, and railway rolling stock. William Staite was one of a handful of Military Policemen who were also travelling on the ship.

In appearance, LST420 was much like the LSTs that had landed tanks on the shores of Normandy back in June the same year. She was already something of a combat veteran, having taken part in the Allied amphibious landings in Sicily, Salerno, Anzio and Normandy.

Plodding along at just 12kts she was a slow vessel, designed to carry 125 officers and crew and about 140 troops, although war conditions meant that the latter figure was often exceeded. She measured 328ft from stem to stern and displaced 4,080 tons when fully loaded. LSTs could also carry a variety of military hardware, ranging from tanks and tank-landing craft to wheeled and tracked vehicles, and from artillery to heavy construction equipment and military supplies

The weather in the Channel had deteriorated overnight and by the time the convoy arrived off Ostend at 1.30pm on the 7th, a Force 8 gale was blowing with a heavy sea. The convoy commander in LST405, Lt-Cdr J.T. Sheffield, RNR, was informed that Ostend

A Sherman tank disembarks from LST517. William Staite sailed on an LST like this one. ***US National Archives***

was temporarily closed to shipping owing to the appalling weather conditions. The five LSTs were ordered to turn about and head back into the English Channel to seek shelter in The Downs anchorage off the East Kent coast, until conditions improved.

At about 3.20pm a massive explosion ripped through LST420. The ship pitched forward and below decks was plunged into darkness when her electrical power failed. She had struck a mine which broke her completely in half at the bridge. Both halves of the ship were ablaze and began drifting apart. Lurching and rolling in the heavy seas, LSTs 405, 367 and 320 came to the aid of LST420.

There were few survivors. Most of those onboard had either been killed by the explosion or were drowned in the ice cold waters of the English Channel. Out of more than 300 passengers and crew, only 5 officers and 26 other ranks were rescued by the other LSTs and a trawler. LST420 lost 55 of her crew, the biggest single loss of any British LST in the Second World War. RAF 1 BSRU was almost wiped out to a man.

LST420 went down by the stern, with her forward section drifting for half a mile before sinking in 15 metres of water. Bodies were carried far and wide by the currents and washed up weeks later on the shores of Holland and Germany, but many like William Staite were simply lost at sea without a trace. Lt-Cdr Everett went down with his ship and his body was never found.

Private William Edgar STAITE
Service No: 5177778; *Unit:* Corps of Military Police; *Died:* 7 November 1944 aged 39; *Commemorated:* Brookwood Memorial, Surrey, Panel 21, Column 3; CC.

IN THE HOUR OF VICTORY

Major John William Poston, MC and Bar, 11th Hussars – Winsley

> 'On 23 December 1941 this officer, in command of his troop, ran into an entrenched enemy position two miles north west of Sceledima. This position had two heavy armoured cars fitted with anti-tank guns as its mobile protection. Lt Poston immediately attacked the position, drove off the armoured cars and forced the enemy to withdraw in lorries, leaving behind three anti-tank guns on the ground. In the pursuit that followed he captured approximately 55 Germans, a lorry load of automatic weapons including anti-tank guns, and he also destroyed a lorry-load of bombs. This action was later reported by the BBC.
>
> 'Lt Poston has performed the arduous and exacting duties of a troop leader in an armoured car regiment since June 1940, his bravery and determination having been a fine example to those under him. I strongly recommend that he be awarded the Military Cross.'

This was the glowing commendation from John Poston's commanding officer for an action at Beda Fomm that resulted in John receiving the Military Cross. The regiment's war diary also commented on his bravery: 'Mr Petch and Mr Poston extremely brave and cool in their work. They showed complete disregard to shellfire which is a hard thing to do.' John, from Winsley, eventually received his Military Cross in the spring of 1942.

John William Poston was born on 16 September 1919 at Alton, Hampshire, the

General Montgomery's trusted *aides-de-camp*, John Poston (left) and Johnny Henderson.

John Poston, Freddie de Guingand, Montgomery, and Johnny Henderson in front of Monty's TAC HQ.

eldest son of Colonel William John Lloyd Poston, DSO, and Marjorie Blanch Poston (nee Dalglish), of Barnes, Surrey. John was educated at Harrow School from September 1933 to Christmas 1937. He was commissioned into the Royal Tank Regiment (Supplementary Reserve) on 29 April 1939 and on 14 January 1940 he transferred to the 11th Hussars in Libya as a 2nd lieutenant.

The 11th Hussars had been in Palestine and Egypt from 1932 until the outbreak of war, so the regiment was already well versed in desert warfare. It was equipped with armoured cars for reconnaissance duties and saw frequent action in the Libyan Desert, at first against the Italian Army and later the German *Afrika Korps*. As part of 7th Armoured Brigade it fought in many of the major battles and minor skirmishes of the early war period, including Beda Fomm/Sidi Saleh in February 1941, and in November that year at Sidi Rezegh, Libya.

The air forces of both the Axis belligerents, the *Reggia Aeronautica* and the *Luftwaffe*, made regular attacks on the regiment, whose men soon realised that their armoured cars offered precious little protection from air attack.

John was commander of 1 Troop, A Squadron, from early in 1940 until well into 1942, seeing frequent action on patrolling duties across much of Libya. He was taken ill on 31 December 1940 and evacuated to a military hospital, but he was back with his regiment on 7 February 1941.

Operation 'Crusader', which began on 18 November 1941, saw British forces aim to destroy as much German armour as possible in Libya. In a running battle that lasted into December, heavy losses were sustained on both sides. Particularly bitter fighting took place around Sidi Rezegh, south east of the besieged port of Tobruk.

On 6 December, John was in command of his troop of three armoured cars when he attacked an enemy force in the Sidi Rezegh area. In the action that followed 3 German officers and 57 soldiers were captured.

Later, on 23 December, John and his troop were involved in a firefight with dug-in German troops near Beda Fomm, and then their subsequent pursuit, for which he was awarded the Military Cross.

In April 1942 the regiment moved from the main battle area to Iraq. A move into Persia followed, but the 11th Hussars were soon back in action in the more familiar surroundings of the Western Desert.

Unfortunately the regiment's war diaries for much of 1942 have not survived, so it is not possible to say for certain what John was doing between February and August 1942. But, on 12 August John was invited to join General Sir Bernard Montgomery (Monty) as an Aide de Campe (ADC) at the general's tactical headquarters. He was with Monty at the Battle of El Alamein in October and remained with him for the rest of the war. After the Allied landings in Sicily in August 1943 John returned home in December to attend the Army Staff College, but later rejoined Monty's staff as a liaison officer just before D-Day.

In the autumn of 1944, John was awarded a bar to his MC. Monty personally recommended him for an immediate award which was conferred by King George VI on 21 December 1944. Monty's handwritten commendation describes how John earned the award:

John Poston's grave at Soltau.

'Major Poston is a GSO2 (Liaison) at my Tac HQ [Tactical Headquarters]. His duties take him daily to the battle area in order to bring me an accurate picture of the fight. In the operation of the Second Army in the Nijmegen-Arnhem area this officer had to proceed daily up the corridor to keep me informed about the battle. On 21 September 1944 the enemy had broken in to the corridor and were astride the road north of Veghel. Major Poston found himself engaged by fire from Panther tanks, but this did not deter him from carrying out his mission and bring me back the information I required. I recommend him for the immediate award of a bar to the MC.

(Signed) B.L. Montgomery, Field Marshal, C-in-C 21 Army Group, 24/9/44.'

John was with Monty and his Tac HQ as they crossed the River Rhine in March 1945 and advanced into northern Germany. On 21 April, Majors John Poston and Peter Earle (who was another of Monty's liaison officers) had been on a fact-finding visit to General 'Bubbles' Barker, commanding the 49th Division in northern Germany. They were returning with a copy of Barker's plans for the Elbe crossing to Monty's Tac HQ camp at Soltau on Lüneburg Heath, by a short cut chosen by John, when they ran into trouble in open heathland. Peter Earle recalls:

'From driving along on a summer [sic] evening, congenial company, dinner and a bottle of hock not twenty miles ahead – the scene suddenly, like a clash of cymbals, changed.

'It was like standing in the butts at Bisley during a rapid shoot. The bonnet had been ripped up and the windscreen punctured, made opaque with bullets, and I found I had been hit in the right arm. The futility of it all; the inevitability of being late… for dinner and my appointment with the Commander-in-Chief. I saw ahead of me the same sordid end that had overtaken so many of my friends... We had both fired our Sten guns from the side of the Jeep until the bullets had run out. We did no damage, but may have kept their heads down. John was crouched down behind the level of the windscreen and I at once assumed – quite wrongly – that he was badly hurt. In point of fact, very sensibly he was taking cover from the bullets which I, as driver, could not do.'

Although wounded in the right arm, Earle managed to drive straight at the German machine gunner ahead of them, killing him, but in the process crashing the Jeep. John lay on the ground wounded and was trying to eat the orders, to prevent them falling into enemy hands, when the Germans closed in on him.

'John was now some three yards on my right; as I was slowly getting to my feet I heard John cry out in an urgent and desperate voice, "N-No-stop-stop". These were his last words and were spoken as a bayonet thrust above the heart killed him instantaneously.'

John Poston died just over two weeks before the end of the war in Europe. It is likely that die-hard Nazis who refused to acknowledge Germany had lost the war and would soon surrender to the Allies, had ambushed John and Peter Earle. They may even have been attacked by the fabled *Werwolf* – a Nazi guerrilla movement. Legend has it that the *Werwölfe* retreated to the Black Forest and the Harz mountains to continue the fight until the late 1940s.

John was the youngest of Monty's liaison officers and had become almost a surrogate son to the general. Monty was inconsolable for many days after his death and would see nobody. The King wrote a personal letter of condolence to John's father, and Monty himself penned an obituary that appeared in *The Times* on 27 April 1945. He wrote:

'There can be few young officers who have seen this war from the inside as did John Poston. He knew everything that was going on; he was in possession of much information that is secret and must remain secret for all time; I trusted him absolutely, and he never once failed me... he was a sterling character, generous, unselfish to a degree, warm hearted, a devoted and loyal friend, and a most loveable person. I was completely devoted to him and I feel very sad; something has definitely gone out of my life.'

John had been buried where he fell by a German farmer, but Monty ordered that he should be re-buried with full military honours. Thus, John Poston was re-buried in the field at Soltau where the Tac HQ caravans were parked. Monty wept unashamedly at his funeral.

After the war, John's remains were exhumed once more and re-buried at Becklingen War Cemetery. There is a road in Winsley village, Poston Way, which is named after him.

In 1945, the Poston family were living at Innox House in Turleigh; John's father, William, was a member of Bradford and Melksham Rural District Council. His wife, Marjorie, was living at Burrough-on-the-Hill, Melton Mowbray, Leicestershire.

Major John William POSTON, MC and Bar

Service No: 87368; *Unit:* 11th Hussars; *Died:* 21 April 1945 aged 25; *Buried:* Becklingen War Cemetery, Germany, Grave 15.C.6; *Commemorated:* Winsley WM.

Chapter 11

Brothers In Arms

Bradford's Sibling Warriors

THE BUTLER BROTHERS

The Butler brothers – Peter Saumarez (b.1916) and Roger Montgomerie (b.1922) – were born into a naval family at Bradford-on-Avon. It is believed that Peter and his brother were the only children of Vernon and Helen Butler. Their father, Rear-Admiral Vernon Saumarez Butler (1885–1954), was a well-known destroyer captain in the First World War who commanded a succession of naval vessels. He was awarded the DSO in 1918 and was also mentioned in despatches. From 1935 to 1937 he was Senior Naval Officer, Persian Gulf, and in 1936 was appointed ADC to the King. Butler was promoted to rear admiral in 1937, in which year he retired from the Navy.

Helen Nancy Montgomerie Butler (nee Tothill, b.1893), the boys' mother, was a daughter of Admiral Sir Hugh Henry Tothill KCB (1865–1927) and Lady Hilda Montgomerie Tothill (nee Beddoe, b.1867), whose home at Bradford-on-Avon was The Chantry. Dr Alex Moulton of The Hall remembers Lady Tothill as 'a great character, very flowery, with great hats'.

As a captain, Sir Hugh Tothill had commanded the warship HMS *Conqueror* at the battle of Jutland in 1916; promoted to rear admiral in 1917 he was appointed 4th Sea Lord of the Admiralty 1917–19; Commander-in-Chief East Indies, 1919–21; promoted to vice-admiral in 1921 and made admiral commanding reserves from 1923 to 1925.

By the Second World War the Butler family was living at Midway House, Ston Easton, Somerset. Peter had joined the RAF in 1937, but Roger was still at school. His turn to join the forces would come soon enough.

DOWN IN THE DRINK

Flying Officer Peter Saumarez Butler, RAF, 49 Squadron

In the last years of peace before the Second World War, Peter Butler trained as a pilot at RAF Cranwell in Lincolnshire. He took a regular commission in the RAF and was appointed a pilot officer on 31 July 1937. Peter's first operational posting was to 49 Squadron, a Handley Page Hampden bomber squadron stationed at RAF Scampton, also

Hampden bomber crews line up beside an 83 Squadron aircraft in June 1940. *IWM CH266*

The 'flying pan handle' in flight. With its slender fuselage and crew grouped together one behind the other, the Hampden shared many design characteristics with German bombers of the period like the Dornier Do 17 and Junkers Ju 88. *Author's collection*

in Lincolnshire. When the first Hampden was delivered to the squadron on 20 September 1938, replacing its ageing Hawker Hind biplanes, it became the first in the RAF to receive this new type of monoplane bomber. Peter was a contemporary on 49 Squadron of Plt Off R.A.B. 'Babe' Learoyd, who as a flight lieutenant was destined to win the Victoria Cross on 12–13 August 1940.

On 31 January 1939 Peter was promoted to flying officer and for a short spell in the summer of that year became squadron adjutant. When war broke out he was one of a small cadre of professional airmen who led the RAF into action. Combat losses quickly ate into their numbers and within several years of war they had become a dwindling band. Fate decreed that Peter Butler was not to survive the first year of war.

Peter's first operational flight was on 26 February 1940 when he was second pilot to Sqn Ldr R.S. Allen in Hampden P1174, on a daylight navigation and reconnaissance flight over the North Sea from RAF Kinloss in Scotland. Their objective was to observe enemy surface vessels and attack any submarines, but their aircraft suffered engine trouble and so they had to return early. On 28 February Peter flew a daylight sweep over the North Sea in L4060, his first as first pilot and captain of aircraft. There followed a round of flying training exercises then two minelaying sorties, on 21 April and again on 1–2 May.

This is the post-raid report that Peter made to the squadron intelligence officer on return from a minelaying sortie on 21–22 April 1940.

> 'We took off at 19.33hrs. At 19.51hrs we crossed the coast at Skegness at a height of 1,500ft and set course for target 'Daffodil' area [the Sound off Copenhagen between Denmark and Sweden]. I was cruising at -2lbs sq in boost and an indicated airspeed of 130, and gained height slowly to 5,000ft, where I increased airspeed to 145mph and flew level. The weather was fine and clear except for a thin layer of cloud encountered at about 4,000ft.
>
> 'At 21.55hrs we crossed the German coast 10 miles south of Nordstrand and set new course for target. While crossing Germany I descended to 2,000ft. Over the Danish islands a small amount of ground mist was observed.
>
> 'As we approached the target we passed below a thin layer of cloud which was lying at about 2,000ft, this obscured the moon but allowed enough light through for the coastline and target area to be clearly distinguished. Weather conditions were ideal for operations.
>
> 'The Drogden light was easy to locate and this indicated the position of the target area. At 23.30hrs I planted the melon [mine] and set course for Skegness.
>
> 'Immediately after leaving the target area we climbed up to 3,000ft and flew as far as the west coast of Germany in cloud. We emerged into clear air over the coast 10 miles south of Nordstrom and then climbed to 7,000ft.
>
> 'The weather was exceptionally fine and clear, and by the light of the full moon the Frisian Islands could be clearly seen several miles away to port. A W/T fix was obtained on 348 Kcs when we were north of Terschelling and a new course set. At 02.20hrs we crossed the coast between Boston and Wainfleet and set course for Scampton on QDMs.

> 'We arrived over Scampton at 02.35hrs but after receiving a series of reds from the flare path, and noticing that the fog was spreading over the aerodrome, I proceeded to Waddington and landed there at 02.55hrs. During the flight no AA or searchlight opposition was encountered. Over Flensburg on the way out my observer [Sgt Harrison] saw two unidentified aircraft burning navigation lights.'

At this early stage of the war enemy defences had not yet evolved into the deadly belts of flak and nightfighters that would soon confront Bomber Command. Unreliable engines, bad weather and navigational problems were more likely to claim an RAF bomber crew.

Peter's first operational flight over Germany came on 21–22 May when he bombed the railway marshalling yards at Julich and Erkelenz, and then again on 23–24 May to the marshalling yards at Aachen.

At 6.00am on 25 May, twelve Hampden crews of 49 Squadron – including Peter Butler – were given a one-hour standby for operations, but were stood down at 1.30pm. At 4.00pm, ten crews were put on standby again for bombing operations against railway communications links between Aachen and Krefeld in western Germany. It was not until 9.30pm that the order was finally given to go and the aircraft took off at 5min intervals.

Peter was pilot and captain of Hampden Mk I, P1318. The aircraft took off from Scampton with its crew of second pilot and navigator Plt Off John Bennett, RAF; rear gunner, Sgt John Harrison, RAF, from Blackburn, Lancs; and LAC George Parsons, wireless operator/air gunner, RAF, 19, from Scunthorpe, Lincs. The aircraft is presumed to have crashed into the sea off the Belgian coast, the cause unknown. The bodies of John Bennett and George Parsons were recovered from the sea and buried at Adegem War Cemetery, Belgium. Peter Butler and John Harrison were never found and are commemorated on the Commonwealth Air Forces Memorial, Runnymede.

Flying Officer Peter Saumarez BUTLER

Service No: 33182, RAF; *Unit:* 49 Squadron, RAF Bomber Command; *Died:* 25 May 1940 aged 23; *Commemorated:* Commonwealth Air Forces Memorial, Runnymede, Panel 5; HT; Ston Easton WM; RAF Chapel, Westminster Abbey.

AMBUSH AT VILLERS-BOCAGE

Lieutenant Roger Montgomerie Butler, 1st Battalion The Rifle Brigade

D-Day plus two, 8 June 1944. Lieutenant Roger Butler, a junior officer in the 1st Battalion The Rifle Brigade, landed with his unit on Gold Beach in Normandy, having sailed from Tilbury Docks. By now the Allies had established their beachhead and were poised for the breakout into Normandy. The 1st Rifle Brigade was a motorised rifle battalion in 7th Armoured Division equipped with M3 half-track vehicles, 6pdr anti-tank guns, and a handful of Stuart M5A1 Honey light tanks. Roger commanded the Anti-tank Section of A Company, its anti-tank guns towed by half-tracks.

On 12 June, during the first days of the Battle of Normandy, 7th Armoured Division's 22nd Armoured Brigade launched a daring right hook deep into German held territory to

Four Tiger tanks of Michael Wittmann's 101st Heavy SS Panzer Battalion on their way to Normandy. *Bundesarchiv 101/299/1804/7*

take high ground at a feature known as Point 213, to the north-east of the small town of Villers-Bocage.

At 6.30am on 13 June, the battalion moved off from their overnight leaguer along the road from Livry to Amay-sur-Seules. Shortly before 9.00am, Roger was among the platoon commanders from A Company, 1st Rifle Brigade, who were driven in half-tracks past the stationary vehicles of 22nd Armoured Brigade in Villers-Bocage to the head of the column, for an orders group meeting at Point 213 with Maj James Wright, CO A Company 1st Rifle Brigade. Thus, Roger and the other platoon commanders (Lts Bruce Campbell, Alfred de Pass, Charles Parker, and Peter Coop) were temporarily separated from their men.

All seemed peaceful. In one of those bizarre situations that can happen in war, the British were unaware of the presence of the German Panzer Lehr Division and advance elements of the 101st Heavy SS Panzer Battalion close by; and neither were the Germans aware of the large British force poised to infiltrate their rear.

A sergeant in A Company, 1st Rifle Brigade, who was heading out of Villers-Bocage to Point 213 in one of the half-tracks, broke radio silence with the dramatic message that a German Tiger tank was heading straight for them.

Shortly after 9.00am all hell broke loose. The British advance led by Cromwell and Sherman tanks of 4th County of London Yeomanry (4th CLY) and 5RTR, supported by Roger Butler's 1st Rifle Brigade, was taken by surprise by the German Tiger tank ace *SS-Obersturmführer* Michael Wittmann of 101st Heavy SS Panzer Battalion. In his 60-ton Tiger I, with its lethal 88mm main armament and co-axial machine gun, Wittmann made short work of the British tanks and half-tracks that were parked up along the main street of the town, many of whose crews were having a brew-up. First he took out the rearmost

Cromwell and then a Sherman Firefly further up the hill, effectively blocking the road in both directions to Point 213.

Wittmann then dealt with the vehicles in the column immediately behind A Squadron 4th CLY, in which were the 1st Rifles Brigade's half-tracks and Bren carriers including Roger Butler's anti-tank platoon. Most of their occupants had quickly dismounted and were desperately seeking cover in roadside ditches and nearby fields. To add to the mayhem, two sapper lorries in the column packed full of explosives were also hit and blew up. Dense clouds of smoke from burning tanks and vehicles added to the mayhem.

In the engagement that lasted no more than 15 minutes, Wittmann destroyed seven cruiser/medium tanks (including one Sherman Firefly), three Stuart light tanks, one Sherman OP, nine half-tracks, four carriers, two anti-tank guns and two sapper lorries. However, Sgt Bray of Roger Butler's anti-tank gun platoon attached to A Company, 1st Rifle Brigade, succeed in scoring a hit on the running gear of Wittmann's Tiger, immobilising the tank and forcing the ace and his crew to bale out and run for cover.

British infantry and tank crews took cover in ditches and hedgerows from German tank and small arms fire. German reinforcements were quickly brought in and for the rest of the day fighting continued to rage in Villers-Bocage and at Point 213. By late afternoon on the 13th, the British realised their position was untenable and once it was dark withdrew from Villers-Bocage to a more secure area nearby.

The total British casualties for 13 and 14 June were high, and amounted to some 378 killed, wounded and taken prisoner. The 1st Rifle Brigade lost 4 officers and 145 other ranks killed, wounded or taken prisoner. Half of Roger's anti-tank platoon was killed or missing. Roger may well have been killed in the initial shoot-out with Wittmann shortly

A heavily camouflaged German SdKfz251 armoured personnel carrier half-track drives past wrecked British M3 half-tracks of Roger Butler's 1st Rifle Brigade on the road out of Villers-Bocage. ***Bundesarchiv 101/494/3376/239***

after 9.00am (possibly with his fellow platoon commanders, 20-year-old Lt Alfred de Pass and Lt Peter Coop, also 20), although it is just possible that he could have worked his way back into Villers-Bocage only to die in the fighting that raged in the town throughout the rest of the day. We may probably never know for sure. Of the whole company, only one officer and thirty other ranks out of more than 100 returned during the next few days.

Lieutenant Roger Montgomerie BUTLER

Service No: 226400; *Unit:* 1st Battalion Rifle Brigade; *Died:* 13 June 1944 aged 21; *Buried:* Tilly-sur-Seulles War Cemetery, Normandy, Grave XI.H.11; HT; Ston Easton WM.

THE HARKER BROTHERS

Few families in Britain were untouched by the carnage of the Great War. It was a conflict that almost wiped out a generation of the nation's manhood, bringing untold hardship and pain to the many thousands of families left without husbands and fathers.

Early in the war Mabel Harker from 44 Woolley Street was told that her husband Frank had been reported missing at Gallipoli. Her three children were too young to understand what this meant. Baby Jack was only a few months old when his mother eventually received official word that Frank had died on 2 May 1915, aged 28, serving with the Royal Marines Light Infantry.

The Harker children grew up in a home without a father figure, where their mother worked hard to put food on the table and keep a roof over their heads. Such was the lot of thousands of young families all over Britain in the wake of the Great War.

Thomas Charles Harker was born at Bradford-on-Avon on 26 June 1913, his younger brother Jack arrived two years later. Their parents were Frank and Mabel Harker who made their home at 44 Woolley Street. Thomas was educated at Christ Church School and at 14 he went to work for Spencer Moulton & Co until deciding to emigrate to New Zealand in the early 1930s. There he was taken on as a farm labourer at Longburn and Karawa. Jack, who worked for Messrs Garlick as a meat rounds man in Trowbridge, Bradford-on-Avon and Melksham, was later employed at the Avon Rubber Mills.

Joyce Wicheard (nee Evans), who was a billettee with the Harkers, recalls her time with the family:

> 'I was 7-years-old when I was evacuated to Bradford-on-Avon from Dagenham when war broke out, with my brother and sister. We were billeted with Mrs Harker at 11 Belcombe Place. She was a lovely woman. It must have been something to have three Cockney kids to look after at her time of life. Her son Jack lived at home and was engaged to be married to a girl whose family had a farm at Conkwell. After he joined the Army we'd see him when he came home on leave. He became a prisoner of the Japanese. Mrs Harker had a card from him saying he was well. When the war ended she had all Jack's clothes and shoes ready for him when he came home. Later, she had a visit from a man who had been in the same camp as Jack. He was with him when he died and Jack had asked him to visit his mother when the war was over.'

BEATING ROMMEL

Corporal Thomas Charles Harker, 25th Battalion New Zealand Infantry

As the Nazis unrolled their Blitzkrieg across Western Europe in the summer of 1940, Hitler's Fascist ally Benito Mussolini was attempting to conquer North Africa. A numerically smaller force of British and Commonwealth troops drove out the Italian invaders, and then added insult to injury by capturing the entire Italian Tenth Army.

Mussolini's ineptitude forced Hitler to send a small military force to North Africa to assist the Duce, the *Deutsches Afrika Korps* under the command of *Generalleutnant* Erwin Rommel. From April 1941 Rommel and the Allies fought many bitter battles across the unforgiving deserts of North Africa. In the two years that followed, the fighting raged back and forth as one side then the other gained the upper hand. At the Battle of Alam Halfa in July 1942, Rommel and his *Afrika Korps* were halted at the very gates of Cairo and the Suez Canal.

When Operation 'Lightfoot' – better known as the Battle of El Alamein – opened on the night of 23–24 October, the 25th Battalion New Zealand Infantry was involved in the assault on the Miteirya Ridge against tanks of the German 15th Panzer Division and Italian *Littorio* Armoured Division.

Casualties from both sides were often treated in the same ad hoc aid posts on or near the battlefield. Tom Harker may have been taken to such an aid post after he was injured at El Alamein. ***IWM E6797***

Tom Harker in pensive mood writes a letter home. *Phyllis Huntley*

Thomas volunteered at Hawera for the New Zealand Army on 30 January 1940. His attestation paper records that he weighed 11st 4lb, stood 5ft 9½in tall, and had a dark complexion, brown hair and eyes. He had tattoos on both forearms and was an experienced horseman. On 17 May Thomas joined the 25th Infantry Battalion and was posted to Egypt in the October. The battalion embarked for Greece on the cruiser HMS *Orion* on 17 March 1941 as part of 'Lustre' Force, the British Expeditionary Force (BEF) to assist the Greeks in repelling an Axis invasion. In the face of an unstoppable Axis advance, the BEF fought a gallant retreat and on the night of 28–29 April the 25th Battalion was evacuated from Monemvasia to Egypt, via Crete, arriving at Port Said on 2 May.

From then until November, the 25th Battalion was engaged in training activities in Egypt before rejoining the Allied offensive in the desert and taking the fight against the Axis forces into Libya. Thomas was then appointed as a battalion anti-tank gunnery instructor and on 1 September 1942 he was promoted to lance corporal, with promotion to full corporal following on 17 October.

The Allies under General Bernard Montgomery made their stand against German and Italian forces in North Africa, 60 miles from the port of Alexandria, between the small town of El Alamein and the impassable Qattara Depression. The 25th Battalion lost 25 men killed in action in the first 3 days of the Battle of El Alamein, with a further 6 dying of wounds received. Among the latter was Thomas Harker.

The Battle of El Alamein marked the turning point of Allied fortunes in North Africa, with Rommel being forced into a long protracted withdrawal westwards towards Tunisia. With the Allied landings in French North Africa in November – Operation 'Torch' – Rommel and his *Afrika Korps* were forced into a war on two fronts, trapped between the converging Allied armies. On 12 May 1943 the Axis forces in North Africa capitulated.

Corporal Thomas Charles HARKER

Service No: 32754; *Unit:* 25th Battalion New Zealand Infantry (2nd NZ Infantry Division, 6th NZ Brigade); *Died:* 26 October 1942 aged 29; *Buried:* El Alamein War Cemetery, Egypt, Grave V.H.11; *Commemorated:* BOA WM; HT.

DEATH RAILWAY

Driver Jack Harker, 198 Field Ambulance, RASC

In 1972, when I was eleven, we moved house from Bath to Westwood. It was here that I learned of an 'old' man who lived alone in a bungalow in the village, and who was said to have been a prisoner of war of the Japanese. To us he looked very old, but he cannot have been more than fifty. He certainly cut a sorry figure and we children were scared of him. I suppose we felt uncomfortable with his odd appearance and shambling gait.

My Great Uncle Jack had been a prisoner of the Japanese, too. He was in the RAF and had been captured at the fall of Singapore in February 1942. Three years of inhuman incarceration in Changi jail had broken him physically, but he was one of the lucky ones who survived to come home. I felt sympathy towards my uncle, as well as harbouring a

Jack Harker and friend Rex. *Joyce Wicheard*

certain curiosity about 'what' and 'where' he had been. On one occasion that I met him I can remember thinking he had suffered the most unspeakable treatment imaginable, and yet here he was, a pretty ordinary looking man, chatting to me as we sat around my grandparents' kitchen table. Even so, the damage to his health had been done and not long afterwards we learned that he had died suddenly from a heart attack.

I wish that I had shown more compassion to the 'old' man in the bungalow. God only knows what he, too, may have been through.

Jack Harker volunteered for the British Army in April 1940, serving in France with the BEF, and was evacuated from Dunkirk. He left Britain on 28 October 1941 onboard the troopship SS *Oronsay* for service overseas. Most of 198 Field Ambulance and the other troops of the 18th Division in the convoy had been kitted out for desert fighting, so the rumour was they were destined for service in North Africa. The convoy headed west to Halifax, Nova Scotia where Jack's unit changed ship (possibly to the troopship USS *Joseph T. Dickman*) and then sailed south in convoy to Trinidad, arriving on 22 November. After taking on fuel they set sail once again, crossing the equator into the South Atlantic and on to Cape Town, South Africa, where they enjoyed some shore leave. It was probably during this stop-over that Jack had a chance meeting with his brother, Thomas, on his way from New Zealand to the Middle East. This was the last time the brothers would ever see each other.

At about this time official notification was received that the convoy was to divert from its original (secret) destination in the Middle East to the Malay Peninsula. The convoy sailed again on Christmas Eve, and after another break to their journey in Bombay they finally arrived in Singapore on 29 January 1942.

Jack was posted missing at the fall of Singapore on 15 February 1942 when the island was surrendered to the Japanese invaders. It was not until February 1943 that his mother received official notification that her son was a prisoner of the Japanese.

Jack was incarcerated in the notorious Changi jail in Singapore. At some time between 5 and 17 May 1943 he was transported hundreds of miles up-country to the Burma Railway as a part of 'H' Force, to work as a slave labourer for the Japanese. Under inhumane conditions of brutality, starvation and disease, he laboured in the Tonchan South, Malay Hamlet and Kurikonta camps on the so-called 'Death Railway' in Thailand, hewing railway cuttings from solid rock by hand and assisting to lay track, until he was taken ill and died of beriberi in Kanchanaburi F & H Force Camp No 1 Hospital on 11 October 1943. He was buried at Kanchanaburi F & H Force Cemetery in Grave 135, before exhumation after the war for reburial in the Kanchanaburi War Cemetery.

Mabel Harker had to wait until December 1945 before she was officially informed that her son Jack had died in a Japanese prisoner of war camp. Two world wars had robbed Mabel and her daughter Helen of a husband and a father, and of two sons and brothers. Their agony must have been unspeakable.

Driver Jack HARKER

Service No: T/175462; *Unit:* 198 Field Ambulance, Royal Army Service Corps; *Died:* 11 October 1943 aged 28; *Buried:* Kanchanaburi War Cemetery, Thailand, Grave 2.A.43; *Commemorated:* BOA WM; HT.

THE SADD BROTHERS

'Eric died in Burma on 25 February – mum's birthday. Ron died of his wounds in Germany on 9 March. Mum received news on the same day that they had both died.' This is how Eileen Sheppard, the last surviving sibling of the eight Sadd children, remembers the day when the telegram boy called at their Frome Road home. She has been widowed for some years and lives alone in Bradford-on-Avon. Despite the passage of more than sixty years, her voice still quavers when she talks about her lost brothers and how their deaths shook the family.

'There were ten of us children originally – five boys and five girls, but mum [Alice Elizabeth Sadd, née Ovens] lost a boy and a girl as babies. We lived up at Tory then and went to Christ Church School, but later we moved across town to a house at 42 Frome Road. Father [Walter Ernest Sadd] was a stone mason for Mr Bowyer. He had been a soldier in the Great War.

'All four of my brothers went into the Army. Before they were called up Ron [b.1917] worked for the Council and Eric [b.1923] for Spencer, Moulton & Co. Vic and Alfred (we called him 'Sam', but never Alfred), who were the eldest, both survived the war.

'Eric was the youngest of my brothers. He was sportier than Ron and was always on his racing bike. He played football for Christ Church Crusaders and Woolley Rangers and liked to swim down at Barton Farm where he loved to jump off the bridge into the river. I can remember him coming down the town hill on his bike so fast that he couldn't stop and he went straight through the front door of the Swan and out the back!'

ON THE ROAD TO MANDALAY

Private Eric Sadd, 10th Battalion Gloucestershire Regiment

Eric joined the 10th Battalion Gloucestershire Regiment in 1941 when it was serving on Home Defence duties in Lincolnshire, shortly after which it was converted to a tank regiment – the 159th Regiment, Royal Armoured Corps (Gloucestershire Regiment). In October 1942 Eric sailed with the battalion for India via Brazil, arriving in Bombay, where they and their tanks were posted to the British 36th Division.

In April 1943 the regiment reverted to its previous identity, the 10th Battalion Gloucestershire Regiment, and training began in combined operations. In February 1944 the 10th moved to Calcutta, by sea to Chittagong, and river steamer to Cox's Bazaar. Then they were told that they would be going to the Arakan Front in Burma to fight the Japanese. They had been sent into the fighting completely untrained for infantry jungle warfare, and what they learned had been 'on the job', on campaign and on the battlefield. Even so, the 10th Gloucesters took part in the re-occupation of Burma in 1944–45, winning battle honours at Pinwe and Myitson.

By the beginning of 1945 the battalion was badly under strength. Seven months of continuous fighting in Burma against a ruthless Japanese foe, combined with the natural

Pte Eric Sadd, Gloucestershire Regiment.
Eileen Sheppard

enemies of blistering heat, pouring rain, leeches and mosquitoes, had all taken their toll on the men.

In early January Eric was with the battalion when they renewed their advance south towards Mandalay after being halted by the monsoon rains. They crossed over the Irrawaddy River at Katha and trekked up the Schweli valley, through the teak forests of the Shan towards Mabein where, on 11 January, they clashed with Japanese forces in a series of short sharp engagements. At the end of the month the newly arrived 26th (Indian) Brigade took over the advance from the 72nd Brigade (which included the 10th Gloucesters).

On 9 February the 26th Brigade crossed the Shweli River some 8 miles to the north without opposition. They occupied the village of Myitson on a bend in the river, but over the next few days came under repeated and heavy attacks by the Japanese. The jungle fighting against a resourceful enemy was fierce and hampered by the tall elephant grass.

A wild and unspoiled region of forested hills and snow-capped mountains, Myitson is in Burma's northernmost state of Kachin that borders India and China to the north and east. The village itself sits on the confluence of two small rivers, the Maykha and Malikha, that join to form the Ayeyawaddy River.

Although weakened by seven months of fighting, with three companies having around 70 men each and C Company down to just 45 men, the 10th Battalion put up a tough fight. The regimental war diary proudly records that: 'At Myitson the 10th fought according to the highest traditions of the Regiment, and D Company in particular, under Capt G.O. Watkins, made an epic stand, cut off and constantly attacked by the enemy for five days.'

On 14 and 15 February attempts were made by A Company to relieve D Company, but they were driven back by determined resistance from the Japanese. When help finally got through to D Company on the morning of the 16th, after four days under siege, the 10th became surrounded. The Battle of Myitson reached a climax the next day when the battalion was heavily shelled by the Japanese, who then launched a concerted attack on Myitson village itself. The Indian Brigade and the 10th Gloucesters put up a vigorous defence and by nightfall the enemy had been beaten, melting away into the Burmese jungle. The battalion had lost 2 officers and 24 men killed.

On 22 February a company of Gurkhas finally relieved the 10th Gloucesters and the next day the whole battalion crossed the Nammeik Chaung.

It is likely that Eric was the one and only soldier in B Company who was killed crossing the NWA Sakan Chaung at Myitson on 25 February. A concealed Japanese machine gun position opened up, killing one man and injuring the company commander and seven others.

So ended the Battle of Myitson and the last active operations of the 10th Gloucesters in Burma. They advanced to Mongmit, thankfully with little opposition, and onwards through difficult mountain country to Mogok. In May the battalion was flown to Mandalay by the RAF and then patrolled on foot towards Meiktila. Then they were flown back to Imphal, in Assam, before moving to Poona, where on 5 December 1945 the 10th Battalion was disbanded.

CLEARING THE WEST BANK

Ronald Sadd, 7th Battalion Somerset Light Infantry

From the heat and humidity of the Burmese jungle, to the cold and rain of wintry North West Europe, the contrast could not have been greater. In March 1945 Eric's older brother Ronald was a private soldier serving with 7th Battalion Somerset Light Infantry in Holland, in 214 Brigade. He and his battalion were among the infantry units clearing the enemy from the west bank of the River Rhine in preparation for the imminent Allied crossing over the river into Germany. German troops put up a fierce and prolonged defence in the west bank villages of Kehrum, Marienbaum, Vynen and Wardt. They were a very determined enemy who had to be cleared house by house, street by street, and from strong points and trenches. The 7th Somersets fought for every inch of ground that was ferociously defended by the regular Heer (Army) as well as fanatical SS troops.

By 4 March, the 7th Somersets, helped by the Cornwalls, Worcesters and sappers of 204th Field Company, RE, had mopped up all of the west bank of the Rhine except for the important town of Xanten, which fell on 9 March to the 5th Wiltshires and 4th Somersets after heavy fighting.

Enemy artillery positioned on high ground above the opposite bank of the Rhine kept up intermittent shelling of Allied vehicle convoys and troop positions around Xanten and Luttingen. Towards the evening of the 9th, the bombardment died down, but a chance shell-hit on slit trenches outside the battalion headquarters caused death and injury among the Somersets' regimental police and several men who were under detention. A succession of shells fell around the headquarters, where one heavy shell struck a tree above one of the slit trenches occupied by battalion prisoners. Two men under arrest were killed, as well as the guard commander and one of the guards. One prisoner and a third member of the guard were severely wounded. The battalion Medical Officer was able to render first aid to the wounded, but one of them died of shock very soon after the shell

Pte Ronald Sadd, Somerset Light Infantry. *Eileen Sheppard*

strike. This man was almost certainly Ronald Sadd.

The Germans had already begun to retreat across the River Rhine on 6 March and their withdrawal was largely complete by the 10th. Allied ground forces began their amphibious crossing of the river – Operation 'Plunder' – late on 23 March, and 24 hours later US forces had established a bridge across the Rhine. At 10.00am on the 24th, a vast aerial armada of 2,931 Allied aircraft, troop-carrying gliders and paratroops, swept over the Rhine in Operation 'Varsity', the greatest Allied tactical air assault yet mounted on Hitler's *Festung Europa*. By the afternoon, Allied ground troops had linked up with their airborne compatriots on the far bank of the Rhine around Wesel and Rees, and by the 27th a bridgehead 35 miles wide and 20 miles deep was firmly established inside Germany.

Private Eric John SADD

Service No: 14579752; *Unit:* 10th Battalion Gloucestershire Regiment; *Died:* 25 February 1945 aged 21; *Buried:* Taukkyan War Cemetery, Myanmar (Burma), Grave 27.D.7; *Commemorated:* BOA WM; HT; AR.

Private Ronald Walter SADD

Service No: 5676107; *Unit:* 7th Battalion Somerset Light Infantry; *Died:* 9 March 1945 aged 28; *Buried:* Reichswald Forest War Cemetery, Germany, Grave 47.D.6; *Commemorated:* BOA WM; HT.

THE DOBSON BROTHERS

The Dobson brothers, Leonard George ('Len', b.1923) and Arthur William (b.1919), were born at Bradford-on-Avon, the sons of Sidney James (b.1882, Bradford-on-Avon), a quarryman, and Augusta Horler Dobson (nee Bishop, 1889–1985), whose home was at St Laurence Road in the town. Both brothers became married men: Len to Margaret, with whom he had twin sons David and Peter who were born in 1942; and Arthur, who was married to Pamela.

Len had worked for Spencer, Moulton & Co, and Arthur at the Co-op outfitters in St Margaret's Street. Both brothers were members of the town's Auxiliary Fire Service before they were called up – Len into the Royal Navy, Arthur into the Army.

STRAY BULLET

Able Seaman Leonard George Dobson, RN, HMS *Elissa*

Able Seaman Len Dobson, RN. *Peter Dobson*

Len Dobson died in an accident on the British Naval Base at Phillipville (now called Skikda) in Algeria, and was buried in Bone War Cemetery. Some time after his burial Len's mother received an unexpected letter from the Admiralty, informing her that her son had been wrongly buried in the officers' plot at the cemetery. It went on to say that Len's body had been exhumed and reburied in the appropriate section of the cemetery. Even in death, so it seemed, there appeared to be a distinction between officers and men.

In 1943 he was a crewmember on HMS *Elissa,* a boom defence vessel in the harbour at Phillipville. The circumstances surrounding Len's death are unclear, but it

Algiers harbour in 1942. *IWM A12721*

is understood that while on guard duty a gun went off by accident and a bullet hit him in the back, killing him.

Able Seaman Leonard George DOBSON

Service No: R/JX 346082; *Ship:* HMS *Elissa,* Royal Navy; *Died:* 22 February 1943; *Buried:* Bone War Cemetery, Algeria, Grave VIII, A.14; *Commemorated:* BOA WM; HT.

L/Cpl Arthur Dobson, Royal Engineers. *Peter Dobson*

MINE CLEARANCE

Lance Corporal Arthur William Dobson, 260 Field Company, Royal Engineers

Arthur Dobson would have seen much action with 260 Field Company, Royal Engineers, following the D-Day landings of 6 June 1944 and the Battle of Normandy that followed. His unit was involved in the dangerous task of clearing mines and making war damaged roads passable to military traffic.

Royal Engineer sappers like Arthur Dobson clear mines on the main street of Tilly sur Seulles, 19 June 1944. *IWM B5772*

In most war zones the clearance of enemy minefields usually falls to sappers of the Royal Engineers. It is not a task for the faint hearted, requiring extreme care, a steady nerve and generous helpings of bravery. The danger did not end there for mine clearance teams because while they carried out their job they were also at risk from ambush, enemy snipers and shell-fire.

So it was that during the Allied breakout from the Normandy beachhead and the push inland, thousands of enemy mines had to be lifted and cleared from the path of the Allied advance. On 4 August, Arthur was engaged with his company in mine clearance operations to the east and northeast of St-Martin-des-Besaces, on high ground at Point 361 in the Bois de Brimbois, and at the village of l'Angotiere, when one man was wounded. On the 5th they had moved 4km south to the town of Le Mesnil-Auzouf where the company's Lt Basil Jeffreys, 22, was killed and 3 men were wounded by enemy shell and mortar fire. The next day, 6 August, things got worse for 260 Field Company when a section was ambushed by an enemy patrol which resulted in the death of one sapper and the wounding of three more. Four more casualties were sustained later that day.

It is not possible to say for sure where, how and on which day Arthur was wounded – the 4, 5 or 6 August, but it is known that his wounds were sufficiently serious to necessitate his medical evacuation to England for further treatment. Arthur was admitted to the Royal United Hospital, Bath, in a full plaster cast, where he died of his wounds on 10 August, with his family at his bedside.

Lance Corporal Arthur William DOBSON

Service No: 2093488; *Unit:* 260 Field Company, Royal Engineers; *Died:* 10 August 1944 aged 25; *Buried:* Trowbridge Cemetery, Wiltshire, Sec AA, Grave 4294; *Commemorated:* BOA WM; HT.

Chapter 12

They Also Served

The Forgotten Soldiers

Eight local men can justly be called 'the forgotten soldiers' of the Second World War. I can find no further information about Arthur Harrison, S. Oliver, and Frederick Wootten. Little is known about Walter Ritchens who died of wounds in Holland, 1944; and Norman Pocock who died in service, 1945. Fred Huntley died in suspicious circumstances in Greece, 1945. Philip Margetts and Herbert Oliver were medically discharged, only to die at home. Once forgotten, but now remembered.

Gunner Philip Charles Henry Margetts, 96 LAA Regiment, Royal Artillery – Bradford-on-Avon

Philip Margetts, Royal Artillery. *Rene Maundrell*

Philip Margetts was a true Cockney, but a Bradfordian by adoption. Born in 1901 at Shoreditch in London's East End, like his father Philip (b.1875, Hoxton, London) and mother Elizabeth Margetts (b.1876, Clerkenwell, London), he was born and raised within earshot of the bells of St Mary-le-Bow church, Cheapside, in the City of London.

Desperate to join the Colours, Philip lied about his age to enlist in the Army and saw military service towards the end of the First World War. When the Second World War broke out in 1939, it was not long before London became the target for German bombers. To escape the Blitz in 1940, Philip and his family were evacuated from their East End home to the relative safety of Bradford-on-Avon. They moved into a cottage on Woolley Street and Philip took work in the town at Spencer, Moulton & Co. It was not long before he was called up for military service and joined the Royal Artillery.

Latterly, Philip suffered from a heart condition that led to him being medically discharged from the Army. He died in his sleep on 21 April 1944 aged 42, leaving his wife (Ada Blanche Margetts, 1901–70), two sons and three daughters.

Gunner Philip Charles Henry MARGETTS

Service No: 11255161; *Unit:* 300 Battery, 96 LAA Regiment, Royal Artillery; *Died:* 21 April 1944 aged 43; *Buried:* Bradford-on-Avon Cemetery, Sec AA, Grave 79.

Lance Sergeant Herbert George William Oliver, Royal Artillery – Bradford-on-Avon

'My mother told me that my father was with the BEF in France and had been evacuated from Dunkirk. Later he turned up at Bradford station and got off the train with loads of other soldiers back from Dunkirk – English, French, Poles. I don't know where they all went after that.' This is how 7-year-old Philip 'Nobby' Oliver, the son of Herbert Oliver, from Middle Rank in Bradford, remembered his father's homecoming from the 'miracle of Dunkirk' in June 1940.

Herbert George William Oliver was born in 1907 at Woolwich, Kent (now in south-east London), the son of Albert George (b.1883, St Leonard, Sussex), a soldier in the Army Service Corps who had fought in the Boer War, and Bertha Rosina Oliver; and the husband of Alice Oliver (1905–79) of Bradford-on-Avon. The family home initially was at 24 Tory before they moved down the hill to live at 5 Middle Rank.

Herbert had lied about his age to join the Army and enlisted at Trowbridge, where he joined the Royal Artillery. He saw service overseas on the lawless North West Frontier of India before returning home, only to be sent to France with the BEF soon after war broke out in 1939.

A few years later, Herbert developed cancer and was admitted to hospital in Bristol for surgery. The prognosis was not good and on 8 May 1943 he was discharged from the Army on medical grounds. He took a job as a bakery van delivery driver for the Coop around Winsley and Limpley Stoke, but eventually he succumbed to his illness and died at home fourteen months later.

Herbert's two brothers, Clifford and Sidney, both served in the Forces in the Second World War – Clifford in the RAF and Sidney in the Royal Navy. Both survived the war.

Lance Sergeant Herbert George William OLIVER

Service No: 1056833; *Unit:* Royal Artillery; *Died:* 23 July 1944 aged 37; *Buried:* Bradford-on-Avon Cemetery, Wiltshire, Sec AA, Grave 90; *Commemorated:* BOA WM.

Private Walter Isaac Ritchens, Army Catering Corps – Bradford-on-Avon

Walter Isaac Ritchens was born in 1911 at Melksham. He married Nell James at Bradford-on-Avon in 1934 and they had a daughter, Margaret, born in 1937. Walter died

Lance Sergeant Herbert George William Oliver, Royal Artillery, from Bradford-on-Avon. *Nobby Oliver*

of his injuries in eastern Holland on 2 February 1945, leaving Nell and daughter Margaret at 13 Crown Court, Woolley, and sisters Mary and Freda at 26 Orchard Road, Trowbridge. No further details.

Private Walter Isaac RITCHENS

Service No: 222408; *Unit:* Army Catering Corps; *Died:* 2 February 1945 aged 33; *Buried:* Nederweert War Cemetery, Netherlands, Grave III.B.6; *Commemorated:* BOA WM; Melksham WM.

Corporal Norman Llewellyn Pocock, Royal Auxiliary Air Force – Winsley

Norman Llewellyn Pocock (b.1914, Melksham) was the only son of Mr and Mrs Pocock (nee Pratten) and the husband of Millie Cook of Nottingham, whom he married in January 1945. The Pococks were better known as the former residents of the gardener's cottage at Rodwell Hall in Trowbridge, in the days when the gardens were visited by hundreds of people. Norman was educated at Trowbridge Boys' High School and as a boy assisted his parents in collecting from visitors to Rodwell Hall for the benefit of Trowbridge District Hospital. Norman joined the RAF early in the war and his postings had all been in England. Latterly he had been stationed at RAF West Beckham, a Chain Home radar station in north Norfolk; and at RAF Ossington in Nottinghamshire, an aircrew operational training unit in 93 Group Bomber Command. Norman was taken ill with pneumonia in early June 1945 and died a few days later on the 5th at Cromer Hospital, Norfolk.

Corporal Norman Llewellyn POCOCK

Service No: 861186, Royal Auxiliary Air Force; *Service:* RAF; *Died:* 5 June 1945 aged 31; *Buried:* Winsley St Nicholas Churchyard, Wiltshire.

'I'M THE MAN YOU NEVER SAW'

Private Frederick Ronald Huntley, 2nd Battalion Duke of Cornwall's Light Infantry – Bradford-on-Avon

'My twin brother Fred walked into his billet in Greece one evening and shot himself. The Army held a Court of Inquiry, but the circumstances of Fred's death remain a complete mystery,' says Dick Huntley. 'We were both called up on the same day, 4 March 1943. I joined the Royal Artillery and Fred the Duke of Cornwall's Light Infantry (DCLI). This was the last time I saw him. After training we both went overseas. I was a Royal Artillery signaller attached to the US 5th Army. Fred was with the Cornwalls in the British 1st Army. We both fought right the way through the Italian campaign.'

Frederick and Richard Huntley were born at Chapel Row Cottages in Winsley on 10 February 1925, the younger set of two pairs of twins to Henry John and Ivy Agnes Bessie Huntley (nee Angell). As children, both Fred and Dick had been members of the Christ Church Crusaders boys' club.

Dick Huntley again: 'When the war was finished we all piled over to Greece because we knew the Russians wanted to get a foothold there. I was sent over there just after my brother was killed.'

Fred Huntley, Duke of Cornwall's Light Infantry.
Dick Huntley

The 2nd Battalion DCLI had been posted to Greece on 13 December 1944. Its duty was to aid the official Greek government in its civil war against the Communist EAM (National Liberation Front) and its military arm ELAS. British troops were kept in Greece after the end of the Second World War to support the Greek free government.

One day, when Dick was sitting in the NAAFI in Athens having a drink, another British soldier came over to speak to him and Dick asked if he knew him.

'Are you in the Cornwalls because I think I know you?' the soldier replied.

'I told him that he may have known my twin brother. "What's his name?" he asked.'

'Fred Huntley.'

'"Bloody hell! You haven't seen me in your life," and he hurried out.'

'Now, why would a complete stranger say that? There'll always be something very strange about this whole business.'

At the time of writing, Dick has requested a copy of his late twin's army record of service, in the hope this will lead to the truth about his brother's death.

Private Frederick Ronald HUNTLEY

Service No: 14557381; *Unit:* 2nd Battalion Duke of Cornwall's Light Infantry;
Died: 20 September 1945 aged 20; *Buried:* Phaleron War Cemetery, Greece, Grave 20.E.5;
Commemorated: BOA WM; CC.

Chapter 13

THE MEN WHO FELL TO EARTH

THE BRADFORD-ON-AVON BOMBER CRASH

'He died not as some men, by degrees, but swift and sure beneath Somerset's trees.'
Inscription on the gravestone of Sgt Norman Simpson, Stretton, Cheshire

Coincidence played a part in unravelling the story of the Halifax bomber, V for Victor, which crashed at Bradford-on-Avon in 1944. I contacted newspapers in Canada where the crewmembers came from, but frustratingly with little success. It was only through a chance contact with the Canadian Air Forces Reunion Association that its organiser, Joyce Inkster, happened to know personally one of the two men who had survived the crash, and she passed my details to him. Since my first correspondence in 1985 with survivor Craig Reid, my family and I have enjoyed a warm friendship with the Reids. We visited them in Canada in 1996, and on several occasions since then we have welcomed three generations of their family as our guests in England.

For more than fifty years Jean Morris, sister of the rear gunner Sgt Graham Evans, had been searching in vain for the place where her brother had died. Official records had noted the crash site as Christchurch, Wiltshire, but there is no such place: the aircraft came down near Christ Church in Bradford-on-Avon, Wiltshire. Jean read my letter in a South Wales newspaper asking for anyone who had known Graham Evans to get in touch with me. She visited me just a few days after reading my letter and I took her to the spot on the hill above the town where her brother had died.

Jean's visit was a troubling experience for me because I was responsible for stirring unhappy memories that had lain dormant for decades. It is something that I worry about with many of the investigations I have carried out in the research for this book and I have often asked myself 'should I be doing this?' One part of me says 'leave the past alone. Let what has happened remain with the past.' But then there's another part that says 'these forgotten events and the men who were caught up in them should not be lost to posterity'. Young lives were given up well before their time, and for causes that today have little or no meaning for most people.

None of these men were born in Bradford-on-Avon, nor had they ever lived in the town. So what is their link to Bradford? Was it by fate or chance, or was it through following orders that they arrived over Bradford in their burning bomber on a spring evening in 1944?

Plt Off Brian Hall, pilot of the Halifax bomber that crashed at Priory Ground, Bradford-on-Avon, on 26 March 1944. *Library and Archives Canada*

Plt Off Don Hernando de Soto Grover, navigator. *Library and Archives Canada*

When Halifax V for Victor crashed into a field near Christ Church it may have been more through luck than judgement that it came down in an open space, away from habitation. The actual chain of events on that disastrous spring evening may never be known for sure.

The townspeople of Bradford-on-Avon believed that the Canadian pilot, 22-year-old Flt Sgt Brian Hall, had valiantly steered his aircraft away from the centre of the town, thereby saving many lives and damage to property. Had the Halifax crashed onto a populated area of Bradford the results could have been disastrous. The aircraft was not carrying bombs because it was on a training flight, but with its petrol tanks filled with high-octane fuel, and with pressurised oxygen bottles and live ammunition on board, the bomber was still capable of wreaking considerable damage if it crashed.

At about 8.30pm on 26 March 1944, in the tiny hamlet of Clivey, near Dilton Marsh, Leonard and Ivy Pickett were pushing their daughter home in her pram from a visit to Leonard's parents. A shadowy form grabbed their attention as it fell from the sky and swept over their heads, falling into a field beside the remote country road.

Several minutes later at Bradford-on-Avon a Halifax bomber was seen circling the town. One of its four engines was on fire and the aircraft trailed smoke and flame. For some time beforehand the aircraft had been seen flying around Bradford, the pilot presumably looking for a suitable place in which to crash-land.

Clearly, time had run out for the bomber and its crew when Brian Hall gave the final order to those left on board to save their skins. Three figures tumbled from an escape hatch in the belly of the Halifax, their barely opened parachutes candling in their wake as they fell to earth, too low for the chutes to open.

Plt Off Roy Porter, bomb-aimer. ***Library and Archives Canada***

From where they were standing on Winsley Road, Sholto Morris and his wife Joan heard the unmistakeable sound of an aircraft in trouble. Looking up into the moonlit sky they saw a black shape breaking through the patchy cloud. The sound of surging engines could be heard as the Halifax dropped out of the sky in a spiralling dive. Several small white discs were seen to fall from the aircraft and drift down towards the town. Within seconds the huge black shape of the bomber was overhead and diving steeply towards the ground. In fear of their lives the Morrises ran for cover beneath a wall.

Brian Hall was still wrestling with the controls and the rear gunner, Sgt Graham Evans, was hunched in his rear gun turret when the bomber dived into a field and exploded. V for Victor had crashed in Priory Ground, a rectangular strip of rough pasture on top of the hill above the town, bounded on two sides by Conigre Hill and Winsley Road, with Christ Church at its eastern end.

Six trailer pumps from Bradford-on-Avon and Trowbridge Auxiliary Fire Service arrived at the scene of the crash. Driver Fireman Stan Green (brother of Fred Green, see page 25) of Bradford-on-Avon Fire Station recalled:

> 'Leading Fireman Bert Brown was outside the fire station and saw the plane was in trouble. Realising it was going to crash he called out the fire engine and part-time crew who were on duty. They tore off looking for the crash. As the engine was going up Mason's Hill they heard the crash. The engine was parked in the Winsley Road close to the pub [the Rising Sun].
>
> 'In the meantime, the two firewomen on duty reported to Fire Service Headquarters that the engine had left the station. Five minutes later they reported the fire. This upset HQ: how can you attend a fire before it's reported?'

Pieces of Halifax V for Victor that were recovered from the crash site in 1944 by Ernie Harris. *Author's collection*

Appliances from stations in neighbouring towns were also called out and quickly came. It took several hours for the firemen to bring the conflagration under control. Rescuers included the Vicar of Christ Church, townspeople and soldiers from the nearby Army billet at Northleigh, who dragged Graham Evans from his gun turret, but he died soon afterwards. Brian Hall was already dead by the time his body was retrieved from the wreckage. The mutilated bodies of the navigator, Don Hernando de Soto Grover, 23, from Haileybury, Ontario; 21-year-old Roy Porter, the bomb aimer, also from Ontario; and wireless operator Harry Newton, aged 22, from Oldham, Lancashire, were recovered and taken to a makeshift mortuary at the ARP post at the town swimming baths in Bridge Street.

Early next morning at Rudge, two herdsmen were on their way to milking when they found the lifeless body of the 20-year-old flight engineer, Sgt Norman Simpson, lying crumpled in a dewy pasture. He had no parachute, which was found several days later hanging in the trees at nearby Norridge Wood. It was plain from the sickening impression in the ground that he had fallen from a great height. The mid-upper gunner, Sgt Bill Cameron, 22, from Edmonton, Alberta, had baled out and survived, landing in a field near Westbury.

Cpl Craig Reid was a supernumerary crewmember – the eighth man (a Halifax normally carried a crew of seven) – but one who should never have been on the aircraft in the first place. Craig was a ground crew radar technician who had swapped places on V for Victor as a favour to a friend on a 'hot date' with a WAAF. Craig took his place to check out the onboard

'Gee' radiolocation and H2S radar systems. With Bill Cameron and Norman Simpson, he had baled out of the stricken Halifax when it got into difficulty over Wiltshire.

The bomber was a Handley Page Halifax Mk III, serial LW693, V-Victor, which belonged to 425 (Alouette) Squadron, Royal Canadian Air Force. It had taken off from its airfield at Tholthorpe in North Yorkshire on a cross-country training exercise. The sortie had taken it on a flight down the length of England to the South Coast, where it had turned north and headed up through Dorset into Wiltshire. It was over southern Wiltshire that the bomber got into difficulties.

The RAF's official accident report mentions that the pilot lost control of the Halifax between 10,000 and 5,000ft, conjecturing that it may have been because he let the airspeed get too low. Craig Reid, who had just changed crew positions inside the aircraft to the wireless operator's seat, beneath and aft of the pilot's station, recalls the moment trouble began:

> 'When the order came "get the hell out of here" I had to crawl through the small hole into the fuselage to the fore of the main spar. Immediately I was pinned to the upper starboard ceiling because of negative "g". I stumbled and crawled to the rest position to find my chute. They were all in a jumble and my search was desperate. Through the occasional flashes of light I was able to read the ID mark on my chute. Again I was pinned to the port ceiling by negative "g", a terrifying and seemingly endless episode.
>
> 'Going aft I found the mid-upper gunner upside down hanging by his entangled harness in the mechanism of his gun turret. After getting him out we both proceeded to the rear hatch. There was the flight engineer waiting. Bill Cameron the gunner lined up first, the flight engineer next and then myself. In the roar of the air I yelled, "I haven't done this before. What do I do?" Bill shouted, "Jump and pull you fool!"
>
> 'The two guys went first and I followed. I recall the shadow of the tail plane passing overhead. I don't recall pulling the cord, but do recall the awfully wonderful crunch of the open chute stopping my plunge. Then the silence – that's when I became aware that I had been praying.'

Len Pickett remembers Craig's sudden arrival from out of the night sky:

> 'We'd been round to my father's place at Standerwick. It was just getting dark and as we got down to the white bridge my wife said "Look at that up there" and we could see the parachute floating. When we got down to the bridge he [Craig] dropped. We called to him and he heard us. He had fallen on his back. We couldn't get over to him because there was no gate into the field so we got down into the ditch and called for him. He came along and together we got the parachute and harness and put it on the pram. Then we helped him up onto the road and virtually carried him back home.

> 'We took him into the house where he told us he was hungry, so my wife made him some tea and cut him some sandwiches. We didn't have much rations but we made him welcome. Then I went along and got the next door neighbour to sit with my wife while I cycled up to the phone box to contact the authorities.'

Craig, who had landed at Clivey much to the surprise of the Pickett family, and Bill Cameron, were the lucky ones. Norman Simpson, the flight engineer, had a habit of flying with his parachute harness loosely strapped which was to cost him his life. He pulled the ripcord after baling out, but instead of floating safely to earth beneath the big silk canopy he slipped through the web straps and became separated from his parachute, falling to his death over the hamlet of Rudge. Len Pickett also remembers the moment when he came across Simpson's body in a dew soaked pasture: 'I went along the lane for about half a mile or so and I looked over into a field next to the road and I could see an airman in a crouched position down on the ground. It was the airman without the parachute.'

The three crew who baled out over Bradford did so too low for their chutes to deploy properly and were fatally injured. Two of them were caught in the propeller blades as they tumbled from the aircraft: one fell into the trees above Mason's Lane and the other into the back garden of a house in Coppice Hill. The third fell though the roof of a house on Market Street.

Four auxiliary nurses under the supervision of a local GP, Dr Beale Gibson, had the unpleasant task of dealing with the bodies of the crew when they were brought to the ARP post at the town swimming baths. They washed the airmen's bodies and made them presentable before they were driven away up the hill to the mortuary at the hospital.

The following morning people who came to stare at the scene of the crash saw only smouldering debris guarded by troops. On the Tuesday they were allowed into the field to see the roped-off wreckage. For weeks afterwards children found Horlicks tablets and barley sugar sweets from the crew's flight rations strewn across the field, as well as pieces of twisted metal and splintered Perspex.

On the evidence available in 1944, the RAF's accident investigators were unable to decide on the cause of the crash. In any case the RAF had more pressing matters to consider when four nights later Bomber Command lost 96 bombers and over 600 aircrew in a night raid on Nuremberg. It was Bomber Command's worst loss of the war. Based on what we know today about the incident, pieced together from witness statements, V for Victor may have crashed because of a technical malfunction that led to a catastrophic engine fire, combined with pilot error. But we may never know for sure.

Several days after the crash, Canadians Brian Hall, Don Hernando Grover and Roy Porter were buried at Haycombe Cemetery in Bath, thousands of miles away from their families and homeland in Canada. The bodies of the three Britons were returned to their families for burial: Harry Newton to Oldham, Lancashire; Norman Simpson to Stretton, Cheshire; and Graham Evans to Ystrad Mynach in the Welsh valleys.

Bill Cameron returned to flying duties and was promoted to flight sergeant, only to be lost on operations over Germany a few months later on 18–19 July when his Halifax was blown apart by flak over the Ruhr valley. He is buried with his crew at Rheinberg War Cemetery, near Krefeld.

Craig Reid survived the war. He went to university, married and raised a family, and went on to enjoy a career as a social worker and as a politician in the city of Calgary, Alberta. Craig often asked himself why he alone should have been spared out of the eight men who flew in V for Victor on that spring night. It was a question that troubled him for more than 60 years. Craig found some answers in his Christian faith, and he made every new day count through his commitment to family and by working tirelessly for his community. He once told me that every morning when he awoke and his feet touched the ground beside his bed, he thanked God for another day. Craig died in 2009 aged 86.

In 1988 I was behind an application by Christ Church Parochial Church Council to the Diocese of Salisbury for permission to place a memorial plaque inside the church to commemorate the crash. The Chancellor of the Diocese, John Ellison, turned down the application and the appeal in 1990 was unsuccessful. Citing legal and ethical arguments to support his decision, he concluded that the reason why nothing had been done in the past was because such a proposal would have been 'mistaken and inappropriate'. He went on to say that 'the erection of a permanent plaque years later involves very different considerations… The sad truth of the matter is that the whole incident was the result of incompetence on the part of Hall, who caused the loss of this aircraft and four of his crew, and who had he lived would probably have been the subject of military disciplinary proceedings.'

The result of the RAF's inquiry into the causes of the crash was inconclusive, so it was disingenuous of Ellison to blame the crash on Brian Hall. He should have known better than to besmirch the name of a dead man who could not defend himself against such a serious allegation.

Several post war fatal flying accidents that involved RAF aircraft resulted in official investigations where full blame was laid on the deceased pilots. In several cases the evidence for such assertions has been flimsy at least and the families of the pilots concerned have mounted vigorous challenges to the 'official' versions of events. In some instances they have been vindicated, but the official verdicts have never been overturned.

Conscious of my frustration and disappointment after several years of hoping for a successful conclusion, my father contacted Bradford-on-Avon Town Council to ask if they would be interested in supporting the project. They were.

Almost fifty years to the day of the crash, at noon on 25 March 1994, a brass memorial plaque was unveiled outside the Town Council offices in Westbury House Gardens to commemorate the crash and the loss of the bomber's crew. The sole survivor, 72-year-old Craig Reid, flew in especially for the ceremony from his home in Calgary, Canada. Jean Morris, the sister of Sgt Graham Evans, the rear gunner, from Ystrad Mynach, South Wales, was also present to witness the unveiling. With other friends and relatives of the crew, and scores of Bradfordians, they watched a flypast by a Lockheed Hercules transport aircraft from RAF Lyneham.

50 years on: Craig Reid (left) and his rescuer Len Pickett return to the scene of Craig's unscheduled arrival at Clivey, 26 March 1994. *Author*

Pilot Officer George Brian HALL, RCAF

Service No: J/89283; *Unit:* 425 (RCAF) Squadron; *Died:* 26 March 1944 aged 22; *Buried:* Bath (Haycombe) Cemetery, Plot 39. Sec. H. Row C. Grave 260;

Pilot Officer Don Hernando de Soto GROVER, RCAF

Service No: J/85140; *Unit:* 425 (RCAF) Squadron; *Died:* 26 March 1944 aged 23; *Buried:* Bath (Haycombe) Cemetery, Plot 39. Sec. H. Row A Grave 248;

Pilot Officer Roy Stanley PORTER, RCAF

Service No: J/89470; *Unit:* 425 (RCAF) Squadron; *Died:* 26 March 1944 aged 21; *Buried:* Bath (Haycombe) Cemetery, Plot 39. Sec. H. Row B. Grave 248;

Sergeant Frank Norman SIMPSON, RAFVR

Service No: 2208949; *Unit:* 425 (RCAF) Squadron; *Died:* 26 March 1944 aged 20; *Buried:* Stretton (St Matthew) Churchyard; *Commemorated:* Stretton WM, St Matthew's Church;

Sergeant Harry NEWTON, RAFVR

Service No: 1480974; *Unit:* 425 (RCAF) Squadron; *Died:* 26 March 1944 aged 22; *Buried:* Oldham (Greenacres) Cemetery, Sec. C. Row 15. Grave 192;

Sergeant Graham EVANS, RAFVR

Service No: 1025594; *Unit:* 425 (RCAF) Squadron; *Died:* 26 March 1944 aged 21; *Buried:* Ystrad Mynach (Holy Trinity) Churchyard, Plot F. Grave 290.

The Commonwealth War Graves plot at Bath's Haycombe Cemetery, the final resting place of three of V for Victor's crew. ***Author***

SOURCES

PRIMARY

Wiltshire and Swindon County Record Office:

The Churchman, Holy Trinity and Christ Church Parish Magazine, various issues; Winsley and Turleigh Womens' Institute Scapbook (compiled 1956).

Trowbridge Reference Library:

The *Wiltshire Times*, *The Times*, trade directories.

Bath Reference Library:

The *Bath and Wilts Chronicle and Herald.*

The National Archives (Public Record Office), Kew:

Army, RAF and Royal Navy Award Citations, Royal Navy, Seamen's Records.

British Army, Unit War Diaries, Second World War:

WO 171/855 – 3rd/4th County of London Yeomanry, August 1944; WO 171/1278 – 2nd Battalion Devonshire Regiment, 8–14 July 1944; WO 171/1287 – 5th Battalion Dorsetshire Regiment, July 1944; WO 171/1358 – 1st Battalion The Rifle Brigade, June 1944; WO 171/1395 – 5th Battalion Wiltshire Regiment, July 1944; WO 171/1608 – 260 Field Company Royal Engineers, 1–15 August 1944.

Royal Air Force, Station and Squadron Operations Record Books, Second World War:

AIR 27/708 – 86 Squadron, October 1943; AIR 27/1121 – 178 Squadron, October 1944; AIR 27/1838 – 425 (RCAF) Squadron, January – December 1944.

MI9 General Questionnaire for British/American ex-Prisoners of War, 1945

WO344/106/1 – Warrant Officer Edward Farrands; WO344/124/2 – Flight Lieutenant Bernard Green.

RAF Museum, London:

Air Ministry Form 1180 – Aircraft Accident Record Cards

Airspeed Oxford Mk I, X6858; Avro Lancaster Mk I, ME584; Avro Lancaster Mk III, ND906; Consolidated Liberator Mk V, FL954; Handley Page Halifax Mk III, LW693; Vickers Wellington Mk II, W5432.

Commonwealth War Graves Commission:

Online records, Debt of Honour Register.

http://www.cwgc.org

Library and Archives Canada:

ATIP and Personnel Records Division – Military Service Records

R147536 Richard James Gregory; J15008 John Ross Robertson; J22099 Burnham John Malcolm Thorp.

Naval Historical Branch:

S6718 – HMS *Mahratta*, Summary of Service 1943–44 (compiled 1964).

WEBSITES

www.awm.gov.au – The Australian War Memorial is a national archive whose purpose is to commemorate the sacrifice of those Australians who have died in war.

www.chrishobbs.com/sheffield.htm – The Chris Hobbs Site, articles with a Sheffield connection.

www.convoyweb.org.uk – Merchant convoys during the Second World War.

www.cwgc.org – Commonwealth War Graves Commission.

www.firepower.org.uk – Firepower: the Royal Artillery Museum, London.

www.hellfirepass.com – all about the Burma Railway ('Death Railway') in the Second World War.

www.hmsmahratta.50megs.com – destroyer HMS *Mahratta.*

www.hmsdunedin.co.uk – cruiser HMS *Dunedin.*

www.hongkongwardiary.com – a project that documents the 1941 defence of Hong Kong, the Garrison, and their fates until liberation.

www.john-pinckney.co.uk – Pinckney Family Tree.

www.netherlandsnavy.nl/Singapore – Singapore convoys.

www.northeasthistory.co.uk – history site for the North-East of England.

www.bbc.co.uk/ww2peopleswar – 'People's War' is an online archive of wartime memories contributed by members of the public and gathered by the BBC.

www.acseac.co.uk – RAF Liberator Squadrons of 205 Group, SEAC, Coastal Command and Commonwealth Air Forces.

www.156squadron.com – cross-referenced transcriptions of 156 Squadron, RAF, operational records, 1943–45.

www.powtaiwan.org – the story of the Taiwan POW camps and the men who were interned there.

www.thewardrobe.org.uk – RGBW Museum, Salisbury, Wiltshire.

www.tna.org – the UK's National Archives.

www.uboat.net – the U-boat war 1914–18 and 1939–45, and Allied efforts to fight the U-boats in the Second World War.

www.ubootwaffe.net – Kriegsmarine and U-boat history.

www.1901censusonline.com – 1.5 million original 1901 Census documents of England and Wales online detailing 32 million people.

www.nationalarchives.gov.uk/documentsonline – Documents Online allows you online access to The National Archives' collection of digitised public records, including both academic and family history sources.

BOOKS, MAGAZINES AND PERIODICALS

Allan, Bob (ed), *1941–1945: The Arctic Lookout – The Russian Convoy Club Official Magazine*, issues 33, 35, 36

Blamey, Joel C. E., *A Submariner's Story: The Memoirs of a Submarine Engineer in Peace and in War* (Periscope Publishing, 2002)

Carter, Nick and Carol, *The Distinguished Flying Cross and How it Was Won, 1918–95* (Savannah Publications, 1998)

Chorley, W., *RAF Bomber Command Losses of the Second World War*, various volumes (Midland Publishing, various dates)

Delaforce, Patrick, *The Black Bull: From Normandy to the Baltic with the 11th Armoured Division* (Alan Sutton, 1993)

Delaforce, Patrick, *The Fighting Wessex Wyverns: From Normandy to Bremerhaven with the 43rd (Wessex) Division* (Alan Sutton, 1995)

Douglas Home, Jamie, and Henderson, Johnny, *Watching Monty* (Sutton, 2005)

Ford, Ken, *Assault on Germany: The Battle for Geilenkirchen, November 1944* (David and Charles, 1989)

Forty, George, *The Desert War* (Sutton, 2002)

Forty, George, *Battle Zone Normandy: Villers Bocage* (Sutton, 2004)

Gill, Stuart, *Blood in the Sea: HMS* Dunedin *and the Enigma Code* (Weidenfeld & Nicolson, 2003)

Graham, Andrew, *Sharpshooters at War* (London, The Sharpshooters Regimental Association, 1964)

Hartwell, G.R., Pack, G.R., Edwards, M.A., *The Story of the 5th Battalion the Dorsetshire Regiment in North West Europe, 23 June 1944 to 5 May 1945* (The Keep Military Museum, 2006)

Hayward, Roger, *Cruisers in Camera* (Sutton, 2000)

Holmes, Richard, *The World at War: The Landmark Oral History* (Ebury Press, 2007)

Holliday, Joyce, *It's a Bit Lively Outside: The Story of the Sheffield Blitz* (Castleford, Yorkshire Arts Circus, 1987)

Hunt, Eric, *Battleground Europe, Normandy: Mont Pincon* (Leo Cooper, 2003)

Kemp, Paul, *The Admiralty Regrets: British and Commonwealth Warship Losses of the 20th Century* (Sutton, 1999)

Lewendon, Brigadier R.J., *Gunners in Java* (n.d., Royal Artillery Institution)

MacDermott, Brian, *Ships without Names: the Story of the Royal Navy's Tank Landing Ships of World War Two* (Arms and Armour Press, 1992)

McNish, Robin, *Iron Division: The History of the 3rd Division* 1809–1989 (Galago, 1990)

Meredith, Capt J.L.J., *The Story of The Seventh Battalion The Somerset Light Infantry, June 1944–May 1945* (1945; Naval & Military Press reprint, 2008)

Middlebrook, Martin, and Everett, Chris, *The Bomber Command War Diaries* (Viking, 1985)

Orde, Roden, *The Household Cavalry at War: Second Household Cavalry Regiment* (Gale & Polden, 1953)

Perrett, Bryan, *Seize and Hold: Master Strokes on the Battlefield* (Arms and Armour, 1994)
Philips, Lawrence, and Sainsbury, Anthony, *The Royal Navy Day by Day* (Sutton, 2005)
Salmond, J.B., *History of the 51st Highland Division* (Blackwood, 1953)
Scarr, Major Desmond, *Recollections* (privately published, 1989)
Sebag-Montefiore, Hugh, *Dunkirk: Fight to the Last Man* (Viking, 2006)
Smith, Colin, *Singapore Burning: Heroism and Surrender in World War II* (Penguin, 2006)
Stephen, Martin, and Grove, Eric (ed), *Sea Battles in Close-up* (Ian Allan, 1988)
Tavender, I.T., *The Distinguished Flying Medal Register for the Second World War* (2000, Savannah Publications)
Thompson, Julian, *The Imperial War Museum Book of the War at Sea: The Royal Navy in the Second World War* (Sidgwick & Jackson, 1996)
Waters, S.D., *The Official History of New Zealand in the Second World War 1939–1945: The Royal New Zealand Navy* (Historical Publications Branch, Wellington, NZ, 1956)
White-Spunner, Barney, *Horse Guards* (Macmillan, 2006)
Who was Who, various editions (A & C Black)
Williams, David, *Wartime Disasters at Sea* (PSL, 1997)
Wingate, John, *The Fighting Tenth: The Tenth Submarine Flotilla and the Siege of Malta* (Periscope Publishing, 2003)
Gibson, Major Edwin and Kingsley Ward, G., *Courage Remembered: The Story Behind the Construction and Maintenance of the Commonwealth's Military Cemeteries and Memorials of the Wars of 1914–18 and 1939–45* (HMSO, 1989)

INDEX

(Note: page numbers in italic refer to photographs)

PEOPLE

LOCAL CONNECTIONS

STREETS, ROADS AND HOUSES

CHURCHES, FIRMS, ORGANISATIONS AND SCHOOLS